RIGHT TURN

*The Coastal Academy for Driver
Education Training and Safety*

MICHAEL WAYNE TEMPLETON

RIGHT TURN

3RD EDITION

FINALLY, A DRIVER EDUCATION AND TRAINING GUIDE FOR THE PARENTS AND GRANDPARENTS OF TEENS AND TWEENS!

DRIVER TRAINING

How to Prepare your Children for Driving in the 21st Century

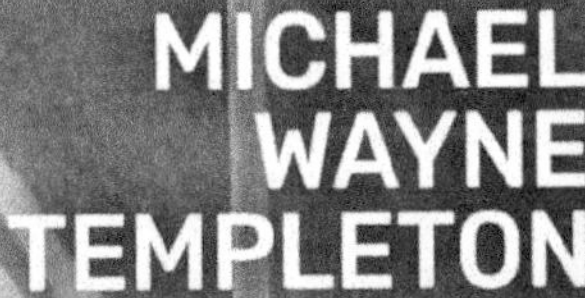

MICHAEL WAYNE TEMPLETON

CONTENTS

APPENDICES

PREFACE

I knew that Albert Francis* was going to be a special challenge. The office manager of the driver education company I was employed in had called me and asked for a "special favor" again. He told me another driving instructor had conducted a first lesson with Albert and had pronounced him to be "untrainable."

After I had conducted my first driving lesson with Albert, I very nearly agreed with my coworker. During that lesson, Albert had used his own unique, "walking- the-wheel" technique to turn the car around corners not very successfully. I also noted that *while his hands were on the wheel*, he fidgeted with his fingers constantly while attempting to drive ... again, not very successfully. He also seemed to be extraordinarily preoccupied with other matters going on in his young brain other than the immediate task at hand, which was driving a three- thousand-plus-pound automobile.

During that lesson, what did strike me was that Albert was trying desperately to please me. He just didn't have a clue how to do so. During our entire first lesson (his actual second overall lesson), we never left the parking lot. During that two-hour period, we worked and worked on his steering, turning, and consistency of the application of foot pressure on the gas and brake pedals. It isn't completely uncommon that beginning drivers require additional time, training, and care in parking lots.

However, it also was apparent to me that Albert had a learning disability.

During Albert's third lesson, I decided to determine the level of Albert's learning disability by training him to Parallel Park. Up to this point, my employer had not informed me that Albert suffered from ADD (Attention Deficit Disorder). His mother had not informed me of this fact either. If they *had* informed me, I'm not sure I could have taken a different approach for Albert's behind-the-wheel training other than the one I chose, but I certainly would have put it into action sooner.

At the start of the lesson, I set up our parallel parking cones and poles. As always, I drove around the parking lot and demonstrated the parking procedure as I had been trained by my employer. Albert got behind the wheel and pulled up near the spot I had indicated.

As he backed, Albert (like many teens, even those without learning disabilities) became confused and turned the wheel in the opposite direction he should have. Albert didn't just bump the front left pole—*he ran completely over it!*

The second time we prepared to parallel park, I patiently explained which way to turn the wheel as we approached the critical spot, and I helped him turn the wheel as we backed in. As we backed toward the back poles, I asked him to stop the car within a foot of the poles. After all, they represent the bumper of a car. Albert misjudged the distance badly and completely *ran over* one of the back poles. After I had him pull forward, I set the poles up again and asked him to pull out of the parallel parking space. On the way out, he clipped the left front pole again and then somehow managed to *run over it* with the right rear tire, scoring a rare "trifecta" during his first parallel parking lesson!

I supposed that if someone from *America's Funniest Home Videos* had been recording this lesson, they would have scored big with it. However, I looked over at Albert, and I can state with absolute certainty that it wasn't funny to him. His face reflected that his dreams of successfully learning to drive a car were beginning to evaporate. Since I was his second driving instructor, one given the special assignment to train him, he knew that if I gave up on him, his parents just might give up on him too. At the end of the lesson, I asked to speak with his mother privately out of earshot of Albert.

We left the parking lot and went into the hall of a shopping mall where we had agreed to meet, and she sat down on a bench facing me. Marshalling all the diplomacy that I could muster, I explained to his mother what had happened. His mother's eyes welled up. I could tell she was about ready to lose it. She looked up toward the ceiling in exasperation and said "Oh Albert" and dropped her head down toward her knees. She had obviously heard this sort of thing about her son before from other sources. Now she was faced with the prospect that her son might never learn to drive a car safely, let alone that little matter of passing a state driving test. This was a public place, as much as she wanted to break into tears; she somehow kept her composure and looked up at me.

She asked me, "Are you going to give up on him?"

I looked at her, swallowed hard, and said, "No, I'm not going to give up on him. If you will partner with me, I think we can teach Albert to drive, but I need your help. First, we need to talk about the medication he is or isn't taking, when he takes it, and how it affects him. Then I need to coach you on how to watch Albert as he is learning and how to reinforce our techniques."

I was already aware that, like many families today, Albert was in a broken home. Albert's father was not going to be a partner in this process. She said, "I'll do whatever it takes as long as you don't give up."

The graduated licensing program in the state where I reside and teach is not like the graduated licensing program in many states. I will discuss just which states have graduated licensing programs later. However, in several states, a fifteen-year-old can obtain a permit, receive state certified driver education, and obtain a provisional driver's license with several restrictions. Our state driver education program requires a *minimum* of eight hours of classroom instruction, six hours behind the wheel with a state certified driving instructor, and at least forty hours of supervised driving with a parent or legal guardian. Some parents need to be reminded of that last part. Later in the book, I will expand further on our state requirements and the requirements of your state, but let's get back to the training of Albert Francis. Between Albert's third and fourth two-hour lesson—yes, we had already exceeded the six-hour minimum without departing the parking lot— I developed a new parallel parking procedure for Albert. It really wasn't all that much different than the old "S" procedure that I had learned in high school decades earlier, still being used religiously by the driver education company that employed me now.

During the early minutes of lesson no. 4 with Albert, I demonstrated my new procedure, just as I had practiced it and written out the steps. Albert watched me and processed the "baby steps" in the order I had provided them. Then he got behind the wheel, and I coached him through each and every independent step.

After an additional coaching sequence, I said, "Now do it on your own, Albert, and tell me each step you are going to execute *before* you do it." Yes, Albert successfully parallel parked that day, and he didn't touch a cone!

Of course, parallel parking is just one of many requirements for learning to drive a car. Some parents and almost all students believe that parallel parking should no longer be included in DMV driving exams.

As a professional driving instructor, I conclude otherwise. Parallel parking requires judgment, timing, execution, and a degree of precision which reveals more about the capabilities of a driver than many parents and students realize.

Now that Albert had conquered parallel parking, it was time to teach him how to drive. The process of teaching teens to drive will be covered in detail in this book. Albert required twice as many lessons as an "average" student.

During his final lesson, we drove on four of the busiest highways in our county. We also entered the expressway, changed lane several times, and exited safely. As we drove the last five miles of our fifty-mile drive that day, I still wasn't entirely convinced that Albert was ready to obtain his driver license and drive safely on the road.

As we rounded the final corner, we approached the mall rendezvous meeting spot previously arranged with his mother, and then it happened.

A reckless driver pulled right out in front of Albert from our right, violated our space cushion, and threatened immediate collision. I lifted my foot to hit the brake on my side of the car, but before I could do so, Albert had already slowed, expertly shifted lanes early to avoid collision, and prepared to make a safe left turn into the mall.

Unlike previous episodes, this time he was cool, calm, confident, and in charge of his vehicle. He even signaled that he was turning left after danger had passed, and he cleared oncoming vehicles properly. When I met his mother, I signed his training certificate and his provisional driver's license application. I informed her of the episode that had transpired just a few moments before. I told her how proud I was of Albert in the way he had handled it. That critical moment was the moment, more than any other that convinced me that he was ready.

People ask me all the time why I got into the driver education business. The first reason was the look on Albert's face. The second reason was the look on his mother's face.

All personal names referenced in this book are fabricated in order to protect the privacy of the innocent and the not-so-innocent. However, we assure readers that each and every anecdote in this book is factual.

FOREWORD

In my opinion, **_Right Turn_** is a gold standard for written text in the field of driver education. It looks and reads like a fine textbook with first-rate illustrations, diagrams, photos, and graphics. While many books have been developed about driver education, driver training, or both, virtually none of them include specific guidance about how to train another instructor, how to improve the driving of an adult, or how to train a student driver in a training car. This clearly was and is not the intent of most driver education and training textbooks. This is where my friend, fellow driving instructor professional, and now author, excels.

This book provides extensive details, performance grids, training aids, and instructional guidance revolving around the science of _teaching_ driver education and training, not only for parents and grandparents but also for any professional or private driver education instructor as well as those who are charged with oversight of them. This makes this book unique among all current driver education books and especially those that have preceded it. It is essentially a train-the-trainer type textbook for professional educators and for parents who wish to gain that level of driver education knowledge.

Michael Wayne Templeton may be unique as a pro- driving instructor. He has had the opportunity to attend several different pro-driving academies and compare their policies, procedures, and teaching practices. He also has trained several professional driving instructors.

I was a corporal of the Surfside Beach Police Department when I attended Mike's Coastal Academy for Driver Education, Training and Safety's 40 forty- hour course. Later I became the lead driving instructor for the Affordable Driving Academy and lead driving instructor for recruits of the Surfside Beach Police Department where I eventually became chief of police.

During the past several years, I have also researched many driver education books textbooks and/or training aids such as those referenced above. Some of these references offer conflicting viewpoints or alternative driver education instruction philosophies.

By definition, the requirements for teaching high speed pursuit law enforcement driving and the requirements for teaching beginning drivers to drive for the first time are different. However, if another current or former pro-driving instructor has compared differing teaching philosophies in an attempt to improve driver education, I have not yet read a comprehensive comparison of these differing driver education training/teaching philosophies published within the same textbook. Under normal circumstance, which is 99 percent of the time, safe driving practices remain safe driving practices and the rules of the road remain the rules of the road.

A current deficiency within the field of driver education that professional instructors are faced with every day is that few parents are even aware of their own role in the driver education process. For example, many parents are not aware that if their child attends professional driver education training, in order for driver education/training to be effective, the parent *must supplement* the professional instruction. This supplemental training should begin during preteen years (before the teen actually begins to drive) and should continue throughout the entire driver education process.

Many parents admit that they were not professionally trained, that their training is obsolete, or that they have simply forgotten some of the basic rules of the road. Of course, all these parents should read *Right Turn*. Meanwhile, many parents who sincerely believe they are qualified to teach their own children to drive simply review their own state DMV manual and then begin the awkward teaching process. *Right Turn* should convince parents that this is a very poor choice.

If professional instruction is not reinforced, parents' unsafe driving practices or the teen's friends' driving habits are reinforced. In addition, even in the small percentage of cases when a parent actually provides appropriate beginning driver instruction to their teen, many of these techniques and the rationale for them are often *not* clearly understood by the teen until they are defined properly by a professional instructor.

This text provides hundreds of nuanced details about the science of safe driving. Any preteen or teen between the age of ten and seventeen, legal immigrant, or senior driver (not to mention parents again) could benefit immeasurably by reading *Right Turn, especially if the parent or grandparent understands the contents sufficiently to reinforce the material in your own words.*

In doing so, you will become essential in assisting the professional driving school of your choice while providing the very best training in this field available today.

We, your driver education and training professionals, don't think you can't put a price tag on saving a human life, especially if that human life is a member of your own family.

Sincerely, Rodney Keziah,

Chief of Police, Surfside Beach Police Department, South Carolina

BACKGROUND

Knowledge may be gained as a result of formal training, informal training, experience, and through a variety of other related means. The owners and operators of the Coastal Academy for Driver Education, Training and Safety Inc. accrued knowledge, skills, abilities, and an education in the field of driver education. However, we also brought training and experience from other safety related fields. Throughout the chapters in the book, when you read the pronoun *I,* you are reading a personal account from Michael Wayne Templeton. When you read the pronoun *we,* you are reading about the policies, procedures, and practices developed by CADETS Inc.

I believe that three different phases of my life have contributed to my understanding of driver education and to the development of this book. The first phase was (and still is) my experiences while driving. I have been driving for over forty-five years now, beginning with my first extended drive at thirteen years old. No, I'm not going to tell an anecdote about every driver who cut me off over the past forty-five years, but there are *some* milestone events that have contributed to my current knowledge of driving as related to driver education.

I also feel I need to highlight at least some of these driving experiences, lest you conclude that since we opened our driving academy in Myrtle Beach, South Carolina, we know nothing about driving in the rest of the country. During my adult life, I have lived in California, Missouri, Georgia, Oklahoma, Hawaii, Virginia, and now South Carolina. During that time, I have crisscrossed the United States via rural roads, super highways, and expressways more times than I can count, even if I wanted to.

Perhaps my greatest *driving* experience gained (while *not* teaching) was earned while living, working, and commuting within the Southern California road and highway system. During more than twenty of my forty- five plus driving years, I drove on Southern California freeways and roadways. Those commutes were within Los Angeles County, Ventura County, Orange County, and San Diego County, or a combination of the above.

When you drive daily in Southern California "rush hour" traffic, you either learn to drive properly, or you get run off the road. The drivers will give you a semi- smiley face as they drive past your dead carcass. In Southern California, the term *rush hour* is an inside joke. It is used for tourists, vacationers, and Hollywood stalkers who were hoodwinked into believing that the chaos they now find themselves driving in really just lasts *one hour*. On Southern California freeways, "rush hour" begins at about 2:00 p.m. and ends at about 7:00 p.m., only if there are no collisions on one of the thirty- five freeways you happen to be driving on and it isn't Friday.

Friday's are even worse, and it's probably worse now than it was then. For every "fender bender" that occurs during a two-hour commute, a driver must add at least another half hour or more to the commute. This of course depends on how many of the eight lanes on your side of the median are occupied by emergency vehicles.

Other states I have lived in had their own unique set of road and highway issues to deal with. For example, I lived and commuted on the Island of Oahu, Hawaii, for four years. It wasn't uncommon to get behind a driver on the H1 "expressway" leading into Honolulu and find yourself screaming along at the astonishing speed of twenty-five miles per hour! Later I found out that there were several reasons for this phenomenon.

For example, I made the mistake of owning a red Corvette during first year in Hawaii. That first year on Oahu, I got a ticket for doing twenty- seven miles per hour in a twenty-five-mile-per-hour zone! Yes, I guess I was technically "speeding," so I was guilty as charged. Then a few months later, I jumped into the Corvette to drive exactly one block to our neighborhood tennis court. Since it was only one block away, I didn't put on my seatbelt. Since that time, I have learned that that was a bad decision for more reasons than just the obvious one. You guessed it; another ticket! It wasn't long after that that we sold the red Corvette. I also changed many of my driving behaviors.

Remember, I wrote that knowledge may be gained through training *or* experience. I haven't had a ticket since that seatbelt infraction in Hawaii in 1991. Now I'll probably get one for doing something equally stupid the day after this book comes out.

I have also driven through about forty of the mainland states to visit family, friends, or for the requirements of my chosen career field. If you spend enough time driving through deserts, mountains, and plains and through rain, sleet, and snow and over ice, you begin to learn what to do. More importantly, you learn what *not* to do.

You also learn a bit about how to coexist on the highways with commercial vehicles like giant eighteen- wheel trucks. Contrary to popular belief, all eighteen- wheel truck drivers are not necessarily nice grandfatherly types. This is especially true if you do not merge properly; you force them to downshift unnecessarily, lane change abruptly, or force them to *attempt* to stop their vehicle in less than the length of a football field while moving at highway speed. There will be more about merging in front of eighteen-wheelers later.

The second phase of my learning experiences as related to driver education involves training delivery, training development, and training administration. The United States army introduced me to training delivery, training development, and training administration at Signal Corps, School Brigade, Fort Gordon, Georgia, after I returned from a year serving in Vietnam. The army essentially said, "You will report to Fort Gordon, and you will teach other United States army soldiers everything you know about aircraft Avionics." And so, I did as I was told by someone that knew more than I did. While I was in the army, I discovered that works pretty well when you try it.

After honorable discharge, I also did some formal training development and delivery for the United States Marine Corps as a civilian. You might be wondering: "What is the difference between formal training and informal training?" Well, in my vernacular, "formal training" is classroom training with a lesson plan. "Informal training" might be "show and tell" with a group of guys standing around looking at a broken machine. During this period of time, I taught digital logics and Boolean algebra. Picture a group of Marines sitting in a classroom learning that from a twenty-three-year old civilian!

The Federal Aviation Administration picked me up when I was twenty- five. I spent the next twenty-nine years there. During the middle part of my career, I completed several training development and delivery courses while employed at the FAA Academy as an instructor.

Examples are Basic Instructor Training, Curriculum Development, Instructional Testing, Computer Based Instruction Development, etc. From 1982 to 1985, I served as an academy instructor teaching automated radar to specialists and engineers. During that period, I also gained valuable experience as a computer-based instruction developer and programmer.

During my final year at the aeronautical center, I served as a staff technical specialist for the FAA Academy Superintendent. Basically, my job was to write persuasive letters for the FAA Academy Superintendent to sign. Once in a while, I was able to do something that was fun. At least, I considered the following project to be fun. My best FAA buddy Ken McCall and I joined forces and transformed our FAA Academy Examination, Control Center from a paper society to a fully automated operation during 1984 and 1985. Ken and I picked a team of superstars to serve on our team, and we completed automating an examination control center process that had essentially had been using the same twentieth-century testing procedures for the previous fifty years.

During the next fifteen years of my FAA career, I moved back and forth between supervisory/management positions and training/management positions. I would like to note here that there *is* a relationship in all this to driver education, although some readers may conclude that FAA safety training and experience is unrelated to driver education safety and training.

In 2001 I received a phone call in my San Diego office from my buddy Ken McCall who I knew was serving on a special assignment at FAA HQ in Washington DC. I always joke with him that he looks just like actor Hal Holbrook; he even did then. Later after Ken retired, he *became* Hal Holbrook because he is an actor now. We won't get into *that* in this book either. He informed me that he had been selected to serve on a long detail (temporary special assignment) as the national training manager for the new Standard Terminal Automation Replacement System (STARS) system.

The new STARS system would be replacing the old Automated Radar Terminal System IIIA that he and I had been trained on years earlier. In 2001 that system (the ARTS IIIA) was still being used to control traffic at virtually every large airport in the country.

He said, "Mike I need your help." We need to get every ARTS II, ARTS IIIA, and some of our EARTS experts retrained for STARS. In my "no- nonsense" way, I said, "Well, what do you need me for? It seems pretty straightforward to me. Just send them to the FAA Academy like we always do."

He said, "You don't understand, old buddy. The Professional Airway Systems Specialist (PASS) Union wants *all* the technical training to be conducted out in the field before, during, and after the installations by FAA National Airspace Systems installation engineers. As an 'experiment,' the Union has reached an agreement with FAA HQ that all the training for the certification experts, at least in this case, would not take place at the FAA Academy in Oklahoma City."

I asked, "Then who are they going to get to conduct the training out here in the field, FAA Academy instructors?" "Well, not exactly," he said. "They want us to train our own cadre of instructors to deliver the training out in the field."

My first response was something along the lines of. "Have all the managers at FAA HQ lost their minds?" Ken responded in his usual diplomatic way. However, since I had known Ken for twenty years by that time, this is basically what I really heard: "Yes, Mike, they have lost their minds. This is why I need your help on this suicide mission career killer. Please come back to Washington DC to help me!" And so I did just like I had learned to do when I was in the army. Well, at least this time I was asked. We trained about thirty instructors during 2001 and 2002.

Each instructor required about a year of advanced training in order to teach STARS to field specialists who were charged with assessing, evaluating, troubleshooting, maintaining, repairing, and ultimately certifying the new Standard Terminal Automation Replacement System, processing automated radar at our nation's largest airports.

In 2002 a colleague from the Western-Pacific Region approached me while I was still at HQ working on STARS. I had once worked directly for him twenty years previously, and I also had once supervised his stepdaughter about seven years previously at Southern California TRACON. His stepdaughter was a bright, energetic young engineer who was eager to make a contribution to the FAA. By the time she was assigned to work with me in Technical Support, I was a grizzled veteran. I had gained about twenty years of experience in FAA years by then, so I was able to help her acclimate.

Although her father and I rarely spoke of her when we crossed paths at HQ, during the few occasions we did, I could tell that he appreciated the way I had treated her years earlier. He and his daughter are "black" or "African-Americans" as the preferred term seems to be these days. I'm not sure that the fact that they are African Americans has any significance or relevance to this narrative other than I want it to be known for my own personal reasons, so I am putting it in the book. We used to call it "the power of the pen" during my FAA staff assistant years.

I thought very highly of both of them, and I have never really had a chance to thank him for what came next. On this particular day, when he stopped by my desk, he said, "We are bidding a new position here at FAA HQ for a National Airspace Implementation Training Manager … for the agency." He added, "I would like to see your name on the bid list." As diplomatically as I could, I asked him about the responsibilities of the manager who would eventually hold the position.

He parried, "We have never had a national training manager for NAS Implementation or for Field Engineering (as was the previous name for the organization for literally, decades previously). We have now determined that we can no longer afford to be without a national training manager." I had never worked directly for NAS Implementation or Field Installation engineering, and he knew that. I felt like I needed to press him for an answer because I knew that bid announcements, especially at HQ, were often vague. "What will the responsibilities of this new manager actually be?"

He replied, "We have about one thousand three hundred installation engineers FAA wide, *most* of them require additional technical training.

We have about three hundred professional airway systems specialists, *all* of them require regular technical training at the FAA Academy. We also have about fifty managers who require *regular* training at the Center for Management Development at Palm Coast Florida." In addition, there are about five hundred contract personnel nationwide who require some degree of additional FAA training or out-of-agency training. I didn't say it, but I thought to myself. *Oh ... is that all?*

During years 28 and 29 of my FAA career, I served as the manager of National Airspace System Training (ANI) at grade level GS-14. I should point out that the person who initially approached me about the position and asked me to apply, *was not* the selecting official. In fact, he didn't even serve on the selection panel. However, if he hadn't encouraged me to apply, it never would have happened.

I once considered writing a book about my experiences in the FAA. Most folks know a little about air traffic controllers (because of television and movies). Some folks even know that the FAA has some aircraft accident investigators. The general public hasn't been informed much about the functions of thousands of other specialists who were and are employed by the Federal Aviation Administration. However, I feel that a current book revolving around the topic of driver education will, in the long run, be more beneficial for our nation's teens and maybe even some of our adults. Snicker if you want, but this is what I believe.

I thought I would take this opportunity in my background section to tell you a little about them. They were and are hard-working public servants. I take my hat off to them. If you are wondering what all this FAA training stuff has to do with driver education, training, and safety, well, please read the rest of my book and you can draw your own conclusions.

Sincerely,

Michael Wayne Templeton

INTRODUCTION TO CADETS AND RIGHT TURN

Our purpose for writing this book is to cause parents, legislators, and educators to have an *epiphany.* If you read this book and you do not have an epiphany, it may mean that you feel that you are already an expert in the field of driver education. However, please consider that even if you feel that you are an expert *driver,* it doesn't necessarily follow that you have become an expert at teaching driver education in the classroom or driver training in an automobile.

It is a far more challenging endeavor than you may initially realize.

If you are a parent, at this point you may be thinking, *Well, my kid is going to take driver education here at the local high school, and he/she will be good to go after that."* Well, maybe. This book should have a large subtitle that says, "Read Me First" on the cover. Let's start with some sobering facts.

The following are a few representative statistics that *must* be acknowledged. Some of these statistics are only compiled and published every few years. Nevertheless they haven't changed much over the past several years. If anything, they are getting worse, not better. Two glaring reasons for the downtrend are DWP (Driving While Phoning) and DWT (Driving While Texting). However, DWP and DWT are only symptoms of the root cause of the problem. The real root causes of dozens and possibly hundreds of driver education-related deficiencies will be critically exposed in this book.

This isn't a book for someone who loves statistics. This may be the last section of the book where you will see them. However, the few statistics that we have chosen to reference do help paint a picture, and it isn't very pretty. These representative statistics (and others like them) should confirm some of your worst fears about the overall state of driver education throughout America *today.*

- *Motor vehicle crashes are the leading cause of death for fifteen- to twenty-year-olds. *(National Highway Traffic Safety Administration (NHTSA), Traffic Safety Facts – Young Drivers DOT HA 810, 817.)*

- *Thirty-four percent of all teen drivers and 25 percent of *female* teen drivers were speeding.

  (NHTSA and the American Driver and Traffic Safety Education Association, ADTSEA).

- *Teenagers make up just 8.7 percent of licensed drivers but account for 14.6 percent of drivers involved in fatal crashes *(NHTSA and the American Driver and Traffic Safety Education Association, ADTSEA).*

- *The fatality rate for teenagers is four times as high as the rate for drivers between twenty-five and sixty-five *(NHTSA and the American Driver and Traffic Safety Education Association, ADTSEA).*

- *Although all states and the District of Columbia have a twenty-one-year minimum drinking law, during a recent year of study, 21 percent of young drivers, fifteen to twenty years old, who were killed in crashes were intoxicated *(NHTSA and the American Driver and Traffic Safety Education Association, ADTSEA).*

- *During a recent year of study, 2,730 more unrestrained (driver/passenger) youths died in crashes than those who died wearing seat belts *(NHTSA and the American Driver and Traffic Safety Education Association, ADTSEA).*

- *States with nighttime driving restrictions or curfews for young novice drivers (Graduated Licensing Programs) report lower crash rates than all states without restrictions *(NHTSA and the American Driver and Traffic Safety Education, ADTSEA).*

- *About 15 percent of teenage drivers are involved in a reportable crash their first year of driving *(NHTSA and the American Driver and Traffic Safety Education Association, ADTSEA).*

- According to the *National Highway Traffic Safety Administration,* during one of the deadliest recent years, *8,155 drivers between fifteen and twenty years old died in motor vehicle crashes!*

If you think the above statistics are bad, please think about this; most of them were compiled *before* DWP (Driving While Phoning) and DWT (Driving while Texting) became so prominent. The following are two more recent statistics:

- A recent National Highway Traffic Safety Administration study found that drivers talking on cell phones were *30 percent* more likely to crash than a driver not engaged in mobile phone activity.

- During the same study, the National Highway Traffic Safety Administration found that distracted and inattentive driving contributed to six thousand deaths across the country that year alone.

Some adult "multitaskers" reading these statistics are probably thinking. *Yes, we need to do something about these teens talking on mobile phones and/or texting while driving.* We agree with that of course. However, we would be remiss if we did not point out that a four-thousand-pound vehicle doesn't know if you are sixteen years old or sixty years old!

Trees, ditches, fire hydrants, telephone poles, six- thousand-pound super SUVs, and trucks that are much heavier don't care how old you are either.

The statistics above are useful only if we learn from them. Please consider that they essentially represent our success rate in the field of driver education in general over the past ten years. Now, many otherwise responsible people throughout the country are also saying, "Oh by the way, it is okay to phone or text and drive too. After all, I do it, and I'm still alive!" We apologize in advance for being so blunt to legislators, state DMVs, public high school driver education programs, professional driving schools, and a few national insurance agencies that *sometimes* talk the talk but don't walk the walk. The reviews are in, and they don't lie. *We have failed miserably!*

We don't pretend to have all the answers to *all* the current deficiencies in driver education. Some of the organizations we will refer in this book have some excellent ideas about modern driver education. We have applied those principles and techniques in the classroom, in the cars, and within this book. However, we believe that we, collectively all of us, can do better. We believe we *must* do better. There is just no longer *any* acceptable excuse for not setting higher standards, achieving them, and sometimes even *exceeding* these higher standards in the field of driver education. The lives of your children and grandchildren depend on it!

As a parent or grandparent, where do you start? You can start by reading this book. One of the many reasons I decided to write this book is that I am aware that there are many related driver education books already out there. I know because I have read them. After reading the books, I became more concerned, rather than less, because it seemed that an inordinate number of them were written by parents who somehow managed to teach their teen or teens how to pass a driving test!

Based on research, observations, and our own experiences conducting thousands of hours of training, we can state the following unequivocally and without reservation: *without professional help, parents are not equipped technically, psychologically, or emotionally to teach their own children how to drive.*

If you accept that statement without taking it personally, you are on the right track for preparing your teen to drive. However, the road to developing your teen or teens to be safe, competent, confident, decisive, knowledgeable, lawful, collision-free drivers for the remainder of their natural lives will be a road filled with pot holes, blind alleys, obstacles, twists, turns, and hazards.

For example, one driver education publication, now in its *fifth edition*, was written by a parent who admitted that his teen failed the driving test the first time and had crashed during her first year of driving! This is not a glowing endorsement of the contents.

As you read this book, you should conclude that we are very, very passionate about the field of driver education. Therefore, as you have already discovered, this book was not written to be politically correct. It was written to deliver a very powerful wake-up call to parents, legislators, and those responsible for delivering driver education.

Therefore, as you read the book, you will (hopefully) realize that while I am hard on everyone, even myself, I am also an "equal opportunity disser." This means if you are a poor driver or you exhibit the behaviors of a poor driver on the road, I am going to diss you regardless of race, creed, national origin, color, age, or gender.

If you are a national driver training organization and you do things we don't agree with, I'm going to write about it in this book. Who am I to do that?

Well, you have to have a healthy sense of self-belief in order to stand up in a classroom and tell twenty FAA engineers and specialists who have been certifying systems for the previous twenty-five years how to do it *now*. Believe me; it isn't for the faint of heart. As leaders at the FAA Academy used to intone, "You better have your story straight."

While *Right Turn* wasn't written specifically to provide a flattering portrayal of all the organizations we have received training from, we will give credit where credit is due. Therefore, we will refer some outstanding driver education resource material that is already available for parents or anyone else who would like to learn more about modern driver education.

For parents in particular, if you are the parent of child, tween, or teen between the ages of ten and seventeen, this book will also help arm you with:

- The latest driver education policies, procedures, and driving techniques.

- How technology has changed driver education since you were trained to drive.

- How to determine whether your teen's high school driver education program or a private driving school is the right choice for you to make for your teen.

- How to partner with the driver education program of your choice to minimize risk, not only for your teen but also for you and other drivers on the road.

- How to become a safer driver and a better role model for your children *as they watch you drive and learn from your behaviors.*

- How to objectively asses the progress of your teen through each critical stage of development.

- How to apply performance standards developed by professional driver education instructors.

- How to recognize when your teen is ready for a more advanced phase of driving and when he/she is not yet ready for the next phase.

- How to minimize risk when your teen is in the driver's seat and *you* are in the passenger seat!

Before proceeding to the first chapter, I feel that I must touch on how the Coastal Academy for Driver Education, Training, and Safety (CADETS) was launched and how we learned so about the industry over the past eight years.

I retired from the FAA at the age of fifty-five. That may sound relatively young unless you take into account that I worked almost nonstop from age thirteen. During three of those years I served in the armed forces, during the following four years, I worked for the Department of Defense as a civilian. As previously referenced, I followed my Department of Defense positions with a twenty-nine-year Federal Aviation Administration career that was under the aviation wing of the Department of Transportation.

When I retired, I decided to take a year off to play tennis and golf. Can you blame me? There are a few places in the country where you can play tennis and golf in the winter. One of the best places is Myrtle Beach, South Carolina!

After a year of playing tennis and golf and not doing much else, a friend of mine got me a part-time job cutting greens on a golf course. The pay was just above minimum wage, but the perks (free golf on nine courses and free tennis) were terrific. Each morning I walked six miles at a very brisk pace behind a high tech lawn mower. During those brisk six-mile "strolls," my mind sometimes wandered away from the task at hand to consider doing something a little more intellectually stimulating.

One day an ad in the paper caught my eye. A nearby professional driver education company was looking for additional instructors.

I knew something about teaching by that time and had driven *most* of the previous forty plus years without crashing. I figured that made me qualified. At this point, I would like to point out that, unlike a surprising number of adults in this country, I did complete both driver education and driver training in high school. I would like to think that during all my years crisscrossing the country in dozens of different vehicles, my high school driver training helped play a part in determining that I *didn't* crash more often.

However, in the interest of full disclosure, I must be candid here; I *did* crash twice … at the age of seventeen.

I have since learned that in the driver education business, we don't call them *accidents*. We either call them *collisions,* or we call them *crashes.* In retrospect, my first incident was a crash, and my second incident was a collision. However, both the crash and the collision could have been avoided if I had received *better* trainingin high school and was knowledgeable enough to apply that training. Those two episodes, still vivid in my mind, are just two of many reasons I decided to write this book. Whether you wish to call them accidents, collisions, or crashes, almost 100 percent of them can be *avoided* if you take proper precautions.

My entry into the field of driver education began with a fairly large company operating within three states in the southeast. Their headquarters were in Charleston, South Carolina. I hadn't received any formal follow-up training in the field of driver education since high school.

I will give some credit to this driver education company that provided me the opportunity to enter the rewarding field of driver education. They required me to relearn to drive cars more safely than I had been driving them for several years. They also refreshed all the training I had received in high school. Boy, did I need that, and I didn't even know it! It turns out that over the years, I had forgotten much of what I had learned in driver education years before. In addition, I quickly discovered that new automobile technology had changed several driver education and driver training techniques that I had learned years before too.

During the period I was in their employ, I attended classroom training presented by two different instructors (same material presented at different times). I requested a second opportunity to attend their eight-hour classroom training in order to observe their best classroom instructor.

The first instructor that I had observed admitted to me that she had never once conducted a single Behind- the-Wheel lesson (abbreviated as BTW for the remainder of this book) in an automobile! I liked her very much as a classroom instructor, considering the material she covered. However, it was the material that she *didn't* cover that troubled me. If a driver education instructor has never trained a real beginning driver BTW, that instructor can't possibly have a complete understanding of all the challenges incurred while teaching an actual beginning driver in a training car.

Professional driving instructors encounter a significant variety of students with differing entry levels, manual dexterity, and far different initial driving capabilities. An experienced instructor can identify many deficiencies within the first ten minutes in the car with a new student.

While teaching in the cars, I quickly determined that I needed to drive using the techniques in which I had been retrained 100 percent of the time, not just when I was teaching. Over time, I came to realize that this was for my own safety, the safety of my passengers, the safety of other drivers on the road, and in order to develop these techniques into habits on display for my passengers and students at all times. While teaching, I eventually realized that the field of driver education is dynamic, meaning it must evolve regularly in order to keep up with new technology and new techniques.

I'm certain my background in aviation safety for the Department of Defense and the Department of Transportation heavily influenced my desire to promote the very best driver education policies, procedures, and techniques that I was able to determine were available in this country. This goal was and still is in the interest of *public safety,* not only for all new driver education students, regardless of age, but also for all other drivers on the road.

One day I happened to call a very good friend and former FAA coworker by the name of John Kurywchak. He and I were each managers at the Southern California TRACON in San Diego during the mid-1990s. Later when I obtained my positions at FAA HQ in Washington DC, he was also promoted into similar positions as an air traffic control manager in the Western Pacific Region. Still later, he was promoted again and became the manager at Oakland California's Air Traffic Control Tower.

During that phone call, I casually mentioned to him that I was thinking of opening a new professional driving school in Myrtle Beach, South Carolina. Of course he wanted to know all the reasons I wanted to do such a crazy thing. So I told him. I'm paraphrasing here just a bit. I answered, "Because I can not only do it better, I can do it a lot better!"

In so many words—air traffic controllers can be quite loquacious so I am paraphrasing here too—he said, "Would you like a partner?" I had forgotten that air traffic controllers can retire at age fifty as long as they have served for over twenty years in the agency.

Prior to our telephone conversation, John wasn't convinced he was going to retire when he reached eligibility that following January, but he changed his mind when he thought about teaching driver education with me.

This may be difficult to explain. (Perhaps John can explain it far better than I.) However, those of us who have served in safety, training, coaching, and mentoring are drawn toward doing something productive with all the training and experience we have acquired. Someone once asked Ringo Starr (long after he could sit in his castle all day without moving a finger) why he still played drums in his All Starr Band. He answered, "Because that's what I do. I'm a drummer."

All that training and experience is just sitting there in our heads. We have to do something with it.

The Coastal Academy for Driver Education, Training, and Safety Inc. (CADETS) was launched in the fall of 2006. The name popped into my head at 4:00 a.m. one morning. Of course, if you have served in the Department of Defense for six years and served within the Department of Transportation for twenty-nine years, you just know the title of your new driving academy *has* to be an acronym, and it *has* to make sense on some level.

Before we opened CADETS, I attended an additional forty hours of training conducted by a different driver education company than the company that had first employed me. The name of that company was and still is Cruise Control. They are located in Summerville, South Carolina, a suburb of Charleston.

The lead driving instructor took me out behind the wheel again and re- verified that I possessed all the skills necessary to teach classroom and BTW driver training.

We also compared training philosophies, procedures, and techniques. We found that we had a great deal in common. He gave me several good teaching tips that I was able to incorporate into the CADETS training program later.

During the week in Summerville, I had the opportunity to meet at length with the Cruise Control office manager.

I must have asked him a thousand questions about driver education, training administration, DMV documentation requirements, budget tracking, marketing, and many other topics related to the business. During the course of that week's training, I also had the opportunity to review all their classroom material. I took advantage of this opportunity by discussing the content of this material at length with the lead instructor.

After I completed this forty-hour course, I was required to travel to Columbia, South Carolina (about two hundred miles from Myrtle Beach) to take a written examination conducted at the state Department of Motor Vehicles. I am perplexed that the state *does not require prospective professional driving instructors to complete a basic DMV driving test.*

In fact, when I entered the state, I was re-licensed for regular driving. I was not required to complete a driving test at that time either. This might not be too shocking, unless you consider that my driver's license was stamped as being valid *for the next ten years!* I completed the fifty-question written test at the state DMV. Although I missed only one question, I remember thinking that it was a poorly written test.

Years earlier while attending FAA Academy Instructional Testing as an academy instructor, I had learned that well-written multiple-choice examinations may be developed to be as "difficult" or as "easy" as knowledgeable authors wish them to be. However, bedded in the distracters should be *one and only one correct answer* for each well-written multiple-choice question. All other distracters should be certifiably false, unless defined otherwise in the stem of the question. No examination is ever deemed to be perfect. However, I'm afraid I must state here that the South Carolina Department of Motor Vehicles examinations for prospective professional instructors revealed some rather obvious deficiencies in the evaluation process.

After I received my teaching certificate, I was certified to teach driver education to other students but not certified to teach or train other prospective instructors … yet. The following year during 2007, **CADETS Inc.** developed a forty-hour classroom and

BTW curriculum that was approved by the state Department of Motor Vehicles.

The approval of our forty-hour professional driving instructor curriculum was significant for several reasons. First, very few state public or private driver education schools acquire this certification in any state.

Second, it meant that we could not only train our own instructors, but we could train any *other* potential driving instructor within the state that required a teaching certification. Finally, prospective commercial drivers who did not require job centered training for a specific CDL certification could receive professional training from CADETS Inc.

Approved state certification for professional training within the state of South Carolina may not seem like a very big deal outside of the state of South Carolina, unless you consider the sources of our classroom and BTW training reference resource material. All of our classroom training material (except our state DMV reference manual) did not originate in the state of South Carolina. They were developed in other states and were very carefully selected. These special training DVDs and other reference materials were developed in Missouri (my home state), Texas, and Florida.

Fortunately, the South Carolina Department Of Motor Vehicles Manual is an outstanding, well-written manual with excellent illustrations. We handed this manual out as *the* primary reference manual our students were instructed to read after every class. Students should have read it *before* class, but we usually determined in the first hour of instruction in the classroom that most had not read it, or they didn't understand what was in it.

All CADETS-trained instructors received in excess of eighteen hours of instruction behind the wheel in addition to all their required classroom training. In addition, at minimum, all CADETS instructors received one-on- one instruction on virtually every element of our BTW performance grid from the lead driving instructor. They were also required to observe a fully certified driver education *trainer* (not just another regular driving instructor) and conduct one or more actual BTW driving lessons for real students in the car.

Each instructor was also *observed* teaching elements of the CADETS BTW performance grid in the car. Finally, they received verbal and written critiques after each classroom and/or BTW training session. We will admit that we provided much more than forty total hours of instruction to our own CADETS instructors. Every instructor who was issued a CADETS graduation certificate received at least forty hours of quality instruction … or more.

The CADETS BTW performance grids are provided for your reference in Appendices No. 1 through No.4.

At CADETS, our instructors only used the full performance grid provided in Appendix No. 4. For the purposes of this book, we decided to include more user friendly versions of the grids for parents and grandparents in Appendices No. 1 through No. 3.

These versions will provide you with more room for notes and observations. However, these performance grids come with a caveat.

Please do not write notes or fill out the grids while your teen or adult student is driving! When a new driver is driving, that driver requires your undivided attention at all times. Complete these grids while you are parked or complete them within one hour of completion of practice. Otherwise, you will be surprised about how much you will forget about the decision making and performance of the driver.

In 2007, the other principal owner of CADETS convinced John and me that she should attend AAA's forty-hour "Driver Improvement" course in Charlotte, North Carolina, *before* we did. She wished to teach this course in the classroom. This was a "suggestion" that neither John nor I could find a graceful way of refusing. So Chief Financial Officer, Office Manager and Owner in Charge Elizabeth Templeton attended the coveted AAA training before we did.

After successfully completing AAA's training, Beth was certified to teach AAA's four-point reduction training (labeled differently in each state), fleet training, and she was also certified to teach mature driver refresher training. Beth is a first-rate public speaker and was exceptional at teaching AAA's "Driver Improvement" syllabus.

After a while, I wasn't sure that I was the lead driving instructor in my own domain (our family vehicles). Too much knowledge is dangerous when you are married to the one who has it. Therefore, in addition to the training I had already completed, I also completed AAA's forty-hour course the following year. This training helped enhance my driver education teaching skills, especially while teaching challenging adult students, many of whom are foreigners.

As already noted, John Kurywchak is a very loquacious, well-educated former air traffic controller. Air traffic controllers are used to telling other people where to go and what to do. Most of the people they tell what to do are pilots of big commercial aircraft. John fit right into the driver education and training program from day one.

I will provide an overview of our classroom training in a later chapter. However, I will acknowledge here that *both* John and Beth are better classroom instructors than I am.

Anyway, I do my best with the personality, or lack thereof, that I am in possession of. You have to dance with the guy that brought you in. Therefore, the kids had to deal with me, warts and all! Sometimes they got sick of me after four hours or even earlier. Sometimes they had to endure me after all eight hours in the early days. When I got home, I didn't want to see anybody; I didn't want to talk to anybody. I didn't even want to smell anybody.

Before proceeding further, I would like to point out that this book isn't only for parents of tweens and teens. For example, after we opened CADETS, John and I attended AARP's eight-hour refresher Driver Education course for seniors. John didn't even qualify (at that time) for the AARP discount, but he sat in there for eight hours with me anyway. We wanted to observe and dissect their classroom syllabus, learn more about physical and mental changes that evolve in seniors as we age, how they presented their material, and how current driver education concepts might be adapted and applied for senior drivers.

This book will also assist spouses or friends of adults just learning to drive. Some adults may find the following statement difficult to believe, but it is nevertheless true: *Far more time, effort, and BTW training is required to teach an adult-beginning driver to drive an automobile than is required for the average fifteen-year-old student!*

One contributing factor to these phenomena is that many of the adults we trained were and are *legal* immigrants. Think about the following please: If an immigrant actually goes through the *legal immigration* process properly and strives to obtain a *legal driver's license,* there must or, at least, *should* be an opportunity for providing quality training for these immigrants. At CADETS, we still believe that America is the land of opportunity. Therefore, we believe that we should facilitate the legal assimilation of legal immigrants on our road and highway system to the best of our ability.

After having successfully migrated to the USA, a significant number of our adult students were either learning to drive the first time or trying to figure out how to navigate through our complex American road and highway system soon after arriving. In addition, most of them are either applying English for the first time or learning English as a second language and attempting to *interpret* our complex road and highway system *while learning to speak and/or read English too.*

Many American teens take their rather limited knowledge (in most cases) of America's road and highway system for granted.

The average adult foreign student does not even possess the knowledge of the basic rules of the road that an average fifteen-year-old American teen possesses. This limited initial knowledge and lack of understanding exists *after* both categories of student have generally been behind the wheel but *before* either category of student has entered formal driver education curricula.

While training immigrant adult students, there are often not only physical issues to deal with but driver education language barriers, cultural differences, and "sign interpretation confusion factors" that influence the training process. Sometimes initial "adventures" in the car are not pretty. That's why we take baby steps.

As of this writing, we have conducted over six thousand hours of behind- the-wheel training. During all this training, we have not incurred a single collision, crash, fender bender, bump, scrape, dent, or scratch inflicted upon the body of a CADETS training car. We have had a few scratches inflicted upon our tire "beauty" rims while students were *attempting* to parallel park the first time. However, after our training is applied, this minor deficiency is corrected too.

Yes, we have been fortunate, and we recognize that we have been so. We also recognize that our auto and personal damage avoidance record could end tomorrow. However, in later chapters, we will explain how we take extraordinary measures when teaching BTW in order to *minimize risk.* Our pristine safety record was not achieved because of blind luck! Frankly, we believe that luck has nothing whatsoever to do with it.

We minimize risk, not only while teaching beginning teen drivers but also any driver, regardless of age. The minimization of risk has everything to do with our safety record.

The American Automobile Association (AAA)'s advanced Driver Improvement Training teaches us that risk is always present, that perceived risk is different than actual risk, that risk is shared, and that risk can be altered. The only sure way to completely eliminate risk for your teen or for anyone else driving or riding in an automobile is to never allow them to drive or ride in an automobile again. In today's world, at least in America, this is impractical, if not impossible.

Some parents believe that waiting until their teen reaches an age (usually seventeen or eighteen in most states) when driver education is no longer required is a *better* choice than enrolling them in driver education as a fifteen- or sixteen-year-old. *Later in the book, we will also explain why this is a very poor choice too ... for a number of reasons.*

The statistics listed earlier indicate very convincingly that the driver education industry requires a fresh look. Some very prominent organizations are taking steps to improve and/or standardize driver education throughout the country. A few of organizations we have already referenced are the National Highway Traffic Safety Administration, the American Driver and Traffic Safety Education Association, and the American Automobile Association. We salute them and applaud them for their efforts.

We must also point out that the techniques and procedures required to *teach a beginning driver to drive an automobile the very first time are far different than those required to train an experienced driver how to drive more safely.* We believe that national insurance organizations should balance their training programs so that far more time and effort is devoted to developing and improving their existing teen driver education programs to match or exceed their adult driver improvement programs.

There is another contributing factor to the poor record of teen driving performance over the past ten years. Many parents have taken on more of the driver education responsibility as they have increasingly become more disappointed in or disillusioned with public driver education.

We must point out that the current common practice of parents teaching their own teens to drive is *not* the answer, not only for emotional and psychological reasons but also for critical technical considerations. The facts are that less than 50 percent of parents and/or grandparents have received formal driver education training. Less than 1 percent has received any formal "train the trainer" driver education training experience. Few possess a written performance standard or would know where to obtain one (not available from your local DMV either).

Parents who have only trained a few of their own children cannot possibly differentiate between teaching a "very good" driver education student and training a "very poor" driver education student.

Fewer yet have any means to determine whether a loved one falls into one end of the training spectrum, the middle of the spectrum, or the opposite end of the spectrum in relative terms in aptitude and capabilities.

We know that parents are concerned about their children's driver education. We hear about it every day. But *how* are you going to develop your own knowledge so that you can effectively determine which driver education program to choose for your children? As a licensed adult driver, *how* are you going to enhance your own skills so that you may assist your teen's driver education instructor in (potentially) *the most important training your teen will receive during these all important years?*

Lest you conclude that this book is for parents of teens in one state or about driver education as it is delivered in one state, let us assure you that it is not. As previously referenced, three of the training DVDs we utilize in the classroom were developed in *Houston Texas, Saint Louis, Missouri, and Heathrow Florida.* Two excellent reference textbooks that were written primarily for new drivers are *License to Drive* and *Today's Handbook Plus.* AAA's *Driver Improvement* textbook was developed primarily for those who have demonstrated in the car that they require refresher training.

Each of these textbooks was authored by cadres of North American driver education and training experts representing dozens of training organizations. I have read each of them more than once, and I have earnestly attempted to apply their techniques. In essence, our formative driver education skills were acquired throughout this terrific *country*, not entirely within any single state. *Right Turn* was written to supplement all this terrific material, not replace it. In addition, as previously referenced, *Right Turn* is a guidebook for parents and grandparents who otherwise may not even be aware that the textbooks exist, much less how to acquire them. This book can help with that too.

The unsatisfactory report card for the application of existing driver education teaching policies, procedures, and practices clearly documents that whatever we have been doing isn't working. *In our opinion, we have nowhere to go but up!*

Apply the material contained in this book, and you will become a safer driver and a better role model, regardless of whether your passengers happen to be your own children or someone else that you treasure, including yourself!

*Statistical references courtesy of the American Automobile Association, the American Driver and Traffic Safety Education Association, and the National Highway Traffic Safety Administration.

The author, Mike Wayne Templeton, was the lead driving instructor for the Coastal Academy for Driver Education, Training, and Safety (CADETS). He holds a certification in advanced instructional methods in the field of driver education and is certified to train professional driving instructors and other professional commercial drivers

CHAPTER 1

How to Select a Driver Education Program for Your Teen

During recent years, a study conducted by Johns Hopkins University for the National Highway Traffic Safety Administration found that states that have comprehensive Graduated Licensing Programs (GDL) programs have (on average) a 20 percent reduction in fatal crashes involving sixteen-year- old drivers. A comprehensive GDL program includes at least five of the following components:

- A minimum age of fifteen for obtaining a learners permit.

- A waiting period after obtaining a permit of at least three months before applying for a provisional or "day" license.

- A requirement to attend driver education (classroom) and driver training (behind the-wheel).

- A minimum of thirty hours of "supervised" driving.

- A minimum age of at least fifteen and a half for obtaining a provisional or "day" state license.

- A minimum age of seventeen for full licensing.

- Nighttime driving restrictions.

- Restrictions on the numbers and ages of passengers.

The word *supervised* above is in quotations that were added by the author of this book, not the NHTSA. The reason for this is that "supervised" driving is not defined in every state in exactly the same way. In fact, the rules for each state's GDL program will vary from state to state. However, forty-seven of the fifty states, excluding Arkansas, Kansas, and North Dakota, have some or most of the elements of the GDL requirements described above. Some of the age minimums also vary from state to state. Please obtain a copy of your state's driver education manual for the specific GDL requirements in your state.

While interacting with our teen students and their parents, we have also gained an understanding of several harsh realities.

This knowledge has convinced us that it is well past time for some tough love for parents too. The following are just ten of many examples that could have been chosen to illuminate a disturbing trend:

- Students who manage to pass the permit test sometimes inform us that their parents never required them to read the DMV manual at all. This reinforces teens' common misconception that the ability to stumble through an easy written test and pass also indicates that they are ready to drive a car.

- Initially, over 80 percent of the students we question in the classroom do not know the answers to the very basic rules of the road questions that we pose.

- Parents regularly misinform their teens about the basic rules of the road.

- Many parents today are not aware that most professional driving schools *no longer* train their students to place their hands on the wheel at ten and two during forward steering.

- Parents rarely coach their teens how to turn the wheel properly.

- Many parents (and most grandparents) are not aware that air bags, ABS brakes, and even power steering have changed a number of teaching/training techniques now employed in driver education.

- Most driving schools calculate proper following distance differently today than the guidance provided by driver education instructors twenty years ago.

- Parents often assume that their preteens are not watching them when they drive. They are! In addition, as preteens progress into their teen years, they begin to comprehend when one parent is a "good" driver and when another parent is a "poor" driver.

- Parents often conclude that they can successfully "sell" their teens on the proper techniques for driving while demonstrating far different behaviors while driving their own family vehicle.

- Parents are not trained to provide professional instruction. Therefore, despite their years of driving experience, they are not equipped to objectively assess the progress of their own children.

In our state, as in many states, eight hours of classroom training is required, and only a *minimum* of six hours of professional driving instruction is required. A *minimum* of another forty hours of supervised training must be conducted by the parent or guardian, and it must be documented on the same form where we document our training.

Driver education begins with knowledge and eventually progresses to applying that knowledge in a comprehensive Behind-the-Wheel (BTW) driver training program. Our experience with thousands of teens and parents has convinced us that (currently) the most beneficial BTW training teens receive is from professional instructors. However, because of the length of the permit period, we are only able to apply that training personally during a fraction of the entire permit period. As previously referred, we train most new students BTW for only six hours. Meanwhile during the entire six- month permit period, your teen may drive with you from a minimum of forty hours to hundreds of hours.

In this state, a teen who is enrolled in school can obtain a driving permit at the age of fifteen. It must be held for a minimum of six months, and the teen may obtain a provisional license under our GDL guidelines at the age of fifteen and a half. Of course we didn't make these laws. However, we have concluded that South Carolina has a better than average GDL program. South Carolina has many outstanding driver education instructors, boasts an excellent Department of Motor Vehicles manual, and trains/employs examiners who care about a new driver's health and well- being.

Some driver education publications (and many parents) insist that a fifteen-year-old is too young to learn to drive. After having successfully trained many fifteen- and sixteen-year-old drivers, we respectfully disagree. We have determined many times over that a fifteen-year-old who is emotionally ready can be trained to operate an automobile safely and efficiently. What they don't have is something that any new driver of any age does not have—*experience.* We also acknowledge that all fifteen-year- olds are not automatically emotionally and psychologically ready to drive. Parents should make that determination before they enroll their teens in driver education, not during and not after.

In most states, including South Carolina, a teen can eventually test for a driver's license *without the benefit of having attended driver education at all.* In South Carolina, the age is seventeen.

Remarkably, a number of parents throughout the country do not enroll their teens in any driver education program believing that the benefit of waiting until the teen is older offsets the lack of formal training. This could (potentially) become a deadly miscalculation. There are several possible consequences and a few very definite outcomes for teens who *do not* attend driver education and for the parents who are responsible for them.

As previously noted, there is little difference in the technical aspects of training a fifteen-year-old, sixteen- year-old, or seventeen-year-old to drive. We will readily admit that there may be differences in the maturity level between a fifteen-year-old and a twenty-year-old.

However, the physical difference in training a fifteen-year-old novice to drive and training an adult of any age who has never driven also has provided us with insight that we have experienced many times over. Each year after age fifteen or sixteen, it becomes progressively more challenging to train the beginning driver. This may be due primarily to the influence of peers.

For example, when your teen enters the teen years, he/she is regularly riding to/from a multitude of destinations with *someone else* behind the wheel. To make matters worse, many of these other drivers are teens who *have not* been trained to drive properly. In addition, your teen may (sometimes) be driven to locations that you are personally unfamiliar with or to a location that you may not be aware exists at all.

Once your teen receives this valuable training and has demonstrated the proficiency that comes with it, have your teen become their friends' *driver* of choice whenever possible. Recognizing that you are not always going to be able to control this, your teen will be far safer by routinely volunteering to drive rather than riding along helplessly with those who have not been trained properly. In addition, your teen can apply peer pressure in a positive way (by demonstrating how to drive safely) rather than responding to peer pressure in a negative way (learning from dangerous drivers).

There are other consequences for avoiding professional driver education. For example, most insurance companies generally do not consider teens and young adults to have advanced past the "high risk" age group until they reach age twenty-four or twenty-five.

Most reputable insurance companies also provide a discount when assessing *your* insurance adjustment for your teen and later for the young adult.

If driver education is not completed, the additional annual premiums that must be paid between fifteen/sixteen and twenty-four/twenty-five usually far exceed the single fee of obtaining driver education for your teen. Of course the most severe consequences of your teen not completing driver education increase in risking collisions of any type. Dings, dents, scrapes, and crunches can be very costly and time consuming to have repaired. Collisions and crashes into other vehicles or immovable object are very costly and may be life altering.

Suppose it's time to help your son or daughter pick out his or her first car. Of course, this may become a reality within a few years of your teen completing driver education. What are some of the factors you would take into consideration while shopping for the car? Let's consider some of the possibilities you might consider:

Reliability	Dependability	Size
Safety	Age	Aesthetics
Economy	Miles	Price/Financing
Insurance Rates	Versatility	Options

These aren't all the considerations of course. In addition, certain decision- making factors may be weighted more heavily by you, and a different set of factors will often influence your teen. In any case, lets' say you and your teen have narrowed the final selection down to two short lists. Let's say your teen's "A list" cars meet or exceed the criteria in ten of the above categories. The cars in listed in your teens "B list" meet the criteria in less than half of the categories but cost a few hundred dollars less.

Would you select a car from your B list? If not, why would you select a driver education program for your teen without regard to the quality of the service? Some parents may not be aware that your local high school driver education program is not your only choice.

In addition, the most obvious local choice may not necessarily be the best choice for you or your teen. That said, the first professional driving school that you contact may not be your best choice either.

However, in order to make a sound choice, you need selection criteria. Most parents are well aware that all or most of the factors above will be taken into account when helping your teen pick out that first car. But what are the criteria you use in selecting a driving school? In addition, isn't the selection of your teen's driver education at least as important as the selection of the car he/she will be driving?

Think about it this way: your teen may keep the car for a couple of years and then trade it in. However, proper training helps substitute for experience or lack thereof, especially when that training is reinforced over and over again. The fact is that selecting the very best driver education program for your teen may be among the most important decisions you will ever make for your son or daughter!

In later chapters, we are going to provide details about the specific topics that may be included in an outstanding driver education classroom syllabus. We will also provide details about an outstanding behind- the-wheel training program. In this chapter, we will explain how to avoid figurative "lemons" and "clunkers."

Many high school driver education and professional driver education programs have flaws. Some of them are very serious. You can't very well avoid them if you remain unaware of what to look for. For a start, we suggest that you become thoroughly informed about the driver education options in your area. If you live in a rural area and do not have direct local access to driver education, find out where the nearest professional school is and determine if you can find a way to get your son or daughter there.

In our opinion, a flawed driver education program is still superior to no driver education program at all. Remember, by following the training practices and principles outlined later in this book, you can effectively supplement a flawed driver education program.

You may be wondering how we determined that there are flawed driver education programs out there. We obtained and verified this information in a variety of different ways.

In addition to becoming trained and certified as professional driving instructors, the principal owners of CADETS attended and/ or monitored several other driver education programs that we were not required to complete. For example, at one point, I attended a full classroom presentation that was conducted by a coach from a local high school. He also worked part time for a local professional driving school.

In effect, this training should have matched or exceeded any other training locally available. I was very disappointed in the presentation. First, the training emphasized crash videos instead of teaching. Second, the videos were at least ten years old. Third, the "eight-hour" classroom day was terminated abruptly after about 5.5 hours of non-training. In addition, the training was not nearly interactive as it could have been or should have been. I expected much more from a professional public and private educator.

Another method we used to learn about local high school and professional driving school practices was to simply listen to our students when they chose to talk about them. A common misconception is that teens do not care where, when, or how they are trained to drive a car. Nothing could be further from the truth. They know a quality training program when they see one. In addition, they pay very close attention to where their friends are being trained and *how* well they are being trained. While it is true that some fifteen- or sixteen- year-old teens believe they are immortal, most of them are pragmatic enough to know that serious mistakes behind the wheel can lead to serious consequences.

Your teen, all teens, deserve the very best driver education program available within a reasonable commuting distance.

The following chapters will provide a fair amount of detail about quality driver education, but this book is not intended to *substitute* for driver education. The chapters were written in order to help you prepare for one of the most important roles you will undertake as a parent. Before you read the chapters concerning classroom and BTW training that we *know* has been successful, we wish to identify some of the more common public and/or private driver education deficiencies that you should take measures to avoid.

Common Classroom Deficiencies

Issue

The classroom program does not have a written syllabus.

Analysis:

If the school does not produce a written syllabus, you have no way of knowing what topics they intend to teach or how they intend to teach those topics.

Issue

The school regularly does not meet the state requirement for the *minimum* number of hours of classroom training required by your state.

Analysis

There are no shortcuts in driver education, at least there shouldn't be. We have had instructors in other schools tell us that they "replace" some of state required classroom training with training in the car. Training in the car can and should reinforce classroom training, but *it is not a substitute for classroom training*. Later in the book, we will explain in more detail why classroom training cannot be substituted for behind-the-wheel training, and behind-the-wheel training cannot be substituted for classroom training.

Issue

The classroom training reference material and/or training videos are older and some of the material is obsolete.

Analysis

Any driver education training videos over ten years old should have been updated within the last five years. In addition, you should *verify* that the contents of the training videos reinforce the contents of the current edition of your state Department of Motor Vehicle manual.

Issue

The "training" program primarily screens crash videos.

Analysis

We are aware that some high schools screen more crash videos than teaching videos. Crash videos lose their impact after you have watched hour after hour of them. Moreover, what good are they after they have already scared the wits out of a beginning driver who is just trying to figure out how to get out of the parking lot? The worst sin here is that for every moment a school is screening a crash video, they could be screening an outstanding teaching video. In other words, instead of teaching teens what *not to do*, let's teach them what *to do* so that they can avoid crashes in the first place.

Issue

Instructors turn on a video and then disappear.

Analysis

In our opinion, a good training video provides the catalyst for interactive training. Each segment (usually no more than five to ten minutes) must be discussed with the students, and each segment must be discussed in great detail. Outstanding training video segments provide the fuel for dozens and hundreds of interactive questions. This can only happen if your teen's driver education instructor is thoroughly engaged at all times. Teens cannot teach themselves this material. Even if they attempt to do so, our experience has repeatedly verified that they will make incorrect assumptions.

When instructors are not in the classroom, students doze, daydream, turn their phones on, text message, flirt, play, and generally find almost anything to do other than do what they are supposed to be doing. Good instructors do not leave their students unattended.

Issue

The classroom material either does not include interactive quizzes and/or tests or they are poorly written.

Analysis

At minimum, the classroom training should repeatedly hammer home all the key concepts included in your state's DMV manual and much more.

Many students do not read the DMV manual and stumble through their permit test anyway.

This gives them a false sense of security in believing that if they are smart enough, they can simply use common sense to drive safely. Potentially, this could be a fatal error in judgment.

When students are asked challenging rules-of-the road questions in class, they quickly learn that common sense helps. However, they also quickly learn that common sense alone will not enable them to correctly answer all questions they are posed. They also begin to realize that, without a concerted effort to learn basic driving concepts, their ability to drive safely will be severely compromised.

When students learn they will be tested, they pay closer attention. This is a basic tenet of any type of training. Tests do not necessarily need to be developed with semi-plausible incorrect distracters (incorrect answers) such that that test results produce regular, unnecessary failures. Instead, they should be developed in such a way as to reinforce learning. Many of these students initially lack confidence about a subject they know little about, namely driving. They need to know early on that if they pay attention, they will not only excel in class and during their permit tests, but they will also be better, safer drivers.

Issue

The driver education program either authorizes or allows the instructor to terminate the class or classes early.

Analysis

This is a common problem. *You* (the parent) can help stop it!

Each state has different classroom training requirements, but states that require driver education also require a specific number of hours of classroom training. In South Carolina, that number is eight hours. Eight hours of potentially life-saving information cannot be crammed into a six- hour day.

Make certain that your driver education school of choice does not short change your son or daughter with this vital training. Insist that if the school of your choice has been contracted to provide eight hours of classroom training, that they provide eight hours of classroom training. This excludes lunch.

Common Behind-the-Wheel (BTW) Deficiencies

Issue

The training cars are not safe and reliable.

Analysis

Most state certified driving schools must have their cars inspected each year, but the standards are often very liberal. We have seen training cars much older than five years old or with many more than one hundred thousand miles. Some of the training cars employed are not really the best cars for teaching driver training. For example, we wouldn't recommend selecting a school that trains students in SUVs, sports cars, Volkswagen bugs, pickup trucks, or vans.

Some of the deficiencies of these cars are obvious, but other deficiencies may not be as obvious to anyone other than a professional driving instructor. For example, sports utility vehicles (SUVs) may be suitable for experienced adult drivers to drive (although that theory is often disproven by many adult drivers). However, teens very often understeer or oversteer any vehicle when first learning to drive. They must be repeatedly coached to correct this deficiency. A top heavy SUV is not the car you want your teen wheeling around an expressway ramp the first time in their life they enter it!

Our training cars have received five-star ratings from the National Highway Traffic Safety Administration. We hesitate to name the manufacturer and model of the cars we employ only because there are many cars from most manufacturers that are suitable for driver education. This brings us to another common practice. Some schools advertise that they train with one car and then substitute a different car for the actual training.

We suggest that you check to see that your teen's training car:

- Has all the safety features required by the state installed. This means a heavy-duty brake on the passenger side and a rearview mirror on the passenger side of the windshield. Driver Training signs should be visible on the sides and the rear of the car, in the unlikely event that other drivers will actually respond appropriately to them.

- Has less than fifty thousand miles or a pristine safety record.

- Is carrying current insurance and   registration documents.

- Has passed the state's driver education safety inspection within the preceding twelve months.

- Does not have any obvious physical deficiencies (balding tires, underinflated tires or overinflated tires).

Issue

Multiple students are receiving "training" in the car at the same time.

Analysis

We are well aware that most high school driver education schools are required to carry more than one student in the car while another student is driving. This is one of the most glaring deficiencies in high school driver education programs. The following are some of the disadvantages of this practice:

- One student receives far more BTW training at the expense of another.

- The BTW log may reflect that a student was driving when in fact the student was merely observing.

- We do not believe that students learn to drive a vehicle properly by observing another inexperienced teen drive.

- Some students are very self-conscious learning to drive with a classmate watching. This is completely understandable because classmates often try to identify any type of real or imagined "learning disability" to ridicule.

- Drivers who have had their permits for six months or longer often believe they are far better drivers than they really are. During early training with a professional, they are usually willing to accept the reality that they are not really as accomplished as they thought they were but are not as likely to respond favorably with peers in the car.

- Drivers who are real beginners are often very timid and frightened by the very prospect of moving the car at five miles per hour in a parking lot! These teens do not want the raw emotions they convey discussed or ridiculed in a high school hallway.

- Most graduated licensing programs limit the number of passengers in a car for good reason. The old refrain that "two's company, but three's a crowd" is true for a training car too. The reason is that deadly word: *distractions*.

- Some instructors require one student to drive while they are preoccupied with something else.

A common practice in high school driver education is to require one student to drive while the instructor is reading a map or GPS and searching for the home address (for pick up) of another. The following truth has been proven to us time and time again: A professional driving instructor must focus 100 percent of his/her undivided attention on the efforts of a beginning driver at all times.

- Additional teen passengers may intentionally or unintentionally distract a driving instructor in the same manner as they distract a student driver.

Issue

Because of severe budget restrictions of the public or private school, the BTW training is restricted to a ten- mile radius around the high school or less.

Analysis

Our BTW Performance Grids are discussed in detail in chapters 5 to 7. The activities listed require about one hundred total miles of actual driving *by each student*. Few public driving schools require that much individual (non-observational) driving. Moreover, the public and private driving schools in your local commuting area may not require that a minimum number of miles be driven by each student and/or or set a performance standard beyond the minimum required to pass a driving test.

The bottom line is that you need to find out *how, when, and where* your teen is going to receive his/her driver education and how it is going to be *documented*. At this time, you need to make a decision. Are you willing to accept the minimum standard for your son or daughter to learn to drive a car?

CHAPTER 2

How to Develop Your Knowledge And Skill

According a recent New York Times Almanac of Record, about *four million teens* become eligible to drive every year. We can disagree about when a preteen or teen actually begins to pay attention to how others drive. However, you can *ensure* that your preteen begins to watch *you* drive and that he/she begins to comprehend the requirements involved in the safe operation of a three-thousand-plus-pound vehicle by explaining *what* you are doing and *why* you are doing it. More importantly, for your safety and the safety of your passengers, you should begin demonstrating safe driving practices at all times *today!* This book will provide you with specific BTW performance standards that you are encouraged to refer to while your teen drives with you during the entire permit period.

When I am introduced to new friends and acquaintances and they discover that I teach driver education and training to beginning drivers, I am regularly asked the same question: "Aren't you scared to death out there on the road attempting to teach teens to drive?" The answer I always provide is: "The drivers that scare me the most are not my students."

Obviously, the issue here isn't that parents do not care about their teens' driver education. Parents know what they know, and they very often know what they don't know and admit it to us. However, some parents remain painfully unaware of what they don't know about driver education and do not take an active role in their teen's preparation and progress.

When a teen enters a pro-driver education car for the first time, responsible, experienced instructors know that they *must assume that each new student has no driving skills whatsoever.* Any pro-driving instructor also should verify every new student has *retained* some basic knowledge of the rules of the road that should have been learned in the classroom.

During our behind-the-wheel program, we quiz students for about fifteen minutes before each and every driving lesson while the car remains parked in the parking lot!

If the new student does not answer the questions correctly, we explain the rule or rules, and then we ask the same questions again later in the lesson to verify that the student knows the answers.

At CADETS, if we believe a student is confused or foggy on the rules of the road, we will continue to ask until we receive the answer we are looking for. Please remember this: if a student answers a question incorrectly while the car is parked, the student could potentially make exactly the same error in judgment while the car is moving!

We also demonstrate how we wish for the new student to drive while driving to the initial training locations. We believe that is very instructive for a new student to observe how a professional driving instructor operates a training car. For example, many new students are amazed at how effortless it appears for a car to be turned around a corner, especially when they attempt to execute the same turn at very low rates of speed. It isn't about speed; it's about control.

This is one of many reasons that we strongly encourage parents to initiate the development of your teen's driver education knowledge during the early preteen years. In order for early the coaching and mentoring to be effective, it should be entirely consistent with the training and coaching of the professional driver education instructors who will follow. Otherwise, the credibility of all those involved in your teen's training suffers.

Perhaps we are very fortunate that we teach driver education in South Carolina. The overwhelming majority of our students are polite, respectful, and surprisingly receptive to our training. Most of them are very eager to learn to drive properly. However, we will acknowledge that many new drivers, not just teens, place a bit too much emphasis on passing the driving test and not enough on safety practices until repeatedly required to do so.

No, it isn't our own student drivers that trouble us the most. As we are riding along semi-helplessly in the passenger seat, carefully monitoring our fifteen- and sixteen-year-old students, the following are some examples of what we see every day. Sometimes we see each of the following during the same lesson:

- Drivers who sincerely believe they can talk on a cell phone and operate a three-thousand- plus-pound machine at the same time. Please believe us when we tell you that you simply cannot drive properly when you are calling, answering, or texting, no matter how well you believe you can multitask.

- Drivers who don't know any "right of way" rules at four-way stops.

- Drivers who do not signal their intentions before turning into your path.

- Drivers who demonstrate their complete lack of understanding of safe following distances by tailgating unmercifully, especially those on cell phones.

- Drivers who run stale yellow lights and then end up in the intersection as the light turns red.

- Drivers who cut diagonally across parking lots at a high rate of speed oblivious to other drivers who are attempting to drive and park safely.

- Drivers departing parking spaces without properly clearing the roadway.

- Drivers demonstrating the common misperception that the "fast lane" was created as an American version of the autobahn with no speed limits.

- Drivers who merge at either ten miles per hour slower than the other drivers they are attempting to merge with or at least ten miles per hour greater than the other drivers they are attempting to merge with.

- Drivers who use a variety of different techniques to complete unprotected left turns during inappropriate times, using unsafe means, endangering all other drivers around them.

Some drivers appear to do these things intentionally near driver education vehicles clearly marked "Driver Training." These drivers qualify for the infamous "Darwin Awards." Driver Education students are being trained to deal with drivers who commit the above infractions and many others, but this doesn't mean that we wish for other drivers to *participate* in our training program.

When these infractions are taking place, the instructor is either taking evasive action or pointing out the offending driver to the student so the student can safely take defensive driving action. Some of these techniques will be explained in more depth later. In any case, please do not show off for a driver education student.

Inexperienced drivers must be trained to respond properly to the hazards of sharing the roads with drivers who have not been trained properly or simply do not care. While students are learning these defensive driving techniques, instructors must often grab the wheel for critical course adjustments and/or apply the brake on the passenger side of a professional training vehicle.

Parents reading this may wonder if you are really up to the task of assisting the driver education process. The short answer is, in most states, *you must.* Graduated licensing programs, in most states, require that only a fraction of the total "supervised" training is to be conducted by the professional. The remainder of the training must be completed by a parent, grandparent, legal guardian, or another licensed driver. For example, in South Carolina, eight hours of classroom training is required, and only a minimum of six hours of professional driving instruction is required after the classroom training.

In addition, a minimum of another forty hours of supervised training must be conducted by the parent or guardian, and it must be documented on the same form where we document our classroom and behind-the- wheel training. Since parents are *required* by law to assist in the driver education process in most states, don't you think you should be armed with knowledge of the driver education teaching techniques we employ?

We know all parents and teens are going to love reading this next suggestion. *Please review your state's DMV manual ... again.* If you are a little foggy on some of the rules of the road, including those for unprotected left turns, four-way stops, right turns on red, or any other rule-of-the-road, quiz your family over the dinner table. All state DMV manuals were not created equally. Frankly, I'm very disappointed in the DMV manual for the highest populated state in the country.

Yes, that would be California where I attended driver education/ training, where I obtained my first driver's license, and where I lived and drove for much of my adult life.

If, after reading this book, you are convinced that your state DMV manual is at least up to a minimum standard and when and only if you have read through the entire manual and are reasonably certain you understand every last word of it, then turn it over to your teen. Again, I suggest quizzing your teen on the contents over the dinner table. If your teen seems disinterested or does not eat with you (which I have discovered is often the case in many households today), I suggest you make it mandatory for your teen to get the keys to any vehicle including yours.

When teens complete the classroom portion of a driver education program, they generally know just enough to be dangerous. They haven't been trained to drive properly yet. When they have also completed the BTW portion of the driver education program, they often attempt to coach the person they ride with the majority of the time. That person is *you*. Teens wait for years to gain knowledge about a topic they believe they know more about than their parents.

We counsel our students that their role *is not* to attempt to teach their parents how to drive properly, especially after completion of only eight hours of classroom training and/or after completion of an entire driver education/training program. Instead, we advise our students to drive safely, proficiently, and within the rules of the road as they have been trained to do at all times.

If a parent or a classmate asks a student why his/her hands are on the wheel a certain way, why the car is being turned with a particular technique, or what the correct traffic rule is, the teen should be able to explain the rationale in a way that a classmate can understand and that a parent can help reinforce. *If not, please check your state DMV manual again before you advise your teen.*

Classmates who have not been trained properly often ridicule their friends for driving safely ... at first. However, when a teen echoes the rationale that the pro- driving instructor has provided, there is little wiggle room for a counter argument. This is one of many reasons that our philosophy of teaching is that we not only explain *what* we do, but we explain *why* we do it.

As previously noted, our impetus for the development of this book is our interest in promoting a partnership with parents. We have had perhaps thousands of discussions with teens and their parents.

We are also on the road all day observing adults drive.

In addition, we closely observe parents when they arrive at training locations before and after driving lessons. We are aware that parents generally fall into one or more of the following categories:

- Parents who never had an opportunity to complete formal driver education.

- Parents who have completed driver education but are not aware that current technology has changed the manner in which driver education is currently conducted.

- Parents who have relocated to a new state and have not had the time or the inclination to review their new state's Department of Motor Vehicles manual.

- Parents who know some of the things they are supposed to do while BTW but lost the will or the inclination to do those things years ago.

Whether you are aware of it or not, your preteen has been watching you drive and has been learning from you. They may not talk about it with you directly unless specifically asked.

However, during their preteen and early teen years, they begin to draw conclusions about the behaviors that are acceptable behind-the-wheel. Therefore, since most children ride with their parents the majority of the time, their early driving behaviors reflect your driving behaviors.

If you exhibit sound driving behaviors, your teen is ahead of the learning curve. If you exhibit poor driving behaviors, your teen is behind the learning curve. Is it too late to do something about it? Never! I'm living proof that someone can actually "teach an old dog new tricks."

Since you are reading this book, this means that you are sufficiently motivated to take the first steps.

What are some of the other steps you can take? This chapter is devoted to providing suggestions to you for ways and means to refresh your knowledge and improve your driving skills.

Remember, high school driver education and professional driving schools only train your teen for about 10 percent of the total "supervised" driving time required by a graduated licensing program state.

In reality, the number of hours of supervised driving time should far exceed the number of hours typically provided by a high school or contracted from a professional driving school.

In order to be effective and credible to your teen, you must not only know more than your teen knows, but you should be able to demonstrate that you know more than your teen knows. In addition, regardless of how thorough the training your teen received, you have something a teen certainly does not have: *experience.* You can use this experience to your advantage while supplementing your teen's driver education.

However, be careful! You must be diligent in verifying that the guidance you provide is 100 percent accurate. Otherwise, your credibility with your teen— often poor because well, as you already know—suffers even more because your teen doesn't believe that you know anything important anyway. If you feed them erroneous information about driving, your previously poor credibility will now be "out the passenger window."

There are several steps you can take to refresh your knowledge about your state's rules of the road and many other topics regarding the safe operation of a motor vehicle. For a start, *read your state's DMV manual cover to cover and be prepared to answer questions from your teen about the contents.*

When teens bother to read the manual at all, they are very often confused and draw incorrect conclusions. If you refresh your knowledge of basic rules of the road, it will help reduce the number of times you provide incorrect information to your teen. You might consider reading at least a couple of additional driver education books, like this one. There many others available, and some of them include helpful suggestions regarding teaching teens to drive. However, please recognize that any book or books not authored by a professional driving instructor should be supplemented with other reference material.

As previously noted, also become thoroughly familiar with the teaching material being utilized to train you teen. You may not have an opportunity to view the actual classroom material prior to presentation to your teen. However, take every step you possibly can to *ensure* that the classroom, DVD material, and all other training aids are consistent with your state DMV manual.

We strongly *urge* you to make a copy of the full CADETS BTW performance grid offered in Appendix 4 of this book. Remember, your teen must take baby steps, then small steps, then moderate strides while leaning to drive.

Keep track of your teen's progress, and do not allow him/her to drive in conditions that are beyond your teen's means. Consult with your professional driving instructor, and listen carefully to the pro's assessment of your teen's progress, *not your teen's interpretation of his/her progress.*

When driving in front of your teen and 100 percent of the rest of the time, make a conscious effort portray safe driving skills. Most driving instructors are trained to avoid portraying one set of driving behaviors for their students and then exhibit a *different* set of behaviors when they are driving alone or with nonstudent passengers.

In order to drive safely in front of your teen at all times, you will need to develop safe driving habits whenever and wherever you drive … at all times. This is going to be painful for some parents. However, there are (potentially) some side benefits to this extreme degree of "torture." You may live longer or avoid injury by employing advanced collision avoidance techniques yourself!

Do not be afraid to question your teen's driver education instructors at length, before the training begins, while the training program is ongoing, and after the training has been concluded. One of our biggest disappointments in the driver education field is the indifference portrayed by some parents. Your teen is going to be driving a three-thousand-plus-pound rocket, sometimes at speeds exceeding sixty miles per hour! Get involved and pay close attention! Your son or daughter's life and innocent victims in other vehicles may depend on it. When arrangements have been made for an instructor to drop a student off at home after training (as is often the case), we have taken note of a disturbing trend. After driving lessons, parents are often unavailable for driving instructors to provide any feedback to at all.

This is one of the reasons, whenever possible, we prefer meeting parents at shopping mall parking lots before and after their teen's driving lessons.

After each lesson, we will provide as much information to a parent about the lesson as the parent appears to accept.

The information from the instructor should be used by the parent to identify the teen driver's need for improvement or practice. In addition, a professional driving instructor can objectively assess a teen's skill level far more accurately than a parent. Our experience has been that many parents believe their children are far more competent and skilled drivers than they actually demonstrate in reality.

Please listen carefully to your professional driving instructor. Your instructor can inform you of traffic conditions that your teen is prepared to drive in; more importantly, the level of driving he/she *is not* yet prepared for.

More often than not, when a teen enters a driver education program, the teen has already been behind the wheel several times with a parent. Many teens tell tales of driving on some of the busiest roads and highways a major city has to offer with no prior experience at all!

These are the same teens that cannot turn a corner satisfactorily for a driving instructor until trained properly to do so. In addition, when many teens are questioned about basic rules of the road in the classroom, they answer incorrectly more often than correctly. Teaching a teen or any beginning driver to drive is a very serious matter. You don't just "throw a beginning driver into a pond" to see if he/she will either sink or swim. Some of them will sink—very quickly!

When many new students are asked how they obtained their information about a particular driving rule, more often than not, rather than referencing the DMV manual, they quote a parent. Of course this means that the parent and teen have already been driving on city roads, oblivious to the fact that they do not understand the right-of-way at a four-way stop or most other driving scenarios.

Lack of understanding of right-of-way laws at four- way stops and a general lack of common understanding of the rules of the road regarding many other driving scenarios may be masked for long periods of time.

However, lack of understanding and comprehension of the danger involved in completing an unprotected left turn can prove to be deadly … the first time! There simply is no margin for error in completing unprotected left turns safely. *Your teen must get this right every time.*

Parents also should be advised that teens do not always respond appropriately to outside stimuli. This is an understatement of course. Any teen who has been driving for less than a few *years* is an inexperienced driver.

Any teen who is still driving with a permit or who is receiving driver education training is a very inexperienced driver. They must be *trained and coached* to respond correctly to other drivers that we in the driver education business call *snipers.*

A sniper is any automobile that potentially could enter your path of travel. Often, a professional driving instructor can see events unfolding ahead from great distance. This is just one of several reasons that students are trained to look fifteen to twenty seconds ahead and to scan the traffic scene.

As potential collisions are unfolding in front of pro instructors, beginning, inexperienced drivers of any age do not typically initiate proper defensive driving action. We coach our students to continually be on the lookout for snipers. When they see them, they have several options, but decision making must take place quickly and efficiently. These are the minimum steps we require:

- Take your foot off the gas.

- Put your foot on the brake and be prepared to stop.

- Look for an escape route and be prepared to steer toward it.

- Honk your horn until the driver of the sniper vehicle turns his/her head to look at you.

- If the sniper does not respond, immediately slow the car or *stop the car* as the situation demands.

As previously noted, professional driving instructors have a brake and a rearview mirror on the passenger side of the vehicle. The mirror is used constantly, and the brake is used more for preventative reasons than for emergencies. For example, when sitting in the middle of an intersection waiting for completing an unprotected left turn, an instructor's foot may be on the brake. When a suitable gap appears in traffic, the instructor may lift his foot off the brake without saying anything to the student but allow the student to complete the turn.

As a parent, riding with your teen while he/she drives, you are not going to have the luxury of having an extra brake on your side of the vehicle! In addition, most parents do not purchase and install a passenger rearview mirror; although they are available at most auto parts stores. We recommend that you purchase one with a suction cup so that it can be removed later. Beginning drivers often have steering deficiencies, so much so that we often must help steer the car from our vantage point near the driver.

Finally, and perhaps most importantly, beginning drivers are often so preoccupied with driving their own vehicle properly that they forget about all other drivers, pedestrians, and potential snipers around them. They often develop a sort of tunnel vision while driving and tend to block out the actions of others while they go about the business of attempting to drive a car properly. This is exactly what you don't want of course, and you must be conscious of the fact that your beginning teen driver is going to be doing it.

How can you help mitigate this phenomenon? For a start, it means you must very cautious and conservative while allowing your teen to progress from the parking lot to the residential neighborhood, to light traffic conditions, to heavy traffic conditions, and to expressway driving. In addition, you must be coaching your teen at all times while he/she is driving. You simply cannot assume that just because your experience tells you the driver ahead is going to do something stupid that your teen driver sees this coming as well; often they do not.

Your selected driver education program's instructor should already be coaching your teen about how to respond appropriately to snipers and how to minimize risk. You should also discuss these techniques with your teen *before* he/she begins each driving activity with you. While your teen is driving, we cannot emphasis communicating with your teen enough. We are not talking about asking about how things are going in school.

We are talking about communicating about the task at hand, controlling a three-thousand-plus-pound beast and watching out for other drivers who can't or won't control their own three-thousand-plus-pound beasts. You simply must stay engaged at all times, and you must watch every move your teen makes and every move every driver around you makes.

During early driving sessions, help train your teen by informing him/her of what you see as he/she drives. As he/she gains experience, have him/her tell you what he/she sees ahead that could potentially require evasive action.

During all phases of your teen's BTW training, develop your teen's defensive driving awareness and help fine-tune the skills required for collision avoidance. If you are concerned about the long-term welfare of your child, there simply is no alternative.

The CADETS beginning lesson grid follows.

If the teen has completed classroom or computer- based instruction training and you are prepared to take every step detailed in this book, you should be prepared to supplement your teen's driving instructor's training each and every time your teen is behind the wheel.

BEHIND-THE-WHEEL INSTRUCTION GRID NO. 1

Student Name:_________________ Instructor:_____________________

ACTIVITY	INTRODUCTION	PRACTICE	MASTERY
LESSON DATE(S)			
Basic Auto Setup			
Figure 8 (R/L Series)			
Right Turn Series			
Left Turn Series			
Wheel Release			
Gas and Brake			
Three-Point Turn			
Backing			
Serpentine or Backing Turns			
ABS Braking			
Basic Rules of the Road Q and A			
Residential Driving			
Cul-de-Sac Maneuvering			
Right-of-Way Confirmation			

ADDITIONAL NOTES

73

CHAPTER 3

Alternate Driver Education Philossphies, Procedures, and Techniques

I decided to include this chapter now, preceding the chapters describing current classroom and behind-the- wheel driver education and training. This chapter is longer than originally intended. In fact, I can use the same descriptor for this chapter that I often use for one of my golf shots immediately after striking my ball. "Well, it could have been worse."

For example, the author of the book *Traffic* required fifteen pages of prologue in ten-point font to describe why he became a "late merger." During those fifteen pages, he never really got around to explaining exactly why he became a late merger. Therefore, later on in the book, he provided five *additional* pages devoted to explaining his rationale for the late merge. Sorry, Tom. I'm not buying it, and I think I can explain our rationale in less than twenty pages.

The late merge versus early merge issue is representative of how various driver training educators disagree, why we disagree, and *some* of the pros and cons of the differing philosophies. At CADETS, while we are aware of the differing techniques, we are not at all ambivalent about which technique(s) we require of our students. In addition, we do not utilize the "because I said so" argument that some educators fall back on as our driver education training and coaching philosophy.

Therefore, early on in the classroom and later reinforced in the training cars, our students are informed that there are specific reasons for *everything* we do. This chapter is devoted to the major differing driver education and driver training philosophies we are aware of that exist. We strive to ensure that our students completely understand the rational for our driver training techniques and that they are entirely consistent with our state DMV manual, as well as other professional driver education organizations we respect.

Obviously, all professional driver education entities do not agree on each and every technique for maneuvering a three-thousand- to six-thousand- pound beast through traffic and keeping it and passengers out of harm's way. While we all seem to agree on most of the basic rules of the road and dozens upon hundreds of fundamentals, there are some key differences, and they are very important.

In addition, unlike some of the other driver education authors who have published books and/or articles, I simply cannot bring myself to pretend that these alternative driver education philosophies do not exist.

Over the course of my driver education career, I have attended classroom and BTW training more times than I can count conducted by variety of different organizations. There are very few books or manuals that provide rationale for differing driver education philosophies within the same book or manual. Perhaps the authors wished to convey that there is one and only one technique acceptable? In any case, we chose to inform you of the strengths and weaknesses of the differing philosophies and allow you to draw your own conclusions.

In addition to receiving training from these differing sources, I have now conducted over one thousand hours of classroom training and (literally) over six times that many hours of training in professional training cars. Ironically, I have a brother who is currently a driver education instructor in and around Los Angeles and vicinity. I also have a brother-in-law and a nephew who are race car drivers and are both advanced driver education instructors too. They teach police officers high-speed pursuit and recovery procedures. Perhaps, in some ways, I am almost in a unique position to compare some of these philosophical differences that

I am aware exists between competing driver education companies and/or insurance agencies.

The good news is that we all agree on about 95 percent of the driver education principles, practices, philosophies, and techniques out there. It's the other 5 percent that we argue about. Don't skip to the next chapter yet because it turns out that the other 5 percent is actually quite significant— that's why these topics are controversial. I chose to cover these topics now so that I wouldn't be required to describe *why* we use certain techniques (at least in this detail) in later chapters.

The following are a few of the primary, alternate driver education training procedures that I am currently aware of that are commonly espoused.

These alternate procedures did not *originate* with anyone I know personally. In some cases, they originated with *insurance agencies*. I have nothing against insurance agencies. In fact, I carry a great deal of it myself, especially for my cars, drivers, and occupants. However, insurance agency instructors primarily provide *driver improvement* training for adults who already possess a driver's license. These drivers usually have at least some degree of knowledge and experience BTW (behind the wheel) and can demonstrate a modicum of skills and abilities for a pro-driving instructor. However, there is a huge difference between improving a driver who has been driving for twenty years and teaching a *true beginning driver* who has never driven anything larger than a golf cart.

If you hear about, read about, or receive training advocating a different procedure within your own state or locale, even if is from a national insurance organization, I urge you to *read your state DMV manual and follow their guidelines*. In the meantime, consider the following:

9:30 a.m. and 2:30 p.m. steering versus 10:00 a.m. and 2:00 or 8:00 p.m. and 4:00 p.m. and handover hand- turning versus push/pull

When our students enter our classroom, at least 80 percent have been coached by their parents to drive with their hands at 10:00 a.m. and 2:00 p.m. as the wheel is referenced on the face of a clock. This is how I was coached in driver education in high school too. Driver education continued to emphasize these grips until new technology required that they be changed. Most but not all professional driving schools now teach 9:30 a.m. and 2:30 p.m. grips or 9:00 a.m. and 3:00 p.m. for forward driving and steering. The reason: *air bags.*

If your air bags inflate from a "fender bender," "minor collision," or "major collision," your air bag is going to be propelled toward you at about two hundred mile per hour, depending on the make and model of your vehicle. If your hands are locked in a "death grip" at 10:00 a.m. and 2:00 p.m., as you anticipate the crash, you could be hit in both eyes by your fists and severely injured! However, if your hands are placed at 9:00 a.m. and 3:00 p.m. or even at 9:30 a.m. and 2:30 p.m. (because of the yoke on most cars), the air bag will simply do its job, and your eyes are spared.

Yes, if you anticipate a crash, you should steer toward the path of least resistance using *any* technique within your means to avoid crashing. Air bags don't inflate when you don't crash. That's why I haven't experienced one in forty years.

Another very significant advantage of 9:30 a.m. and 2:30 p.m. grips over other steering or gripping techniques (especially the single hand at twelve o'clock) is that prior to almost all *potential* crashes your hands are *already* in position to execute severe swerves in *either* direction to avoid them. In an emergency, the car may be quickly turned from as little as a few degrees to over 90 degrees so that the rear of the vehicle strikes the other vehicle or object. Yes, at least two laws of physics (inertia and centrifugal force) must be overcome.

Let's stipulate from a representative scenario that a car pulls out of an intersection in your immediate path while you are barreling toward the car and driver at sixty miles per hour. The faster you are driving, the more powerful the force of inertia is. According to Sir Isaac Newton, a body that is in motion "wants" to remain in motion … in the same direction that it is already traveling in. If you are driving at sixty miles per hour and another driver suddenly pulls out in front of you from an intersection, your next move could mean the difference between life and death … for you and the other driver and/or all passengers. You may not have time to move your hands into position to save all drivers and passengers unless your hands are already there!

Your escape route should have already been assessed before the driver pulled out. Now is the time for quick and decisive *execution*. The path of least resistance (danger) is going to determine where you steer the car. If a driver is headed toward you from the opposite direction, that option is obviously not available. If you have an emergency breakdown lane on the right of the highway, obviously that option is available. However, what are you to do if a car is broken down and already occupying that space?

If you are within fifty yards of the sniper (a term driver education instructors use for drivers entering your pathway), you may end up crashing into him anyway. However, instead of steering head-on into a collision with the driver approaching on the left or allowing your vehicle to "T-bone the offending driver's door," you may end up saving his life and other passenger's lives in *both* cars by ABS braking into the driver's left rear bumper with your left front bumper.

If your left hand has turned the wheel from the 9:30 a.m. position to 1:00 p.m. and you do crash, yes, the front air bag is going to inflate at about two hundred mile per hour, and it may drive your left forearm into your forehead.

In addition, at least one of the side air bags (if you have them in your vehicle) should inflate to protect you. You may incur a broken left arm, a very sore forehead, or a few relatively minor injuries. However, this should be a survivable crash for both drivers and all occupants as long as all of you are wearing seat belts!

My own experience as a passenger with thousands of different adult drivers over the years (the majority of whom *were not* students) is that very few drivers control the vehicle particularly well with one hand. As a result, our students are not allowed to *steer* with one hand at any time. As we carefully and repeatedly inform our students, *proper steering requires two hands on the wheel, and proper turning requires one hand at a time, not the other way around.*

When adult drivers do not drive with their hands at 9:30 a.m. and 2:30 p.m., they typically drive with the left hand at or near 11:00 a.m. when banking right and the right hand at or near 1:00 p.m. when banking left. Push/pull drivers who claim to drive with their hands at 8:00 a.m. and 4:00 p.m. typically drive with their left hand at or near 7:00 a.m. The right hand is usually observed somewhere on or near the console when it isn't busy doing something else.

A national insurance association and several police academies teach the technique called push/pull. During the first several years that I taught driver training, push/pull was not even mentioned in many state DMV manuals (including this state's DMV manual) as a viable alternative at all. However, in a nod to the technique many parents were trained to use during our driver training eras, in many state driving manuals, 10:00 a.m. and 2:00 p.m. steering is *still* mentioned as an *acceptable* steering technique.

In October of 2008, a revised version of our state DMV manual described push/pull as a *possible* alternative to 9:00 a.m. and 3:00 p.m. or 10:00 a.m. and 2:00 p.m. but not specifically endorsed. It remains referenced in this manner to this day. However, I'm not aware of any pro-driving school in our state that specifically teaches push/pull. The largest pro-driving schools in the country (besides insurance companies) do not teach that technique either.

Some readers may not be familiar with the push/pull steering and turning technique at all and wonder what I am talking about. When using push/pull, the hands begin at 8:00 a.m. and 4:00 p.m. or (as some practitioners state) 7:00 and 5:00 p.m. When completing a left turn, the right hand pushes the right side of the wheel up.

Meanwhile, the left hand slides up to grasp the wheel at or near 11:00 a.m., and then pull the left side down to 8:00 a.m. Of course, this process is reversed for right turns.

One of several driver education training courses I attended taught the push/pull technique. By chance, one of my fellow students in that class was also one of my former instructor/students. He was and is (as of the writing of this book) a police officer. At the police academy he had been taught push/pull.

However, when he attended our CADETS forty-hour instructor training course, I required him to switch to 9:30 a.m. and 2:30 p.m. for forward steering and utilize the hand-over-hand technique for turning. These techniques are still being used by this instructor to conduct driver training for his own driver education students to this day.

There are a few myths about push/pull that are espoused by push/pull advocates as a means for them to provide justification for using push/pull or teaching push/pull. Let's expose the myths and stick to the facts:

Myth No. 1

When a driver incorporates push/pull, the hands are always on the wheel.

Fact No. 1

By definition, the driver must alternately slide the hands while turning the car more than 30 degrees in either direction. When one hand is pushing the wheel, the other hand is moving to a different location on the wheel. The fact is that (similar to hand-over-hand), only one hand actually moves the wheel at a time. We do acknowledge that both hands are a bit closer to the wheel if the technique is employed *exactly as demonstrated by a pro*. However, we would be remiss if we did not point out that most drivers we have observed using this technique regularly drive with only their left hand at7:00 p.m. while their right hand is on a radio or cell phone.

When both hands *are not on the wheel,* the push/pull technique is effectively neutered until the right hand is placed back on the wheel. More significantly, almost all beginning drivers do not employ actual push/pull even when they are attempting to execute a version of it! Instead, as they attempt to steer their cars toward their intended targets or attempt to turn their cars around corners, they often "walk the wheel."

"Walking the wheel" is *not* push/pull. It is an inefficient, inaccurate method of executing a turn. "Walking the wheel" is *less* effective than actual push/pull and far less effective than hand-over-hand once a teen or any new driver is trained to apply hand- over-hand properly.

Myth No. 2

While using push/pull, the hands never move above the 10:00 a.m. and 2:00 p.m. positions.

Fact No. 2

This is only true if the driver never turns the car more than 30 degrees. Take a push/pull driver to any cul-de- sac (as we require of all our beginning drivers). Either the driver will run over the curb, or his/her hands will move up past 10:00 a.m. and 2:00 p.m.! Our beginning hand over hand students execute this turn extremely well, usually after it has been demonstrated for them. Beginners who insist on walking the wheel or using push/push quickly realize why we teach hand overhand.

Myth No. 3

When driving a slalom road course, the push/pull method provides better "balance" (less weight shift) than simply steering around cones utilizing 9:00 a.m. and 3:00 p.m. steering.

Fact No. 3

The above assertion defies the laws of physics! If both drivers drive the same model/make car, drive the same speed and travel the same path, using two different steering techniques, there cannot physically be a *difference* in weight shift.

Myth No. 4

Turning a car utilizing the push/pull technique is more efficient than using the hand-over-hand steering technique.

Fact No. 4

During the week of training, the police officer and I were graded with high marks for how we navigated the slalom road course utilizing the push/pull technique. We know *how* to use the technique if and when we choose to do so.

However, the same road course may easily be navigated using 9:30 a.m. and 2:30 p.m. without the hands leaving the wheel at all. The reason for this is that slalom turns are not much more than 30 to 40 degrees, very easy for an experienced 9:30 a.m. and 2:30 p.m. driver. The hand over hand is not actually required until the left hand passes 1:00 p.m. during right turns, and the right hand passes 11:00 a.m. during left turns.

Myth No. 5

Some race car drivers use push/pull to steer.

Fact No. 5

Not at the Indianapolis 500!

I watched the race intently this year to look for things that the average viewer doesn't care about. Many (now possibly all) of these specially designed race cars are designed with *pre-molded* grips on the steering wheel that may be designed a bit differently for each driver's arms, legs, torso lengths, and (most importantly) collision avoidance training. I didn't see *any* driver whose hands were below 9:00 a.m. and 3:00 p.m. the majority of the time even while making pit stops at a much lower speeds!

At two hundred miles per hour plus, the slight movement of a steering wheel on a race car can make a huge difference in the behavior of the car, and it needs to happen in a fraction of a second. These drivers have their hands molded at 9:30 a.m. and 2:30 p.m. for a reason. When the network replayed the cockpit camera's video of each driver's expert collision avoidance reactions, I watched all the replays very carefully on high definition video. I was looking at how the hands moved the steering wheel or moved on the steering wheel.

At two hundred plus miles per hour, when the left hand is moved from 9:30 a.m. to 2:00 p.m. and right hand is moved from 2:30 p.m. to 6:00 p.m., it forces an extreme turn in a race car. The force of the turn of the wheel is imparted to the drive train in order to overcome a combination of inertia and centrifugal force.

One of the very best driver training books in North America is entitled *Today's Handbook Plus*, an unfortunate title but an outstanding book. The book describes emergency evasive action steering that *may* require the driver to turn the vehicle so severely that the forearms actually touch.

This permits as much as a 180 degree turn unless you are driving a race car at two hundred plus miles per hour. Think about it this way: suppose you are traveling on a rural highway at sixty miles per hour. This is not unusual.

Let's say a driver "A," looming at the intersection, simply doesn't see you and pulls out in front of you two hundred feet ahead. If you are traveling sixty miles per hour, *it takes about three hundred feet or about the length of a football field to stop your vehicle.* If you have been trained properly and you know this, you immediately launch into emergency evasive collision avoidance mode. If you have a large enough shoulder, you can possibly have something air traffic controllers affectionately call a near miss. A *near miss* is actually a *near hit.* You don't want to have very many of them if you are a professional air traffic controller; otherwise, you won't be one for very long.

Suppose you were changing a CD when this happens, and you are just a fraction of a second late in recognizing the danger. Now you *must minimize the crash!* If you turn the wheel until your forearms touch, the rear of your car may impact the sniper, but you saved your life, his life, and the lives of your passengers.

If a race car driver moving at two hundred plus miles per hour turned the wheel that severely, the car would flip and somersault down the race track! Race car drivers know this of course; therefore, with their hands at 9:30 a.m. and 2:30 p.m., when confronted with a certain crash, race car drivers typically turn the steering wheel in order to force the hurling missile to strike a glancing blow with another car or strike the wall. There simply isn't sufficient *time* for a race car driver to use push/pull *or* hand over hand in an emergency. There isn't sufficient *time* for you to bring a wayward hand up from your console to 2:30 p.m. either.

Your hands should *already* be in emergency collision avoidance position at 9:30 a.m. and 2:30 p.m., just like the hands of a pro-Indy 500 driver!

Readers may be wondering why push/pull is taught anywhere at any time at all. There are two primary reasons:

1. Most police officers and many other commercial drivers do not drive with two hands on the wheel. The right hand may be used for the police radio or another handheld push-to-talk device, and the left hand is used for driving. In fact, watch any push/pull driver in action, and you will note that 90 percent of the time only one hand is on the wheel.

2. Comfort. This is the only advantage for push/pull that I will acknowledge.

Since I have driven very long distances for extended periods within about forty states, I am aware that comfort is a strong motivation, for any driver. For this reason, when our students are coached to drive briefly on an expressway during their final lesson, they are allowed to *slide* both hands to 8 + 4 until they must change lanes or exit. At that time, they are required to revert back to 9:30 a.m. and 2:30 p.m. for their full lane changes and exit.

There is another advantage to 9:30 a.m. and 2:30 p.m. that must be acknowledged by even the staunchest push/pull advocate. While driving with the left hand positioned at 9:30 a.m., the right hand must (or at least should) be positioned at or near 2:30 p.m. as a counterbalance. When training teenage student drivers, this advantage for 9:30 a.m. and 2:30 p.m. over push/pull is *immeasurable.*

Student drivers soon learn than most pro-driving instructors will not allow them to drift out of their lanes for a moment. When driving in rural communities or medium-size cities or on almost any two-lane highway, drifting out of your lane for even a few feet can be disastrous. Our student drivers control the vehicle much, much better steering the vehicle with their hands at 9:30 a.m. and 2:30 p.m. than any other technique we have observed.

In coming years, there will no longer be a viable reason for any driving school to teach any driver to use push/pull at all. Reason: Bluetooth or other similar available technology.

I have Bluetooth installed in my personal vehicle. In training vehicles, I do not accept calls or make them. However, utilizing Bluetooth, a driver can accept a call in a fraction of a second. The driver can make a call in the same fraction of a second.

In either case, if the driver is driving in heavy traffic or is merging into heavy traffic (to use two examples), the driver need not accept or make calls utilizing Bluetooth either. Sometimes when I am driving (not teaching), I *still* do not accept calls using Bluetooth technology. As I explain to my students, current technology allows you to capture the caller's number on your mobile phone. Why not call them back when it is convenient *and* safe for you?

Center-Angle Side View Mirror Adjustment versus Wide- Angle View

Most state DMV manuals describe using the center view method for adjusting the side view mirrors. We do not require additional justification for using this method versus the wide-angle view. However, I will provide additional justification here. First, the center view calls for adjusting the left mirror so that the left rear fender is just visible when your head is in its normal driving position. The right mirror is adjusted so that the right rear fender is just visible with the head in the same location.

With the two side-view mirrors adjusted in this manner, when glancing at either mirror, the lanes that potentially pose the greatest danger to you may be observed, namely the lanes to your immediate left and right. Yes, you still have a small blind spot on each side of the car. However, our state DMV and most state DMV examiners require the driver to glance over each shoulder *before* making a lane change. In our state, if you don't appear to glance over the shoulder before a lane change or any change of position of the vehicle, the driving test penalty is severe. In a regular driving scenario, the penalty may be even more severe.

The wide-angle side-view mirror adjustment procedure calls for adjusting the mirrors for the same view (rear fenders barely visible) but with your head moved all the way to the window for the left mirror and over the center console for the right mirror. If you adjust the side mirrors in this manner, the center of each side- view mirror will reflect the *second* lane removed from the lane you are driving in.

There are a few advantages to this procedure, but most pro-driving instructors believe that the disadvantages far outweigh the advantages. The argument goes that there is no discernible gap between the reflection in the center rearview mirrors and the two side mirrors.

This is true, but there also is no discernible gap between center and side mirrors when the side-view mirrors are adjusted for center view that most schools instruct either.

The problem isn't the nonexistent gap for either method; *the problem is the blind spot next to the car.* If someone is tailgating you (following closer than three seconds behind), the potential always exists that the driver will change lanes at precisely the moment you turn your head to look in your side-view mirror.

If you will resolve to use the procedure we teach— *a*ssess, *p*repare, *e*xecute (APE)—if the tailgater behind you is changing lanes at that precise moment, you will pick the driver up with your peripheral vision during your very brief over-the-shoulder check.

We will concede that during merges onto expressways that have more than three lanes, the wide- angle view helps determine where vehicles are positioned *two lanes* over. However, you can accomplish the same thing by simply moving your head from your normal driving position a bit toward your left shoulder *after* you have cleared the lane of greatest danger to you (the lane *next* to your car). The second most dangerous threat when you are merging is the vehicle directly behind you.

If you are merging at the proper speed—this is the speed the majority of the drivers are traveling at in your merging lane—there is always a possibility that a very aggressive driver directly behind you will attempt to steal your merging space. If the rearview mirror and left side-view mirror are each adjusted properly, you will see this driver immediately as he/she makes a move.

Experienced expressway drivers do not allow aggressive tailgating drivers to steal their merging spots. If you make a habit of allowing aggressive drivers to steal your merging gap, you will often be forced into late and awkward unsafe merges whether you want to deal with them or not. You may be required to bring your vehicle to a complete stop! This can lead to disaster when merging onto busy expressways. Even the most powerful cars on the road cannot accelerate 0–70 in .5 seconds! A much safer practice is to merge safely in the first place.

Another problem with the wide-angle view adjustment is that 90 percent of the time you are looking at a lane that is of no immediate danger to you.

In addition, when the left side-view mirror is adjusted for the wide-angle view, you cannot see the boundaries of your car in relation to the lanes next to you. Furthermore, you can only see 50 percent of the lanes next to you! One additional comment that pertains to this topic: If you have a special convex mirror installed on your vehicle and you know how to use it, the mirror *may* help you see *both* *l*anes on either side.

However, a beginning driver *cannot* use a convex as an excuse for not using the regular lane change procedure during all-lane changes throughout a driving test.

Therefore, you will be a better driver and a safer driver if use the complete APE procedure (as we describe again, later in the book) for all- lane changes, merges, and any change of position beyond cornering within your own lane. At CADETS, we teach the Department of Motor Vehicles center angle view technique only.

Later in the book, an entire chapter will be devoted to early merges versus late merges because of a bestselling author advocating one of these two procedures in his book. No, I don't agree with his misguided philosophy. I will explain in great detail why I and other professional driving instructors do not advocate late merges, and we certainly wouldn't teach any student to intentionally merge "late."

Backward Perpendicular Parking and Angle Parking Versus Forward Parking and Exiting

A common alternative method of parking is to drive forward across a perpendicular boundary line and park backward. The rational for this (for those who teach it) is that upon exiting, you may pull forward with increased visibility while you exit. We acknowledge that a driver *may* have better sight lines when pulling forward rather than backing. However, drivers who attempt to park using this technique unwittingly unleash a host of other related unintended results. These unintended consequences far outstrip the original anticipated advantage gained by pulling forward and parking in the wrong direction in the first place! A few examples follow:

- When a driver drives into the front space and pulls forward to the next adjoining space, he/she cannot see the back of his/her own vehicle. (This area is called the void area.) This usually results in the car being parked with the rear bumper (sometimes the entire trunk) hanging over the rear boundary line of the parking space.

- If the driver is conscious (this is debatable) of not leaving the rear of the car hanging out there, he/she will often overcompensate by pulling too far forward, leaving the front of the car out in the roadway. Of course, drivers can see firsthand how poorly they parked as they exit the vehicle, but few reenter the car to fix the hazard they have now created.

- Let's say that the driver is very fortunate that day, and after returning to his/her vehicle after shopping, no one has crashed into his/her improperly parked car. Of course, the purpose of parking *backward* is to allow the driver to pull *forward* while exiting.

- By design, when a car is moving forward, it does not have its backing lights on. If the exiting driver actually signals here, it helps. However, watch almost any driver pull forward and turn left or right in this manner, and very few have turned on a turn signal for intent. In addition, drivers who are driving in the roadway (that this driver is about to enter) are not expecting a vehicle to suddenly move *forward* between parked cars and enter their roadway.

- If a driver parks in a parking lot configured such as those designed at Wal-Mart (for example), the driver has one of two choices: *neither of which is very desirable.* The first is to exit left, in which case the driver is *driving the wrong way in the roadway.* Now any other unsuspecting driver who turns into that roadway will not have sufficient room to steer around the exiting driver. This results in some very awkward, embarrassing, and unnecessary maneuvering by both drivers.

- If the driver exits right, the driver must execute a *very sharp* right turn of approximately $(90 + 45 = 135$ degrees) without sideswiping the car parked on his/her immediate right.

- Poor drivers cannot execute this turn exceptionally well, especially if another poor driver has parked improperly in the next adjoining space. Now, when Mr. Magoo puts an eight-foot gash in his car from scraping his neighbor's right rear fender, Mr. Magoo has to decide if he is going to stop and leave a love letter or continue merrily along his way.

- Some Mr. Magoos simply keep moving, oblivious to the fact that they have just caused $2,000 damage to your car and $2,000 damage to theirs. This is one of several reasons you need to be very careful about where you park your car and how you park it.

- I have also seen drivers attempt to back into spaces between parked cars. When a driver backs into a parking space between parked cars, this results in one or more of the results above, plus at least one more opportunity for a crash. When a driver backs into a parking space between two parked cars, by definition, the drivers of those two cars either are not in their cars, or they do not have their cars engaged to move. This means they can't take *any* evasive action to avoid Mr. Magoo; even if they see him backing toward their vehicle right before their eyes!

Angle Parking

Angle parking is actually far easier than perpendicular parking when executed properly. Most but not all angle parking spaces will be on your right. However, as previously referenced, Wal-Mart and some other business parking lots generally have angle spaces that may be pulled into by turning right *or* by turning left because they designed to be one way though may not be marked on the pavement as such. *Do not pull forward across the front bumper boundary* no matter if you turn right or left. If you do this, you are asking for all the trouble defined in the perpendicular section.

Also, take care that you do not leave your right bumper hanging over the right front boundary. If you do this, you are practically inviting another poor driver to crash into it. Do not leave the back of your car hanging out in the roadway; if you do ... well, you get the idea. Backing out of an angle parking space is actually a bit easier than backing out of a perpendicular parking space. Backing out of an angle parking space requires essentially the same technique as backing out of a perpendicular space except, due to the angle of the vehicle in the adjoining space; you can usually turn your wheel just a bit earlier ... without crashing.

Perpendicular Parking

Enter any parking lot of any shopping mall and take a close look at the cars. If you know what you are looking for, you will note that at least 60 percent of the cars are parked incorrectly. An incorrectly parked car can and often does have one or more obvious deficiency. The front, left right, or rear of the vehicle will usually be hanging over a white parking boundary line.

As we explain to our students, if you leave a section (even a bumper) of your car hanging over a boundary line, you are inviting another poor driver to crash into your car.

If another poor driver crashes into your car or scrapes your car while you are shopping, the chances are not good that the "Good Samaritan" is going to leave a note informing you. Even if the driver does leave a note, your car still needs to be repaired, and you must wait for your car while it is being repaired. Some time ago (long before I entered the driver education field), one of my personal vehicles was damaged so badly in a parking lot (no, I did not park poorly) that the entire door required repainting. The body shop did not initially match the color properly, and my car door required repainting a second time.

Let's concede that we all agree that it is much better for the health and well-being of your car to park it between the boundary lines. This brings me now to state the obvious. At CADETS, we train all our students to pull in from the front, every time, and not to drive over or turn over white boundary lines at any time.

Therefore, the CADETS procedure requires pulling in frontward every time and not backward at any time. In preparation for exiting, the procedure requires clearing back left and right *before* moving, keeping the *foot on the brake* and not the accelerator while moving at idle speed, and *stopping half way out or earlier* (when you can see clearly) to double-check over each shoulder before moving out into the roadway.

In addition, when a driver engages reverse before moving, *the backing lights miraculously illuminate.* This provides an opportunity that many drivers underestimate; *the measures that other drivers who have been properly trained will take to avoid crashing into you.* If you are a poor driver, you may never know how often this happens. However, if you are a poor driver, it may not happen quite often enough, someday resulting in a crash of some sort.

The "S Swerve" Procedure for Parallel Parking

The old "S swerve" is the technique most drivers have used for years to parallel park. In fact, it is the technique I was trained to utilize in high school. The problem with the "S swerve" isn't that it doesn't work. It does work very well when executed properly.

The problem is that a sixteen-year-old beginning driver (or any student driver for that matter) must begin the *S* at precisely the right spot, reverse the wheel at precisely the right spot, and reverse the wheel again at the right spot, all the while "guesstimating" speed and distance accurately. Oh by the way, the student driver must do this during a period of mild stress (taking a driving test) with a glowering stranger in the passenger seat evaluating every move.

Most of the moms who bring their teens to our parking lessons (without being prompted) freely admit they cannot parallel park. The fathers usually claim they can parallel park (also freely offered, although we don't ask) but also admit that they are thrilled that they don't have to teach their teens how to do it.

Many of the adults I have observed parallel parking somehow manage to "shoehorn" their car in there but leave the car parked in such a way that it wouldn't pass a current department of motor vehicles driving test anyway.

I have heard parents and teens complain bitterly about parallel parking even being included in a modern- day driving test because "no one parallel parks anymore." Of course this is not true. It isn't that no one parallel parks a car anymore; it's that no one *wants* to parallel park a car anymore. Parallel parking is generally required "downtown" (and in many other locations) in even the smallest towns in every state.

I tell my students that mastering parallel parking isn't really about mastering *parking*. Parallel parking requires observation, judgment, technique, recognition, an awareness of the dimensions of the car, and an accurate sense of the boundaries the driver is parking his/her vehicle within. Examiners are well aware that if a new driver cannot parallel park, there is also a strong probability that the new driver cannot *drive* safely either.

The CADETS exclusive parallel parking technique is outlined in Appendix 5 and described in detail in another chapter.

The CADETS parallel parking technique also requires the new driver to demonstrate skills in virtually every category of the preceding paragraph.

We want them to possess those skills before they are turned loose on the masses.

However, the CADETS parallel parking technique does not require the new driver to exhibit all the above skills while the car is *moving*. There is plenty of time for that. *Speed* is not required on examination day, *precision is required.*

Early Merges versus Late Merges for the Advanced Driver

Entire chapters of various driver education books have been devoted to merging. In his book, *Traffic,* author Tom Vanderbilt opines that the majority of merges take place in construction zones, therefore altering normal traffic flow. We must start by disagreeing with this initial incorrect premise. Over 90 percent of the merges required are routine, do not involve construction equipment, and do not feature construction workers directing traffic. It may *seem* otherwise on a single highway or expressway under heavy construction; however, during your routine travels, most of your merges will be ... well, routine, especially if you know how to merge.

At CADETS, we train our students to scan the traffic scene as they are approaching any merge. This is required regardless of whether a yield sign is posted at the corner of your feeder lane or not. Part of the assessment while approaching is determining the relative speed of the vehicles you are merging with. If your target lane is populated by cars traveling at sixty miles per hour, that speed is also your ideal merging speed. If cars in the target lane are moving at forty miles per hour, that speed is also your target speed. If your target lane is stacked with cars in "stop-and-go" mode, I'm afraid that in order to merge safely and efficiently, you must also merge at that same "stop-and-go" speed.

If a yield sign is visible in your feeder lane, the yield sign is giving you several messages in advance. First, that heavy traffic is common at that location. Second, the feeder lane is very short or shorter than optimum for an ideal merge. Third, you may have to yield to a complete *stop*.

Late merge advocates (including Tom Vanderbilt) claim that a late merger is entitled to scream down the feeder lane (and sometimes the shoulder itself) at seventy-five mile per hour, and at the end of the line, a benevolent driver will then feel compelled to let you in. There are several problems with this assertion, not the least of which is that he failed to acknowledge that there just might be a yield sign in your lane.

Let's stipulate that there is not a yield sign in your lane and you are on your own to merge however best you can execute the merge. First, anytime one lane is moving at ten times the speed of the adjoining lane, there is vast potential for some unfortunate "co-mingling."

When cars moving at seventy-five miles per hour comingle with cars moving at five miles per hour, some very bad things can and do happen. Second, a late merger never really knows when his fleet of folly is going to come to a screeching halt. The fact is that the driver of the last car in the feeder lane directly in front of you *may not even have the brake lights of his car illuminated*. The driver of that vehicle may have been sitting there so long that his/her foot may not be resting on the brake, or the car may be creeping along at one mile per hour while you are screaming alongside at seventy-five miles per hour!

From a quarter mile distance away, the car directly in front of you may *appear* to be moving at the same speed as traffic in the target lane, but he/she may not be moving near that speed at all.

Imagine the surprise for some late merge screamers when they discover that the driver they are bearing down on at seventy-five miles per hour not only *is not merging* at that time, but *he isn't even moving* at that time!

Then there is the merge itself. Late merge advocates either expect or demand that *each and every* driver of each car in the target lane politely stop and whisper "after you" in their cars after they have just watched a late merger wiz by their jam packed lane at seventy-five miles per hour. All the experienced mergers reading this can answer the following question: Has this been your experience? I didn't think so, and it doesn't matter which city you live in.

If late merge advocates are correct, then each and every late merge requires that each driver in the target lane create an *artificial gap* (by braking) when a gap is not naturally there.

Late merging also requires (or at least *should* require) that the driver of the late merging car create an additional gap for following distance. In stop- and-go traffic, we can debate whether or not three-second following must be maintained.

However, for comparison purposes, let's stipulate that early and late mergers desire to create three-second following distance. Let's also stipulate that both early mergers and late mergers each require about five seconds of time to actually complete their merges. Keep in mind that utopia would have to be in existence for each and every late merger to require only five seconds.

Some merges can require much more time than five seconds for a variety of reasons, but we will use five seconds for fairness in our comparison. Let's do some simple math. If we stipulate that a late merger in stop- and-go traffic requires five seconds per vehicle, then in sixty seconds, 60/5=12 cars merge. Most large cities have several locations that experience stop-and-go traffic before lasting an hour or much longer during peak traffic periods.

The magic number to beat then if we compare an early merge philosophy rather than the late merge is approximately twelve cars per minute. Remember that twelve merges take place only if everyone cooperates as expected, and all twelve late mergers are allowed to enter during each and every five second interval.

Sir Isaac Newton's first law of motion states that "an object in motion will stay in motion, and an object at rest will stay at rest unless acted upon by an external force."

Although we must remember that objects behave a bit differently in space than they do under the influence of heavy gravitational pull (such as here on Earth), we must also recognize that Newton's laws of motion are used to explain many things here on Earth that are common in our everyday lives.

For example, trains require a very long time to get them moving and a very long time to get them stopped. Another example is the initial movement of a very large lumber truck. Some of the heaviest lumber trucks in Oregon (and many other parts of the country) carry very heavy payloads weighing in excess of one hundred thousand pounds! Those vehicles are going to take significant *time* to get moving and significant *time* to get stopped.

Typical eighteen-wheel trucks, midsize trucks, commercial pickup trucks, and SUVs will not weigh as much as a lumber truck, but they will weigh more and sometimes much more than a regular passenger vehicle. Newton's second law states that "f = ma." This means that force = mass x acceleration. It has been years since I completed calculus and physics. However, my former physics professor may be called upon to help me reiterate that acceleration is (partly) determined by force over mass.

There are some other factors involved in determining the rate of acceleration of course.

However, when a truck driver is stuck in stop-and- go traffic with the rest of us, the first thing involved in getting his truck moving is *perception*. He needs to perceive that something has changed in front of him, and he needs to initiate action to get his vehicle moving. This takes precious *time* (especially if the driver is distracted). If the driver is talking on a cell phone or a CB (Citizens Band) radio or just looking out the window in sheer boredom, his perception time may be adversely influenced.

Let's examine the early merge. One of the several advantages of early merging is that (in most cases) three seconds following distance will be created *naturally* by the laws of physics. Most commercial vehicle drivers must drive using manual transmissions, especially if they carry large payloads. It takes precious time to engage the clutch and *begin* the acceleration process. These vehicles do not stop on a dime—we will cover that later—and they do not accelerate like a sports car either. In fact, in many cases, sports cars with manual transmissions do not always accelerate like sports cars either. It depends on who is driving them and what the driver's initial perceptions and intent are.

Traffic moving at stop-and-go speeds within a given one-mile stretch of expressway or highway may have as many as ten commercial vehicles in varying sizes in the target lane. No matter how quick their reaction times may be, these drivers must reckon with the laws of physics. They simply cannot physically get their vehicle moving as quickly as the little "puddle jumper" sports cars in front of them. In addition, if they are carrying a somewhat fragile payload, they must do something I ask of all my students. They must accelerate and brake smoothly. The drivers of these vehicles create natural merging gaps, whether they wish to do so or not.

These are not dangerous gaps to merge into. In fact, they are among the safest. Let's consider that our merging time begins when the driver in front of one of these vehicles begins moving. Within three seconds that driver may move as much as three car lengths. Those three seconds often take place while the trucker was going through his "perception" phase. The next three seconds take place while the trucker is going through his much slower acceleration phase. During that time, the gap between the truck and a typical family sedan in front opens up three more car lengths of space.

Well-trained drivers moving along safely in the feeder lane (at no more than five miles per hour) are looking for a safe opportunity to merge.

These natural "gaps" created by the above laws of physics create safe merging spaces. Safe, patient drivers now have at least six car lengths of merging space to merge into in front of each and every large commercial vehicle as well as many smaller vehicles; especially those with manual transmissions.

While each late merger is merging in single file at rate of one merge every five seconds, *multiply that number by at least ten to calculate the number of early merges that may take place at the same time!* Here's why. Let's look at what is transpiring along the other sections of this hypothetical one-mile strip of highway. A mile is 5,280 feet.

Let's say that there are eighty passenger vehicles in the target lane and each passenger vehicle takes up approximately fifty feet of space. In stop-and-go traffic, these vehicles would normally be packed in much closer, but it doesn't matter for the purpose of our illustration. Let's stipulate that there are also ten commercial vehicles of varying sizes and length in the target lane. However, we are going assign an average of *one hundred feet* of space to each of these vehicles.

Eighty passenger vehicles multiplied by fifty feet each is equal to four thousand feet. In addition, ten commercial vehicles multiplied by one hundred feet for each requires approximately one thousand feet of space. The total space required of these ninety vehicles including their space cushions is five thousand feet. Just under the total distance for a mile. The feeder lane need not *also* be five thousand feet long for our example. Feeder lanes vary a great deal in length. However, for the purposes of our example the feeder lane need only carry ten passenger vehicles at a time. Most expressway feeder lanes will carry at least ten or more vehicles at a time

Every few seconds, there is a chain reaction move forward of the train of ninety vehicles in the target lane beginning in the front and ending with the ninetieth vehicle in back. Because of perception delays and the natural laws of physics, every surge of the chain results in ten gaps of varying sizes in front of the ten commercial vehicles.

During the late merge example analyzed earlier in this section, we stipulated that each merge requires about five seconds. During our early merge comparison, we will also stipulate that each merge requires about five seconds. However, early merging may enable as many as ten or more merges to take place *concurrently*.

Let's concede that *more* traffic is moving into the target lane within a *shorter* period of time during early merging compared to late merging.

(This is precisely our point.) Drivers who were already in the target lane often move to the left after experiencing repeated merges into their former lane. In addition after the initial ten merging vehicles have safely merged, there isn't any limitation that requires these ten mergers to remain in the original target lane for the remainder of the stop-and-go mile! Safe lane changes may be executed to the left.

Because of the *initial* gaps in traffic, approximately ten vehicles are merging concurrently in front of ten heavy vehicles every five seconds and *one hundred twenty* vehicles may merge per minute. However, we can also take into account that for every ten vehicles that move into the target lane, another ten will make a lane change and provide an additional gap every time they do. While this may also happen for late mergers, they can't take advantage of it because their gaps don't naturally occur at the end of the feeder lane. Recall that during late our late merging example, one vehicle merged every five seconds, and only *twelve* vehicles merged every minute.

If 10 additional vehicles from that lane have moved over to the next lane or lanes, the net result would be that potentially *ten times* as many vehicles cars can also merge into those gaps every minute in addition to the ten that are already merging in front of the commercial vehicles. The net result is that every five seconds from 10 -20 vehicles could possibly change position on busy expressways. Meanwhile late mergers only merge once every five seconds regardless of what is happening along the chain. We know we don't live in a perfect world, and we know that drivers do not drive like robots. In addition, there are dozens of variables here that we haven't explored. I know; I have experienced most of them myself.

But if you concede that the early merge strategy may only be *half* as efficient as described above in certain circumstances, then "only" sixty cars merge every minute versus twelve merges per minute during the late merging alternative.

Some readers may opine that they do not wish to merge in front of an eighteen-wheeler or any other trucker. For a variety of reasons, at least in stop-and-go traffic, merging in front of an eighteen-wheeler is probably one of the safest locations for you to merge! Truckers with huge payloads (especially fragile ones) cannot afford unnecessary jackrabbit starts (even if they could execute one), and they certainly cannot afford unnecessary applications of their air brakes. They also cannot afford to crash into you, under *any* circumstances.

A wise trucker is going to give you plenty of space and gradually slow the pay load as he/she slows the vehicle behind you. Besides, you are not staying in that lane for more than five to ten seconds anyway, are you?

There are at least two *additional* advantages to early, simultaneous merges that have to do with two important topics: public safety and the psychology of your fellow drivers. Many late mergers barrel down the "late merge" lane, traveling at speeds as high as seventy-five miles per hour or higher. Some of them drive their cars using a common scanning technique we call tunnel vision.

If it is within the rush-hour or rush-hour(s) period, some of them are in full, advanced, rabid road rage mode. However, even a blind squirrel finds an acorn once in a while. These drivers sometimes notice that a huge gap sometimes miraculously appears in the target lane. As previously noted this phenomenon is not a miracle at all but happens because of the laws of physics and other matters related to driving commercial vehicles and autos with manual transmissions. Often, late mergers "switch teams" and suddenly become "early merge" advocates after this occurs.

This *Charger* now attempts to "dock" his rocket in the gap that has suddenly miraculously appeared. As he rams his rocket in there, he realizes that the laws of physics must be reckoned with again. Rockets traveling at seventy-five miles per hour don't "dock" particularly well with a stopped vehicles being "driven" by an unsuspecting drivers; simply sitting there minding their own business in the queue. Well, enough of the metaphors here. I'm certain you get the idea by now.

The other remaining issue is the psychology of your fellow man. The drivers sitting there in the queue in your target lane are watching all the expectant late mergers whiz by. This may be a mild form of entertainment for some, but it is a bit more common that a mild form of irritation sets in. As late mergers scream by them at seventy-five miles per hour, the drivers in the other traffic lanes watch brake lights regularly appear up at the end on the late merging line. In many cases, the abrupt rise of the rear of some of the expectant late mergers tells all the other drivers that the "late merge" didn't go exactly as planned.

Some of these stops cannot only be very "abrupt" but very dangerous for any driver or pedestrian on the shoulder.

After all, an abrupt emergency stop requires employing seeking of an escape route. Sometimes an escape route does not exist or the escape route endangers others. Now these dangerous drivers are asking all the safe drivers to politely create a hole so that they may merge *in front* of them in the target lane.

Since this is not a natural gap, it must be created artificially. Many drivers (quite understandably) will not create artificial gaps for reckless late mergers.

Meanwhile, the early mergers, creeping along at safe speeds from one to five miles per hour safely merge as the gaps appear naturally. In addition, when cars begin to accelerate in the target lane, these drivers accelerate equally to keep pace.

The gaps appear more frequently, and they are larger, creating more opportunities for safe, early merging. Meanwhile, most of the late mergers are still sitting in the same spot, while a mild or advanced case of road rage sits in. If a driver is sitting at the end of the feeder lane, waiting endlessly for a gap that seems as if it will never materialize, this reality can and often does have an impact on the driver's emotions which can lead to an abrupt change in his/her behavior.

This change in behavior may be manifested by an exhibited increase in mildly *aggressive driving* or into an exhibition of an advanced state of *road rage*. These two topics will be covered in greater detail in chapter 9.

Remember, you not only have absolute control over your own behaviors, but you have more control over the behaviors of other drivers nearby than you may have ever believed possible.

CHAPTER 4

The Classroom

What actually takes place in an outstanding twenty-first- century driver education classroom? I strongly recommend that all classroom driver education material be replaced and/or updated at least once every *ten years or earlier.* The reason: New technology requires that driver education standards, practices, and behind-the- wheel techniques be upgraded every few years. Even the very best driver education curriculums, be they public or private, cannot teach the same techniques utilizing the same material decade after decade.

In addition, as you research the local public and private driving school options in your state, you should *verify* that the contents of all classroom and behind-the- wheel training materials reinforce the *current* edition of your state's Department of Motor Vehicles manual. Note that we didn't suggest that you merely research the driving schools in your local commuting area. If you are planning to send your teen to college and you wish to *help ensure* your teen reaches the age to attend and graduate, we suggest that you take as much care in selecting a driver education program as you would in selecting a higher learning institution for any other purpose.

For a start, I believe that a sound driver education curriculum requires an outstanding textbook. In addition, in my opinion, good training videos provide the catalyst for interactive training. Each segment (usually no more than five to ten minutes) must be discussed with the students, and it must be discussed in great detail. Outstanding training video segments provide the fuel for dozens and hundreds of interactive questions.

This can only happen if your teen's driver education instructor is thoroughly engaged at all times. Teens cannot teach themselves this material. Even if they attempt to do so, our experience has repeatedly verified that they will make incorrect assumptions.

When instructors are not in the classroom, students doze, daydream, turn their phones on, text message, flirt, play, and generally find almost anything to do other than do what they are supposed to be doing. Good instructors do not leave their students unattended.

At minimum, the classroom training should repeatedly reinforce all the key concepts included in your state's DMV manual and much, much more. Many students do not read the DMV manual and stumble through their permit test anyway. This gives them a false sense of security in believing that if they are smart enough, they can simply use common sense to drive safely. Potentially, this could be a fatal error in judgment.

When students are asked challenging rules-of-the road questions in class, they quickly learn that common sense helps. However, they also quickly learn that common sense alone will not enable them to correctly answer all questions they are posed. They also begin to realize that, without a concerted effort to learn basic driving concepts, their ability to drive safely will be severely compromised. We suggest that you ensure that all classroom material is very thoroughly reinforced and understood by your teen.

The three principal owners of CADETS have received various types of training in a variety of different classrooms for at least a third of their lives.

As for me personally, an FAA friend of mine once calculated that I had trained in FAA classrooms for about twice the amount of time that an average engineer spends in the classroom receiving formal classroom training. Then there's the six years I went to college at night. During these different training circumstances and in different training venues, the training was delivered by employing a variety of different training methodologies.

During these periods, I also received training in field of training development, training delivery, training methodology, and training administration. Currently there are many choices for training delivery available including lecture, correspondence, performance-based, and a variety of automation-based tools that may also be employed. Two automation-based alternatives are computer-based instruction and automated simulators.

Classroom training, online or computer-based instruction (CBI), correspondence study, and driving simulators all have their advantages and disadvantages for being employed *before* student drivers enter an actual training vehicle. The intent of this publication is not to debate the relative merits of each type of training methodology.

The CADETS driver education curriculum included interactive classroom training, interactive training videos, a sophisticated driving simulator, an approved textbook, supplemental handouts, and of course our actual five star NHTSA training vehicles. Various teaching or presentation techniques may be and often are employed in driver education. Many educators agree that a "picture is worth a thousand words." A well-designed, produced, and directed training video segment is invaluable! This is one reason why videos have proven to be far more reliable than eyewitness accounts in other fields such as crime reconstruction.

In our opinion, the best driver education instruction videos combine action/reaction video segments, graphics, interactive questions, 3-D animation, multi- angle views, and virtual reality reenactments. These types of videos were not developed for a teen to stare at in a zombielike state for hour after hour. Most of the video segments last from five to ten minutes, and all of them (in our opinion) require student interaction. Intensive and frequent student interaction helps prevent daydreaming, dozing, flirting with classmates, doodling, and attempting to text message underneath tables or desks.

Peer pressure still seems to be alive and well in classrooms, and sometimes it works in a positive way.

Our classroom will often include students from three or more local high schools, Christian schools, homeschooled students, students from private schools, or adults just learning to drive. Most students wish to demonstrate to their classmates that they know the answers to our questions; therefore, they also know how to drive. Even though the video segments are outstanding as stand-alone teaching tools, we have also verified that they must be augmented with this interaction. This is just one of several reasons that classroom instructors must be engaged at all times.

When students recognize that they simply must pay attention to the videos in order to answer correctly, they pay attention to the videos.

We do not train our instructors to provide lengthy college style lectures. We also do not encourage our instructors to tell lengthy anecdotes revolving around their various personal driving experiences. There simply isn't time for that. Instead, we ask very specific questions about each and every video segment the students are required to watch. Sometimes we place the video segment in pause and ask questions about the video while it has been paused.

We have calculated that we ask our students nearly five hundred questions during each classroom day. Although the videos are worth ten thousand words, our questions and answers provide clarification, comprehension, reinforcement, and sometimes initiate additional student questions. These teaching techniques are not new. We are merely verifying that they must be employed in the driver education field in order to facilitate thorough understanding and learning.

We are proud of the videos we have selected for our classroom training. However, these videos are not the only driver education videos that may be employed in a successful driver education program. Moreover, the three principal training videos that we use were developed by three different organizations in three different areas of the country. One was produced in Houston Texas, a second in Saint Louis, Missouri, and a third from either California or Florida.

At this point, I feel I need to provide a disclaimer. The remainder of this chapter *is not* intended to provide a replacement for classroom training. This chapter, like all other chapters in this book, summarizes the material that we feel should be provided in a driver education program. Therefore, each of the paragraphs below provides a *very brief* overview of the subject matter we presented during each training segment. As previously referenced, most states require at least eight hours of classroom training or equivalency to eight hours classroom training for teen driver education. This chapter actually requires a relatively short period of time to read in its entirety.

In an actual classroom, the following topics typically include video instructor/student reenactments in a training vehicle, supplemental animation or graphics, and a question/answer period. During each training segment, an emphasis is placed on safety practices, performance, and the achievement of the desired final results.

A knowledgeable instructor, well versed in interactive training, may actually find it to be a challenge to determine which material to cram into an eight-hour instruction day and which material to cover in more detail later in the car (often in a parking lot). This is just one of multiple reasons that most training programs developed for professional driver education instructors require at least forty hours of instruction.

However, for the teen driver education program in our state, the following is typically presented during one eight-hour day or two four-hour days.

Introduction

During this period of instruction, it is important to define *what* will be covered during the entire course, in the classroom and BTW. We also explain *when, how,* and perhaps most importantly why each approach will be employed. It is also an opportunity to get to know the students. I usually start by asking each student why they wish to get their driver's license. Fifteen- and sixteen- year-old students provide some interesting and sometimes humorous answers to this question. It helps to get the students thinking that this isn't going to be a lecture class.

Basic Auto Setup, Void Areas, and Blind Spots

It is important for a beginning driver to observe how a car is prepared for each individual of a different height, size, and shape to drive it. These video segments may also provide 360-degree view of void areas and blind spots before beginning drivers are depicted moving the car. The sequence for all pre-driving adjustments and checks are discussed, including the seat adjustment, the mirror adjustments, and the verification that students know where the major controls and indicators are located.

Basic Operation of Gas and Brake

A video segment with a driving instructor and student reenacts how a safe driver moves the right foot between the gas and brake and applies pressure to each smoothly under standard driving conditions.

Basic Steering

The hands are shown at 9:00 a.m. and 3:00 p.m. or 9:30 a.m. and 2:30 p.m. during forward steering. Turns that are less than 45 degrees *generally* may be completed while both hands are on the wheel.

Basic Turning and Three-Point Turns

Hand-over-hand turning is depicted while the vehicle is in drive. Turns that are greater than 45 degrees (turns around corners or U-turns) *generally* should be completed hand over hand.

New drivers may see this, and many other basic maneuvers depicted in the classroom before they drive. Later, the behind-the-wheel instructor may demonstrate many basic maneuvers (again) in the car. Determining precisely when to convert from forward steering to hand- over-hand turning is a function of the BTW instructor.

The three-point turn is shown using step-by-step reenactments and/ or animation. A three-point turn may become necessary in a variety of circumstances such as reaching the end of a single lane dead-end road where there is insufficient room for a U-turn. Most driving examinations include a three-point turn. Like virtually all driving examination maneuvers, there are specific actions that examiners look for. For example, signaling before moving toward the curb, looking over the left shoulder before moving back into the roadway, and signaling again before reentering.

Targeting and Wheel Release Exiting Turns

The driver should be looking in the direction he/she intends for the car to travel. While the actor/student driver is shown exiting turns around corners, the wheel release is demonstrated so that the hands don't actually leave the wheel more than a fraction of an inch while exiting these turns. Instead, when executed properly, inertia allows the wheel and tires to return to their natural positions (straight) as car and driver exit these turns. Students are informed that if they hold on to the wheel too long after a turn, the car *continues* to turn. If they release the wheel too early, they will allow the car to *drift* into the opposing lane. The car is shown exiting turns in the proper lane at all times.

Residential and City Driving

Students should observe driving demonstrated by outstanding student drivers before viewing any videos of poor student drivers. We believe in positive reinforcement.

Lane Changes, Right and Left Turns

In our classroom, the SMOG lane change procedure is discussed and demonstrated. SMOG stands for signal, mirror, over the shoulder, and go.

At intersections, right turns may only be completed after a full stop, unless turning right with a green arrow or a green light. Even then, it is advised to clear the intersection before entering. At red lights, drivers must stop and clear before entering.

Unprotected left turns (all those without a green arrow) are the most dangerous turns on the road. Some left turns are completed without a light, with a yellow light (if your vehicle is *already* in the intersection), with a green light, and with a green arrow. In all cases, we teach our students to ensure that a safe distance from oncoming traffic is maintained at all times, and that an accurate assessment of the speed of oncoming traffic has been completed *before* initiating any left turn. We also teach that some dangerous left turns are best avoided completely. *Three safe right turns equals one extremely dangerous left turn, or a different left turn location may be selected.*

Perpendicular Parking

This video segment may include instructor/student reenactments in a training vehicle, supplemental animation or graphics, and a question/answer period. The emphasis is on safety practices, performance, and the achievement of the desired final result. New drivers shouldn't park between cars until they are provided with BTW instruction, and they have had an opportunity to park between vacant spaces repeatedly.

Backing and Angle Parking

While backing, the left hand is placed at twelve o'clock with fingers pointed toward roof of car. Drivers of noncommercial vehicles (standard passenger vehicles) must look out of the back window while backing. Proper angle parking is reenacted. New drivers shouldn't park between cars until they are provided with BTW instruction, and they have had an opportunity to park between vacant spaces repeatedly.

Parallel Parking

It is beneficial for beginning drivers to see safe and efficient parallel parking depicted in a classroom before they enter an actual training vehicle for their BTW training. The classroom videos allow the parking to be reenacted in slow motion, in multiple angles, or in stop- and-go so that all steps are clearly understood. It shouldn't be necessary to repeat here that BTW training and practice will be necessary later.

We utilize cones and poles in our training vehicles during our second BTW driving lesson that includes parallel parking. However, where does a beginning driver practice? Most DMVs allow parking practice on weekends when no testing is taking place.

We take advantage of this during a typical Saturday or Sunday final driving lesson by having the student drive to the DMV and previewing the driving test with a student. The driving exam only requires about fifteen minutes, but our advanced driving lesson requires a total of two hours of advanced driving.

Reading Intersections and Yielding

During this Q and A interactive lesson, a heavy emphasis is placed on the rules of the road and safety practices. Most collisions occur at intersections. Merging is covered at length in a later section and during at least two BTW sessions in the car.

Turnabouts and More

Cul-de-sacs and other types of turnabouts may be discussed here. Out in roadways, some unsafe U-turns have signs posted and directed toward the driver warning that a U-turn at that location is not only unsafe; it is illegal. It is amazing how many drivers ignore the signs. Those locations are often the locations that police officers stake out, for more than one reason. In addition, there are many unsafe U-turn locations in the country that have no warning signs at all.

Our classroom training and later our BTW training is intended to provide our students with an appreciation of the speed and distance required for a moving vehicle to stop at different speeds. For example, an approaching passenger vehicle or a large SUV moving at sixty miles per hour requires a football field or more in distance to come to a complete stop.

When a new driver is determining a safe location for a U-turn versus an unsafe location, this must be taken into account along with several other factors at that specific location. Students are cautioned to assess speed and distance of approaching vehicles. If unsafe conditions persist, proceed to a different U-turn location or a regulated intersection.

Three-Second Rule, Point of No Return, and 1-2-3

The three-second rule is now used for following distance instead of one second for every ten miles per hour.

Pick out a fixed object when the car in front passes that location, and then count one thousand one, one thousand two, and one thousand three. If your car passes the object before you count to three, you are following too closely.

The point of no return refers to approaching an intersection when the light turns yellow. The point of no return is the point where the speed of your vehicle and the distance of your vehicle from the intersection at that precise moment (when the light turns yellow) have determined that you continue moving. During the video segments, students are shown that good drivers do not "speed up to beat the light," do not skid into the intersection at the last moment, and do not intentionally enter intersections during "stale" (long) yellow lights. However, the precise point of no return varies with speed and distance.

If and when any beginning driver, or any driver for that matter, is within the boundaries of the intersection when lights turn red, the point of no return has *not* being judged properly! This means that when the solid yellow light first appears and your car may be stopped safely before entering, you must do so and execute the stop *without* skidding into the intersection.

The 1-2-3 count refers to a situation when you are the first car in line at an intersection waiting for a green light to proceed. When the green light flashes, remember that another driver approaching from the left or the right may not have observed the point-of-no-return rule properly and may be barreling toward you! The 1-2-3 count allows you to very quickly *look left, right left* before you move. If there are no approaching drivers or they are clearly stopping, then move immediately. If not, this quick double-check just may save your life.

You will see many drivers who violate "stale yellow lights" and even "fresh red lights" rules of the road and enter your intersection when you should have had the "right-of-way." Remember, it is better to make the impatient driver behind you beep at you (as if you don't see the light) than it is to have a sniper T-bone you as you enter a violated intersection.

Gap Selection

Gap selection is explained in great detail in the merging chapter. However, it is also part of the learning process for beginning drivers to complete unprotected left turns. We typically do not have our beginning drivers complete unprotected left turns until the final lesson, unless we are certain they can safely do so a bit earlier than the final lesson.

Even then, we are talking to them while they approach any unprotected left turn and especially if we must wait for "a gap" in oncoming traffic in the middle of an intersection.

Remember, pro instructors have brakes on our side of the vehicles, but we rarely wish to put ourselves in position where we must use them while moving. An ounce of prevention is worth a pound of cure. We suggest you work out a system whereby you assess your teen's understanding of speed and distance while *you* are driving first. Later, when your teen is driving, make certain you and your teen agree on a code word for the completion of unprotected left turns.

Start with very basic left residential driving and then gradually move to very light suburban driving and then on to moderate and heavy traffic. Take "baby steps" at first, even if you don't call them baby steps when you talk to your teen.

Passing

We do not encourage beginning drivers to pass on two- lane highways within city limits. However, they must know the rules of pertaining to solid double lines, broken lines on your side of the road, and broken lines on the approaching driver's side of the road. Beginning drivers must be trained to understand that there is a significant difference between a section of road where it is *legal* to pass and a section of road where it is *safe* to pass.

Special Situations

Special situations may include responding properly to all emergency vehicles. Several reenactments of drivers responding to emergency vehicles may be presented here.

Expressways, Freeways, and Turnpikes

This section should depict how to merge properly, how to pass, how to lane change, which lane to drive in during different periods, how to prepare for exiting, and how to exit safely.

In addition, most beginning drivers do not know the difference between an interstate, an expressway, and a highway. Interstate highways cross state lines but may not be an expressway, freeway, or turnpike during the entire length of that highway.

Most U.S. interstate highways, state highways, and parkways have at least one thing in common; they were all constructed with intersections. Freeways are more common out West, and turnpikes are more common in the East. Certain states in the Midwest (i.e., Oklahoma) use both freeways and turnpikes in their road and highway system. Freeways do not typically have toll booths, but there have been some exceptions. Turnpikes typically have toll booths for entering and exiting with some toll booths in between the entrances and exits during long stretches.

In the classroom, we use the generic term *expressway* for freeways and turnpikes. We also use the term to clearly distinguish them from regular highways and parkways. Expressways, freeways, and turnpikes all have one thing in common too; they do not have intersections. Yes, the posted speed limits are usually a bit higher on freeways and turnpikes than on some highways, but that isn't always the case. For example, out in the middle of some of the large Midwestern states, the posted speed limit on rural highways may be as high as on the posted speeds of the freeways or turnpikes in town.

Rural Driving

Rural roads or driving conditions often include hazards that are common with city driving but sometimes include hazards that are far more common in the "country." For example, flashing yellow lights are often employed for cross traffic at busier roads and highways and/or at those locations where visibility is poor.

Approaching vehicles may be difficult to see *and* traveling at high rates of speed. Extra caution must be observed at these intersections.

Out in a rural community, it may be common for very slow moving tractors to be creeping along in your lane. Safe passing may be completed in accordance with the markings on the roadway *and* your assessment of the speed and distance of oncoming traffic. Current weather conditions and a variety of other factors (the condition of your car) should be taken into account before you pass as well.

Heavy Traffic

Many young students have never seen eight lanes of "expressway" backed up in stop and go traffic much less having had the experience of driving in it. They must be informed about what, when, how, and why many driving practices must be adapted for very heavy traffic. Many scenarios may be presented in the classroom before beginning drivers are exposed to these types of actual driving conditions.

For example, one of our training videos includes an overhead camera angle of very busy "expressway" in Houston Texas. The cars are moving in stop and go.

Students are asked, "If the cars are moving at only three miles per hour, approximately what speed should you merge at when you reach the end of the ramp feeder lane?" The answer is approximately three miles per hour. At the same location at a different time of day, the merging speed may be as much as sixty miles per hour or more if the cars are moving at those speeds!

Advanced Highway Driving Concepts

The paragraph above is an advanced driving concept of course. There are potentially hundreds upon thousands of advanced driving concepts that may be presented and discussed in a classroom. This is one of many reasons that time in a classroom is precious and choices are important. We choose not to use crash videos (other than our single "Aftermath" segment) because we feel that after one or two segments, they are counterproductive. The kids get it that there are things they are not supposed to do, and there may be horrible consequences for driving recklessly. Beginning drivers want to know what *to do* to avoid crashes. This is the *primary* focus of all our classroom material.

Road Testing

Students want to know how their state's DMV test is conducted. While our emphasis is always on safety, we also recognize students are keenly interested in how best to prepare for the DMV test. Some beginning drivers have previously been led to believe that the only thing they really have to worry about is parallel parking. We explain otherwise very early. If a beginning driver is an expert at parallel parking but cannot drive safely or drive in accordance with the rules of the road, there are many short-term consequences as well as long-term consequences.

During the classroom training, virtually all aspects of the driving examination are reenacted during the DVD segments. We include a video reenactment from one video in the morning and another in the afternoon.

Like all our video segments, we may pause and freeze frame, discuss, ask questions, answer them, and explain in detail exactly what the examiners are looking for because we know. We also describe in detail the examination material that will be covered during our BTW driving lessons and which procedures will be required again during their driving examinations. We reinforce how the evaluation process relates to actual safe driving practices.

ABS Don't Let Up

Many drivers of any age do not know what ABS stands for or why almost all late model cars are now manufactured with ABS installed. ABS stands for anti- lock braking system and was originally designed for the landing/ braking gear of aircraft. Like many inventions, it worked so well in one industry that it was adapted for another. ABS was originally designed for aircraft landing wheels to assist the slowing/braking process in slick conditions (rain, sleet, snow, and ice) but also has a function in normal landing conditions.

When ABS is installed in a car, if and when the car is about to enter a skid, the ABS computer pumps the brakes faster than a humanly possible. The driver can keep his/her foot on the brake without letting up. The ABS either reduces the skid or eliminates the skid entirely. Also, students are trained to steer their cars away from danger.

This is a corrective action that is far more effective in a vehicle that has ABS installed than a vehicle that was manufactured pre ABS. We also have a video segment that depicts drivers skidding in non-ABS vehicles in the rain, on snow, and on ice. Students are trained to steer in the direction of the skid and reduce pressure on the brakes when a non-ABS vehicle has entered a skid.

The Aftermath

This segment deals with the aftermath and consequences of impaired driving, distracted driving, and several other categories of reckless driving.

As previously noted, some driving schools screen multiple crash videos during the teaching day, chewing up valuable teaching time in the process. Other schools have a police officer speak to the class. Either approach may be beneficial if not overdone.

Our training video segments provide examples of all the above, but more importantly, they were developed to educate impressionable young drivers about all of the above. When preparing a driver education classroom syllabus, I am conscious of the fact that each minute of time in the classroom is valuable. Each minute of time devoted to a topic should be assessed in advance for maximum effectiveness without compromising the instructional purpose of that block of instruction.

Road Signs, Highway Signs, and Signals

All state Department of Motor Vehicles manuals are not created equal. Fortunately, the South Carolina state DMV manual is outstanding. If your state DMV manual has excellent illustrations of road signs, highway signs, and traffic signals, this is a good time to reference the manual. If not, I would find a different textbook to reference in class. One of our training videos also has a Q and A section pertaining to road signs. The road sign is displayed, and the students are urged to either collectively or individually define the message of the sign.

City and Residential Driving

The training videos should provide examples of safe driving practices in virtually all common driving circumstances. Students should be encouraged to ask questions here. In fact, they should be encouraged to ask questions all day.

As an instructor, I ask at least five hundred questions during a classroom day. Sometimes the questions are rhetorical, but in all cases, the questions are intended to keep the students focused and alert.

The Driver's Exam

See "Road Testing" above. New drivers are also informed of the questions most examiners will ask before the car is even moved out of the parking lot. We do the same thing before each of our BTW driving lessons. In addition, we take great care in setting up our training vehicles for each individual driver.

Examiners will not only verify that a new driver knows how to operate the controls properly, but they will also observe the beginning driver as he/she sets up the vehicle for safe operation before driving. Beginning drivers are encouraged to learn even more about their own family vehicle than they know about a training car.

They are encouraged to read their owners' manuals front to back and ask questions of their parents when they have them. If a parent isn't certain about the answer to a question, ask your local mechanic.

Training for Normal Driving Conditions

In most cities, in fact in many rural communities, "normal" driving is hazardous every day. This is one of the reasons that the development of sound defensive driving skills is heavily emphasized in the classroom. Many beginning drivers drive with a certain amount of "tunnel vision." They must not only be trained to scan the traffic scene, but they must also be trained to recognize when *potential* hazards have been introduced.

Many examples of collision avoidance in otherwise routine driving conditions should be introduced and discussed.

Training for Hazardous Driving Conditions

The only difference between this block of instruction and the previous block is the severity of the initial traffic condition. The hazard may be rain, sleet, snow, construction, or a variety of other hazards. New drivers are trained to respond appropriately to these hazards. The posted speed limit may not be the safest speed for the hazard.

The passing zone may be legal, but is it safe? The construction zone may have a flagman. Obey the speed limit, or obey the flagman?

Virtual Driver for Defensive Drivers

This is one of the most effective segments in one of our training videos. A driving scenario is reenacted, and a hazard is introduced. The video then pauses and asks a multiple-choice question in the stem of the question. Four possible distracters are presented, some of them plausible. This creates student interaction and dialogue. The correct answer isn't always the most plausible or more obvious initial answer. This is an opportunity to explain why certain traffic laws are what they are rather than what we sometimes *wish* them to be.

I have heard some students declare that the response to most driving scenarios is the application of "common sense." We agree that being in possession of "common sense" helps. However, we emphasize that the application of "common sense" is realized before, during, and after driving a vehicle.

This means becoming well versed and knowledgeable of the rules of the road, consistently applying those rules, driving safely, and applying defensive driving skills as presented in an outstanding training program. When passengers of any age observe other drivers, they must clearly understand cause and effect. These are also the skills that *you* must possess and display at all times to your teen.

Searching for Clues to Motor Vehicle Conflicts

Most drivers "tip off" other drivers as to what they are going to do before they do it, even if they don't signal. The "clue" may be the driver's eyes, the direction of the driver's head, or the direction the wheels of the car are turned. Traffic conditions may also provide a clue. For example, in heavy traffic, a driver may "lane jump" believing that any lane other than the lane he/she is driving in *must* be faster. Our students are trained to look for these clues in advance while developing their defensive driving skills.

Positioning and Timing at Intersections

This is a critical skill set, especially before completing unprotected left turns.

If a driver immediately in front of you enters an intersection to make a left turn under a yellow light, you should remain behind the white line until the next light rotation. When two or three drivers are sitting out there, the first driver may complete his/her left turn under yellow as oncoming traffic slows to a stop, but any additional vehicles will be turning left under a red light. This is illegal, holds up cross traffic, and is dangerous to you and other drivers.

Risk Management

Virtually, every aspect of the entire training program could be identified as contributing to the development of the new drivers' risk management skills. As stated earlier in the book, the American Automobile Association (AAA)'s advanced Driver Improvement Training teaches us that risk is always present, that perceived risk is different than actual risk, that risk is shared, and that risk can be altered. That last phrase "risk can be altered" is especially important.

There are reasons that some drivers drive vehicles that are marred with multiple dents, dings, hanging parts, scrapes, and evidence of minor and major damage etc.

Other drivers seem to drive thousands of miles over decades without incurring so much as a dent in their vehicles.

While there is such a thing as being in the wrong place at the wrong time, good defensive drivers take proactive steps every day to manage their risk. These preventative measures are taken before they drive, while driving, and during all aspects of the decision making process and routinely includes advanced collision avoidance actions.

Basic Vehicle Upkeep and Maintenance

Beginning drivers may not be aware of how important regular upkeep and maintenance of an automobile is. In fact, this is part of risk management too. For example, if the tires are not inflated properly, it affects the safe performance of the vehicle and may also alter fuel mileage, braking distance, and life of the tires. All fluid levels must be checked and/or changed in accordance with the owner's manual. Our training videos explain basic maintenance procedures as well as how to change a flat tire and how to safely jump-start a vehicle.

Drug and Alcohol Prevention

This subject is covered at length in the "The Aftermath" section for teens. For underage teens, we basically teach that "an ounce of prevention is worth a pound of cure" and the consequences of acting irresponsibly can be life altering or life ending. The Coastal Academy for Driver Education, Safety, and Training (CADETS) was in possession of a very sophisticated driving simulator. The simulator could be programmed to simulate thirty different driving scenarios for drivers with ten different levels of possible "impairment" levels to simulate. We determined that there wasn't sufficient time in a fourteen-hour training program (eight in the classroom and only six BTW) to employ the simulator for drivers who were underage to drink legally anyway. However, we did take the simulator to several universities, state colleges, and community colleges, and even a few high schools that requested us. This material is covered in chapter ten and may be enlightening for parents of college-age students who believe any young adult over the age of eighteen already knows how to drive.

Highway Patrolman Commentary

As previously noted, a few of our video segments are either introduced by a highway patrolman or narrated by a highway patrolman. Most of the other video segments are narrated by professional driving instructors for good reason.

We are conscious of the fact that law enforcement officers have different responsibilities and skill sets than professional driving instructors. Their focus is on law enforcement; our focus is on teaching.

When arrangements can be made for a patrolman or other law enforcement officer to enter the classroom, it is helpful to have them reiterate the rules of the road and the consequences of driving under the influence of drugs or alcohol. Police officers will help explain in detail what *not to do*. The instructors can provide a follow-up analysis to explain in detail what *to do* to exhibit safe and lawful practices at all times.

Positive Reinforcement Test

Some driver education schools do not administer any type of written examination in the classroom. Years ago while I was employed at the FAA Academy as an instructor/developer, I attended a course called "Instructional Testing."

At that time, I learned that a well-crafted multiple choice quiz could be a valuable training aid in its own right. In addition, by that time, I had already learned that multiple choice tests could be written to be very "difficult" for an average student or very "easy" for an average student.

As a result, our CADETS twenty-five-question final quiz was carefully crafted. Our test was not designed to fail students; the test was designed to verify that students had listened to the material, absorbed the material, and understood the material, and we as instructors had met our own objectives. Our classroom test also included some questions that we believed were *essential* that our students know the answers to when they finished our program. Most of those questions are asked again in the parking lot before each driving lesson began.

Tests are graded in private, and we do not expect students to reveal their scores during a review process. However, the feedback to students and instructor during the review of the test is actually part of the learning process.

When a student struggled with determining the correct answer to a question during the review segment, *it was often another student who explained why the correct answer was correct and why the other distracters were incorrect.* Sometimes a peer explains it more effectively than the instructor! This is why peer understanding and comprehension is so important. The instructor can and should also verify the correct answer by referring to the DMV manual again or by having further clarifying discussion.

When students perform well on the written test (the overwhelming majority of them do), it increases their confidence before they enter the car for their first BTW lesson. In any case, beginning drivers are encouraged to reread their DMV manuals before entering our training cars for their initial BTW lessons. In addition, they are encouraged to complete our course critiques for all classroom and BTW training. Parents are encouraged to complete the critiques with their teens. Instructors need feedback too! This is how we improve.

Classroom Summary

The objectives of the training day are repeated here.

In addition, this is a good opportunity to explain how coordination of all BTW training is to be conducted. Students are again encouraged to ask questions during this period and during all periods of the classroom day.

When you begin to search within your own local commuting area for your teen's driver education program, we suggest you compare their classroom syllabus to topics listed above. Other similar segments may be utilized of course, but this chapter will give you some guidelines. In the field of driver education, new drivers of any age must (figuratively) be allowed to take baby steps before walking, small steps before striding and long strides before running. If the classroom training is bypassed, much of this material is also bypassed.

We suggest you select a program that is not overly dependent on crash videos. A crash video is not particularly effective if you are dealing with a new frightened student-driver who is just trying to navigate the car around a parking lot properly. Most beginning drivers are just trying to follow instructions as best they can.

By the time they finish with the classroom training, 99 percent of them are well aware that they are not expert drivers or even accomplished drivers.

Most of the topics we referenced in this chapter will be referenced again during the behind-the-wheel chapters. As we instruct our students, all the classroom training is directly applicable to the behind-the-wheel instruction. Students cannot exit the classroom and then perform a "memory dump" as they exit the classroom door. Instead, they are instructed to commit the information to memory as best they can and expect to be asked about what they learned again during their BTW lessons. Once they enter the car before each driving lesson, our teens are genuinely amazed at how much they remember from the classroom training and often admit how much they didn't know before attending.

You will see all the above topics referenced again later in the BTW performance grid chapters for each lesson. The BTW grids will be discussed in a fair amount of detail during chapters 5, 6, and 7. We stress to our students that only about 20 percent of successful, safe driving revolves around the application of their motor skills. We explain to our students that 80 percent of successful, *safe* driving involves correct decision making.

Proper decision making cannot take place if a student simply has no clue of what to do. Therefore, we saturate the students with the rules of the road in the classroom *before* they enter the car and again *before* they drive. When students do not answer correctly, we tell them again and then ask them again, until they answer correctly.

This may sound more intense than it really is. Almost all our graduates refer younger siblings to us when they are old enough, and they also refer their friends to us. They know we are firm, but they also know we are fair. Virtually, all of them completely understand that we have their best interest at heart. When teens enter our program, we tell them that we have three primary goals:

- We have a short-term goal to provide them with every tool in our tool box to ensure that they are prepared for the DMV driving test and pass it the first time.

- We have an intermediate goal to provide them with the knowledge, the driving skills, and the demonstrated ability to drive safely and within the rules of the road at all times.

- We have a long-term goal that each of our students drives collision free for the remainder of their natural lives.

CHAPTER 5

Basic Driving Skills

As previously noted, our impetus for the writing this book is our interest in promoting a partnership with parents. We have had perhaps thousands of discussions with teens and their parents. We are also on the road all day observing adults drive. In addition, we closely observe parents when they arrive at training locations before and after driving lessons. Through research, observation, and discussion, we are aware that most beginning drivers have at least one parent:

- That never had an opportunity to complete formal driver education.

- That completed driver education but is not aware that current technology has changed the manner in which driver education is currently conducted.

- Has relocated to a new state and has not had the time or the inclination to review their new state's Department of Motor Vehicles manual.

- That knows some or most of the things they are supposed to do while driving but lost the will or the inclination to apply safe driving practices at all times years ago.

Whether you are aware of it or not, your preteen has been watching you drive and has been learning from you. He/she may not talk about it with you directly unless specifically asked. However, during their preteen and early teen years, they begin to draw conclusions about the behaviors that are acceptable behind the wheel. Therefore, since most children ride with their parents the majority of the time, their early driving behaviors reflect your driving behaviors.

Remember, high school driver education and professional driving schools only train your teen for about 10 percent of the total "supervised" driving time required by a graduated licensing program state. In reality, the number of hours of parent-supervised driving time should far exceed the number of hours typically provided by a high school or contracted from a professional driving school.

In order to be effective and credible to your teen, you must not only know more than your teen knows, but you should be able to demonstrate that you know more than your teen knows. In addition, regardless of how thorough the training your teen received has been, you have something your teen certainly does not have: *experience.*

You can use this experience to your advantage while supplementing your teen's driver education. However, be careful; you must be diligent in verifying that the guidance you provide is 100 percent accurate. There are several steps you can take to refresh your knowledge about your state's rules of the road and many other topics regarding the safe operation of a motor vehicle. For a start, *read your state's DMV manual cover to cover and be prepared to answer questions from your teen about the contents.* After teens read the manual, they are often confused and draw incorrect conclusions.

When you interact with your teen's driving instructor, ask them questions! Adults are often surprised by how much they have forgotten and/or how much has changed. In addition, if you refresh your knowledge of basic rules of the road, it will help increase the likelihood of you providing your teen with correct guidance at all times. It will also help reinforce the training he/she is receiving from the professional instructor.

If your state's driver education program is as thorough as the CADETS driver education program, you might be wondering why we are emphasizing the "partnership with parents" at all. The answer lies in clearly defining the word *mastery* as identified in the last column of our BTW performance grids. A pro instructor in any state only has a finite amount of time to work with a student driver. A specific predetermined amount of *formal* BTW (behind the wheel) training time is required in forty-seven of fifty states for the completion of driver education

However, in our state as in many states, a permit may be obtained before a single driving lesson. In addition, in our state as in many states, the permit period is six months in duration. After that, renewal is possible. This may mean that certain habits and procedures may have been coached during the first five months or even longer, and then the teen may arrive for eight hours of classroom training and six hours of BTW training just a few weeks before becoming eligible to take the driving test.

I am often asked which approach is best for initiating formal driver education for their teen. Should parents enroll their teens in driver education before they have driven at all, or should parents enroll their teens at the end of the permit cycle? As noted earlier in the book, some parents even allow their teen to receive a permit, waive driver education, and allow their teen to reach an age where driver education is not required at all.

Of course, we have recommendations based on our experiences with hundreds upon thousands of teens, but it may not apply to your specific teen. If your child has a learning disability or some other physical or mental limitation, the following recommendations may not apply. However, for the majority of teens, we recommend the following:

We recommend that you abide by the graduated licensing program in your state, obtain a permit for your teen soon after becoming eligible, and have your teen complete driver education within the first three to six months of eligibility. If you wait longer than six months after eligibility, the chances increase that your teen will receive "informal training" from an older "friend' or family member who did not complete driver education. Your teen's safety will be also be jeopardized by the fact that he or she is often riding along helplessly with an unsafe driver and isn't even aware of it. This isn't a function of age. We haven't seen significant performance differences between fifteen-, sixteen-, and seventeen-year-old students *except the performance differences are related to the new driver having received proper training verses improper training.*

If you take your teen out for some BTW coaching, we recommend that you begin in a large vacant parking lot. You should be very cautious and conservative in determining when your teen may "graduate" to residential and/or rural driving. After four or five very basic driving lessons, this would be a good time for the new driver to receive formal classroom training and the first BTW driving lesson from a pro-driving instructor.

When a student driver enters a training car for his/her first driving lesson, it is imperative that a professional driving instructor establishes how much the new student knows about driving and if that knowledge can safely be applied to the training car. Some students who display exceptional skills in the classroom are not prepared physically to drive a car. Other students who are not exceptional classroom students may (eventually) display outstanding physical skills while operating a motor vehicle.

Both types of students and all other students must be developed to an acceptable standard. What is an acceptable performance standard? Well, that's a key question, isn't it? We expect this book to help define acceptable BTW performance standards. While doing so, we will also describe BTW performance that is not acceptable. By the end of the book, you should be able to draw a very clear distinction between safe driving practices and unsafe driving practices.

In describing typical student drivers entering the car for their initial lesson, it is far easier to define what the majority of them *cannot* do properly than what they *can* do. The following is a partial list of characteristics and behaviors that are common in students that have *already held their permits for a period of time.*

- They do not know all the set up procedures for preparing the car to drive.

- They cannot execute a figure 8 in a parking lot without oversteering or understeering.

- They cannot accurately steer the car toward a defined target.

- They cannot turn a corner without drifting out of their intended path.

- They often cannot smoothly accelerate and brake.

- They do not know the difference between steering and turning and have their hands in the wrong location for each.

- They do not know how to release the wheel such that the car is precisely headed in the correct direction after exiting a turn.

- They cannot execute a proper three-point turn (formerly known as a K turn).

- They cannot back the car in a straight line in the intended path toward a target.

- They are confused about which way to turn the wheel while backing in order to move the car in a different direction.

- They cannot simulate stopping the car in the shortest distance possible in preparation for semi- emergencies and/or future emergency braking.

- They remain confused about the basic rules of the road.

- They cannot (initially) safely operate the vehicle in any venue other than a large vacant parking lot.

- They do not signal for their turns, until repeatedly coached to do so.

- If and when they are given the opportunity to drive the car into a cul-de-sac and exit the backside, they will severely understeer the car until coached to turn the car more efficiently.

- They do not stop at stop signs in accordance with DMV requirements (rolling stops are common).

- They are not aware of the safe and legal procedure for clearing a blind intersection

I need to be very clear here. Most of these students are not actual "beginning" drivers in the strictest use of the word. At least 70 percent of the drivers described above have already had their permits and have already been driving with a parent, legal guardian, grandparent, uncle, older sibling, or someone else over twenty-one with a driver's license. Moreover, most of them have already been allowed to graduate from the vacant parking lot and have already been driving on the road. If an overhead camera was trained on the first figure 8 attempted by most new student drivers, it would appear that most of them were in a drunken stupor!

This fact should give you at least a token measure of concern, especially if you have already allowed your teen to drive in traffic. The above are just a few of many reasons that no matter how well a parent says his/her teen can drive, a well-trained and experienced professional driving instructor typically begins the first driving lesson in a vacant parking lot. If there is any assumption to be made by a pro instructor, the initial assumption is that virtually all new students cannot operate a vehicle safely until coached by a driver training instructor.

If the initial training location is different than the pick-up location, our driving instructors drive to the parking lot and explain what we are doing and why while we are driving to a safe training location. HS parking lots and frontage roadways are notoriously dangerous. As a result, we don't allow our students to drive immediately if we pick them up at a HS.

New drivers are often so nervous about how to operate a three-thousand- pound beast and make it behave the way the instructor just demonstrated, that initially they forget some of the valuable classroom training they previously received. It comes back to them after they are reminded of the training repeatedly.

True "beginning drivers" fall into a completely different category than do drivers who are simply inexperienced. At CADETS, we classify a true "beginning driver" as a driver who has received less than five parking lot lessons with a parent or other licensed driver. In addition to the examples of untrained driving skills provided on the previous page, actual beginners typically exhibit one or more of the following *additional* deficiencies:

- Some of them do not know whether to place their right foot or their left foot on the brake.

- They have never adjusted mirrors in a car and do not know where the mirror adjustments might be located, much less how to adjust them.

- They place their hands on the wheel incorrectly while adjusting the bottom seat and seat back.

- They cannot steer the car in a straight path, much less steer it toward a target.

- The first application of the accelerator is usually a "jackrabbit" start.

- The first series of the applications of the brakes are far too hard for routine braking and far too soft for semi-emergency braking.

- Without proper coaching, almost all new drivers of any age or gender cannot turn a car around a pole in a parking lot without drifting off course.

- Initial steering toward a target is characterized by severe oversteering.

- Initial turning around a pole (vacant parking lot) is typically characterized by severe understeering.

- Most beginning drivers initially look over the hood of the car.

- Most new drivers attempt to "walk the wheel back" after completing all turns, resulting in "understeering" the car while the car exits figure 8s and most other turns.

- Beginning drivers are struggling to control the car to such a degree that they are often oblivious to other potential hazards around them, much less how to respond to them.

The good news is that most good students remember far more from the classroom training than they initially realize. Many students just need to be reassured and reminded that the tremendous load of information that they were saturated with in the classroom now needs to be applied in the car. Through proper coaching, they also begin to realize than there are valid reasons for everything we say, everything we demonstrate, and everything we expect them to mimic. This is why our coaching philosophy includes the following protocol during all lessons preceding the final lesson:

- We demonstrate each driving procedure, technique, or skill and describe what, why, and how it is being performed while executing.

- We give the student the opportunity to mimic and/or duplicate our techniques while the instructor is coaching the student through the process.

- We require the student to demonstrate if and when he/she has "mastered" the procedure, technique, or driving skill by the student executing the procedure satisfactorily *without* coaching.

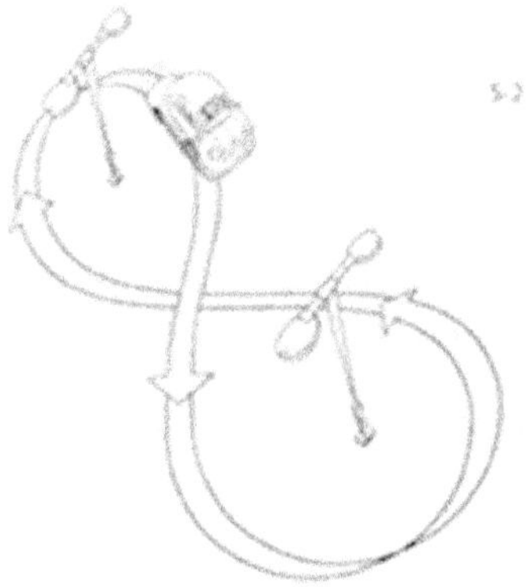

After teaching hundreds of students for thousands of hours, we have verified remarkable correlation between the proper execution of a figure 8 in a vacant parking lot and the proper execution of *other* basic driving skills required later during the same lesson.

The figure 8 must include the application of a proper wheel release (the wheel sliding through the fingers) as car exits each turn. The instructor should point out a target in the distance to steer toward while he/she is demonstrating the figure 8. Once the student takes the wheel, the student must accelerate, steer, slow into each turn, turn around the pole, accelerate, and when prompted, brake properly at the end of the series of figure 8s. The student must read and react to the vehicle's direction as the car is targeted before the turn as well as precisely where the car is targeted after the turn.

Of course, many other driving skills may be developed in a parking lot. For example, the instructor and/or parent may coach the new driver to back the car in accordance with the DMV test and safe driving practices.

If an untraveled entrance road is available, the three- point turn may be mastered. All performance grid activities that can be initiated in a parking lot should be initiated in a parking lot. Once basic parking lot skills are mastered, the student driver is ready for very basic residential driving. Some beginning drivers may not be ready to leave the parking lot after a single lesson.

However, most of our students are ready for very basic residential driving during the second hour of our initial driving lesson. Here, many of the activities in the parking lot are repeated, reinforced, and applied to residential driving. Before departing for the neighborhood, we complete a question-and-answer session regarding scenarios we know will be included in the lesson. However, in residential neighborhoods, there are many other hazards that must be dealt with safely:

- Right and left turns are completed at intersections.

- Two-way or four-way stops are common.

- Pedestrians are common.

- Parked cars must be navigated safely.

- Dogs, cats, children may cross in front of a vehicle unexpectedly.

- Commercial vehicles may be parked in the roadway.

- Blind intersections are common.

The first lesson or lesson(s) of the no. 1 instruction grid is shown on the final page of this chapter and repeated in Appendix 1. A well-trained driving instructor can train a reasonably good student (about 70 percent of new students) to complete all fourteen of the listed activities satisfactorily during the first two-hour lesson. A true beginner typically requires at least one additional lesson. However, true beginners can master virtually all the elements of our entire three-lesson grid in the standard number of lessons required in most states.

We are going to define the word *mastery* here to mean that the student has executed the proper task, maneuver, or driving skill at a performance level defined by a state DMV and a pro-driving school.

However, in order for the new driver to be successful *and* safe, these skills must be demonstrated by the new driver every time he/she drives and *reinforced* on a daily basis when the beginning driver drives with a licensed driver in the passenger seat.

In addition to new skills that must be addressed and developed in the neighborhood, a residential development should be used to confirm the following:

- The student driver is able to successfully turn the car around a cul-de-sac without driving into the gutter or too close to the curb. New student drivers must often be coached in repetition in order to achieve a minimum standard of performance.

- New student drivers can now be coached to release the wheel upon exiting a cul-de-sac such that the car is pointed in exactly the correct direction (the driver's lane) rather than the curb on the right or any potential approaching driver's lane on the left.

- Student drivers must be coached to execute *precise* left and right turns to/from roadways and around corners so that vehicles do not drift from intended path.

- Residential neighborhoods have two lanes, even though they are rarely marked with diving lines. Beginning drivers must be coached to drive such that the left lane belongs to approaching drivers. Approaching drivers have the right-of-way until or unless the lane is cleared.

Of course, the goal is to train a student so thoroughly that each maneuver, performance task, or driving skill becomes repetitive *and* habitual.

However, there simply isn't sufficient time available to ensure that a student can perform each and every maneuver, task, or driving skill ten out of ten times during each lesson.

Will you be satisfied if your child can safely execute an unprotected left turn across a busy highway eight out of ten times? Would you be assured if your daughter turned six corners in a row without drifting out of her lane but, while turning that seventh corner she drifted out wide over the centerline and overcorrected as she steered the car back? If your son cleared that nasty blind intersection in your neighborhood properly nine times in a row, but on the tenth approach, your son decided "that stuff is only for beginners," wouldn't you want to know that you had taken every measure of precaution to ensure otherwise?

Through proper coaching of these techniques by an instructor and follow- up repetition, most new drivers are able to execute safe, efficient, accurate hand-over-hand turning of the car around even the sharpest corners. The majority of our students are able to demonstrate this proficiency by the end of the first two-hour driving lesson, along with several other skills that are required in that lesson.

Parents must be fully engaged with the pro instructor throughout every phase of the training. You can initiate this process by rereading your state's DMV manual and being prepared to answer your child's questions about driving correctly every time. In addition, you can read the following overview of our first lesson and take steps to verify your understanding of each topic. Remember, you and your driving instructor must be "on the same page." If not, your coaching of your teen may be counterproductive toward his/her actual progress.

Each of the following grid elements listed on the last page of this chapter will be described briefly below. The methods used for providing driver BTW training will vary from pro-driving school to pro-driving school. However, the result should be consistent. If you have access to a large vacant parking lot, we suggest that you purchase four rubber cones and four six-foot sections of plastic PVC pipe to fit inside. These training aids can be used to practice many basic driving skills in referenced in our first two performance grids.

Following, we will provide a brief review of each grid element that we teach in the car during the first two- hour lesson. Most of the subject matter was referenced in the classroom. Virtually, all the classroom material is preparation for BTW instruction.

Basic Auto Setup

All driving controls are defined by the instructor. The student is coached to adjust every driving control properly for the personal size and shape of the driver. Specific guidance is provided for adjustment of seat, seat back, headrest, side mirrors, rearview mirror, and operation of the transmission. Proper operation of accelerator and braking systems are discussed before moving demonstrations.

Figure 8 (R/L Series)

Most good performance instructors demonstrate how to do something before they ask a student to imitate their actions. When a student observes, they are often amazed at how easy it looks and equally perplexed by how (initially) difficult some of the drills are to execute. Each grid element has a purpose. Some of the grid elements are obvious. Some are not as obvious.

The purpose of the figure 8 has already been described. We suggest setting up one cone/pole and one end of the parking lot and another at the other end with room to drive around each unless you are lucky enough to have large light poles spaced at great distance in a huge lot. Students who successfully perform a figure 8 in accordance with previously described objectives are ready to proceed to other skills.

Right Turn Series

Sounds simple unless the student does not use hand over hand. The figure 8 requires right turns to alternate with left turns around poles. Watch for drifting out of the intended path or steering too close to the poles.

Left Turn Series

Left turns are okay for beginning drivers in parking lots, but actual left turns in traffic are not safe during a first driving lesson. During the second half of the lesson, extreme caution should be taken for left turns in residential neighborhoods. This lesson is intended to introduce or reinforce the basic operation of the vehicle. More advanced driving will be covered later.

Wheel Release

The proper wheel release as the driver exits each figure 8 into straightaway or after each right/left turn will determine if the car is targeted in the proper direction.

The student should be coached to release the wheel such that the car is pointed precisely toward the correct target line with little or no margin for error. Student drivers must be coached to recognize that this requirement is extraordinarily important.

Gas and Brake

Very smooth acceleration and braking is the standard.

No "jackrabbit" starts or stops. Only the right foot is to be used for each function at all times. Proper acceleration out of figure 8s and proper deceleration *prior* to each turn will help build the confidence of the new driver. Successful repetition will help the confidence of the new driver grow and will help you assess that the new driver is in complete control of the automobile at all times before you move on.

Three-Point Turn

The three-point turn is employed when the car must be turned 180 degrees in the opposite direction and when there isn't sufficient room for a U-turn, and there is no other obvious location of a turnabout, public driveway, or parking lot in the vicinity. The primary elements of a properly executed three-point turn includes but is not limited to the following:

- Signaling before slowing to the curb

- Performing a SMOG (signal, mirror, over the shoulder, and go) before reentering the roadway

- The new driver turns the wheel in the proper direction before each step

- The driver gently lifts the foot off the brake during each step unless the three-point turn is completed on a hill

- The driver looks behind the car while backing during the second step

- The driver does not bang into a curb and/or does not drive over the grass when conducting three-point turns where there are no curbs.

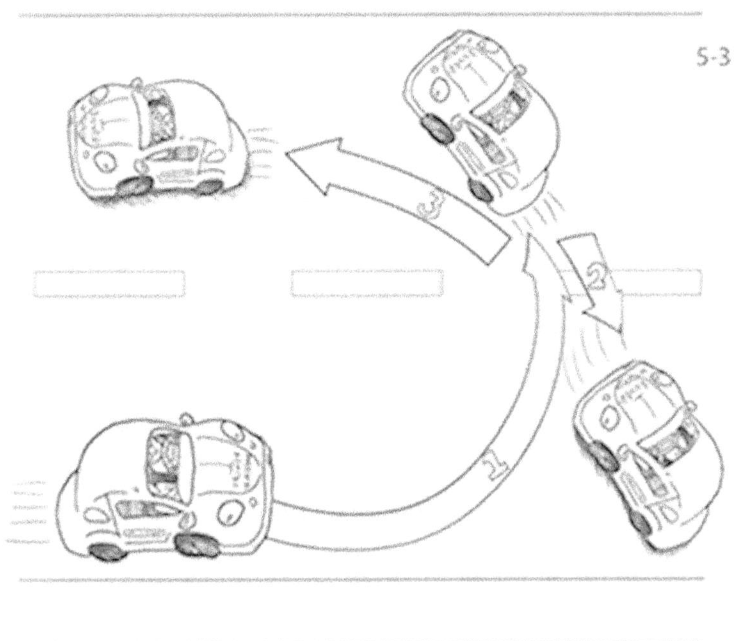

Backing

New drivers must be able to back for at least one hundred feet in their own lane without drifting toward the grass or the middle of the road. The left hand is at twelve o'clock with the fingers pointed toward the sky and the right hand is behind the passenger seat. This forces the driver to look behind the vehicle while moving in that direction. The right foot should be on the brake while backing unless backing on an inclined hill.

Serpentine or Backing Turns

If backing is conducted in a large parking lot, serpentine backing is constructive to determine that the new driver always knows which direction to turn the wheel in order to move the car in one direction or another. Later in a residential neighborhood, this understanding should be verified again by having the student back such that the wheel must be turned full right out of a driveway and full left using only the left hand.

The right hand should remain behind the passenger seat while backing.

Some beginning drivers believe they cannot turn the wheel with one hand while backing, but almost all are able to do so after they have been coached properly. The car must be moving at idle speed (foot lightly on the brake) unless backing up an inclined driveway.

When the car is backed with the fingers pointed toward the sky, the wheel may be moved either full right or full left in a "window washing" motion while the car is moving at one mile per hour. If a beginning driver *must* use two hands to turn the wheel, the car must be stopped when the driver turns around to use the right hand. DMV examiners do not want your body facing forward while your car is moving backward unless testing in a commercial vehicle.

With practice, most drivers will be able to turn the car sufficiently with the left hand.

ABS Braking versus Non-ABS Braking

Beginning drivers must be trained to recognize the difference between routine braking, semi-emergency braking, and emergency braking. If you will seek out a parking lot or unused roadway with a gravel surface, all three braking procedures may be "simulated." Beginning drivers are sometimes confused about how much pressure to apply to the brakes and when. A vacant parking lot provides excellent opportunities to demonstrate that they cannot "break the brakes" by attempting to lock them.

When training in a car that was manufactured with ABS installed, this is an opportunity to convince the new driver that the car will not skid, and it also allows the student to feel the ABS pulsing. Otherwise, in an actual emergency, a new driver may feel that the ABS brakes are malfunctioning! If the parking lot is large enough and vacant, also introduce steering away from danger while the car is slowing to a stop.

If the family car does not have ABS installed, this is an opportunity for the new driver to apply "threshold pressure" such that the car does not skid. In a large parking lot, evasive collision avoidance steering while applying threshold pressure may be simulated as well.

These techniques will be discussed again in later chapters.

Basic Rules of the Road Q and A and Right of Way

While the car is parked, we miss few opportunities to ask refresher questions of the student before each driving lesson and at various times when the car is parked during the driving lesson. We avoid asking questions while the car is moving. Instead, while the car is moving, we are speaking.

We point out what the student should be looking for as he/she drives and the actions that should be taken in advance whenever possible.

When an instructor enters a car with a student for the first driving lesson, we are in possession of the classroom test results in our training folder. Any questions that were missed in the classroom are asked again before we drive. In addition, the maneuvers and procedures that are required for each driving lesson are considered. Questions are asked about each activity before the student is asked to perform each maneuver.

The student is also encouraged to ask our instructors questions while the car is parked. If necessary, a clarifying question may be asked by the student while the car is moving, but we attempt to keep our answers very short and very specific. Even the wording is important. For example, we wouldn't say "turn right ahead" and assume that the student knows precisely where we wish them to turn. We would clarify exactly where we wish the student to complete a right turn.

During first lessons, we also ensure that the student has registered when traffic signs or signals are looming and is responding accordingly. Before departing the parking lot for residential driving, we reconfirm all the right- of-way rules of the road we expect to encounter in the residential neighborhood. If we feel that the student isn't responding appropriately to our questions at that time, we would prefer to remind the student at that time rather than be required to apply our brake on the passenger side of the vehicle later. We have learned to take very little for granted.

Residential Driving

Most residential neighborhoods have posted speed limits between fifteen miles per hour and twenty-five miles per hour. More significantly, most residential neighborhoods have dozens upon hundreds of routine hazards and some that are not routine. After virtually all the basic driving skills have been verified in parking lots, it is time apply the classroom training and the parking lot training. However, a true beginning driver has not yet responded to hazards and responded appropriately to them. We prefer to use a neighborhood that we are very familiar with in order to reduce, if not eliminate surprises.

We also wish to reiterate the rules of the road at four- way stops, three-way stops, intersections with no traffic signs, and blind intersections. In addition, now the student much deal with approaching drivers on narrow streets, pedestrians, bicyclists, pets, commercial vehicles parked in the street, and many other real or potential hazards. In a training car, the passenger brake is used more often here for instructional purposes than anywhere else.

If you are practicing with your teen in the family vehicle, we suggest that you define what is expected as you approach each intersection from a distance, not during entrance. In addition, professional driving instructors are not bashful about placing a hand on the wheel for a course correction. While your teen may not appreciate it, a relatively "minor course correction" is preferable to scraping a parked vehicle or running a hapless pedestrian off the road. If necessary driving instructors apply the passenger brake, usually for cautionary or preventative reasons.

Residential neighborhoods are also used to develop smooth acceleration and braking skills during most driving periods and semi-emergency or emergency braking when and if necessary. Collision avoidance is initiated here.

Driving, steering, and turning at the safe speeds for the driving conditions are each reinforced here.

Since you don't have a brake, you must ensure your teen responds immediately to either the word *slow* or the word *stop* and responds appropriately to each word.

You must scan the traffic or pedestrian scene at all times, and you must be ready to ensure your teen responds appropriately to each situation presented.

Cul-de-Sacs

Most residential neighborhoods have at least one cul-de- sac. If your practice neighborhood doesn't include a cul- de-sac turnabout, we strongly recommend that you locate a neighborhood that does have a cul-de-sac. We describe the requirement of our students to navigate simple cul-de-sacs as one of our more valuable verification tools that we employ during the first lesson.

Take your new driver to a cul-de-sac that does not have a parked car at the curb and ask your teen to drive around the cul-de-sac and exit at a safe speed. The first time a student encounters a cul-de-sac, most beginning drivers exhibit one or all the following:

- The new driver will approach too fast.

- The new driver will not slow sufficiently.

- The new driver will drive in the gutter or bump the curb.

- The new driver will not exit with the car in your lane on the right side of the road at all times.

- The new driver will not release the wheel properly so that the car exits the cul-de-sac in your lane at all times.

Obviously, many beginning students experience a degree of difficulty in navigating cul-de-sacs initially. This is an excellent opportunity to refresh the rationale behind hand-over-hand steering and the safe and efficient wheel release while exiting a turn. We find it is often beneficial to get back behind the wheel and demonstrate the procedure again ourselves. Once we demonstrate every aspect of entering, navigating, and exiting a cul-de-sac, the majority of our students have little trouble with cul-de-sacs. Beginners who insist on walking the wheel or using push/push quickly realize why we teach hand over hand. Most importantly, this helps prepare them for more advanced turns at a slightly greater speeds later on.

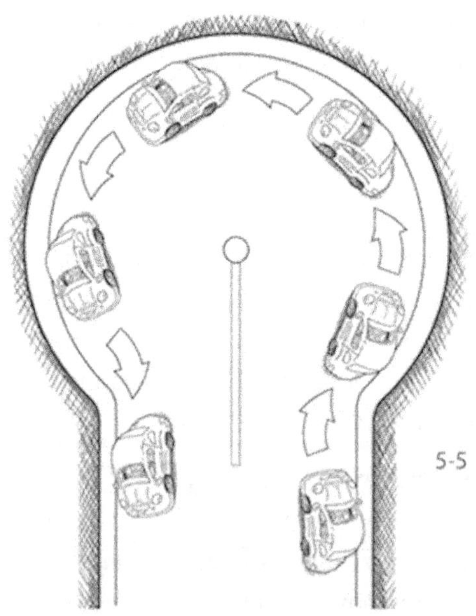

5-5

BEHIND-THE-WHEEL INSTRUCTION GRID NO. 1

Student Name:_________________ Instructor/Parent:_______________

ACTIVITY	INTRODUCTION	PRACTICE	MASTERY
Lesson Dates			
Basic Auto Setup			
Figure 8 (R/L Series)			
Right Turn Series			
Left Turn Series			
Wheel Release			
Gas and Brake			
Three-Point Turn			
Backing			
Serpentine or Backing Turns			
ABS Braking			
Basic Rules of the Road Q and A			
Residential Driving			
Cul-De-Sacs			

ADDITIONAL NOTES

CHAPTER 6

Perpendicular, Angle, and Parallel Parking Behind the Wheel Grid No.2

Before proceeding to the topics of angle, perpendicular, and parallel parking, it should be noted that a training car or a family car must (of course) be *driven* to the parking locations and driven in and around the parking lots. Either driving environment has the potential to be very dangerous for new drivers. Beginning drivers may have driven no more than a few times with a parent. Our second lesson is conducted after only two hours of formal instruction has been provided. Most beginning drivers require reinforcement of most of the material covered during lesson no. 1 and an introduction to new material that will allow them to drive in busy parking lots safely.

At CADETS, we often teach angle and perpendicular in a mall parking lot that has both parking configurations. A different location is often used for parallel parking instruction. There will be more written about parallel parking later in the chapter. We will also discuss parking lot driving toward the end of the chapter.

We select an area of a parking lot mall parking lot that is rarely used and/or vacant. Initially, we do not ask our students to park between parked cars. However, we train them to park as if parked cars are present, or cars will be parked in all the adjoining spaces later. If a car were to be scraped while a beginning driver is learning to angle park, perpendicular park or parallel park, the repair expense could potentially run into thousands of dollars for either car or both cars.

At the end of the parking sequence, space should be visible between each side boundary line, and no part of the front bumper should be hanging over the front boundary. If a student has not achieved this standard, the student is required to back up safely and adjust the location of the car. Then we repeat the entire sequence from start to finish again. As we explain to our students, if you leave a section (even a bumper) of your car hanging over a boundary line, you are inviting a poor driver to crash into your car.

Even if another driver does leave a note, your car still needs to be repaired, and you must wait for your car while it is being repaired. Some time ago (long before I entered the driver education field), one of my personal vehicles was damaged so badly in a parking lot—no, I did not park poorly—that the entire door required repainting.

Fresh out of the army with no job yet, I still remember that the offending culprit was the driver of a very beat-up old red Karmann Ghia. My Firebird was parked squarely between parking lines, even way back then. It had a huge red gash in the driver's door where the driver of the Karmann Ghia had obviously flung open his door carelessly.

Back then, I hadn't attended "Interpersonal Behavior in Problem Solving." I hadn't attended "Human

Relations in Supervision." I hadn't yet attended "Conflict Resolution." Hell, I hadn't even attended "Mediation Techniques for the Common Man." He had damaged my precious Blue Firebird, and now, as I was looking at the Karmann Ghia I literally and figuratively "saw red." I hauled off with one of my size 10 jungle boots and kicked a big dent in the side of the Karmann Ghia, and no, I didn't leave a love letter on the window. Back then, I may have been dumb, but I wasn't stupid. I drove my car away semi-happy and thought to myself, *Well, I guess the jungle boots are still good for something.*

I paid for my precious Blue Formula Firebird to be repaired out of my own pocket. The body shop did not initially match the color properly, and my car door required repainting a second time. Park poorly and you increase the odds that someone like "you know who" will park next to you. Sometimes they do it no matter how you park.

As previously referenced in chapter 3, at CADETS we train all our students to pull in from the front every time (rather than backing into a parking space), and we instruct that they not drive over or turn over white boundary lines at any time. Enter any parking lot of any shopping mall and take a close look at the cars. If you know what you are looking for, you will note that at least 60 percent of the cars are parked incorrectly and inviting damage. In most cases, the reason that tires and/or vehicle body parts are sitting on or hanging over adjoining parking spaces is because drivers did not approach the spaces properly in the first place. Sometimes other drivers do it on purpose.

As referenced in chapter 3, many drivers pull in backward in order to exit while driving forward. This potential advantage is negated when the car is parked incorrectly.

When properly trained drivers prepare to exit angle and perpendicular spaces, they alert other drivers by signaling intent before moving *and* by their backing lights illuminating as soon as the transmission is placed in reverse. If instead if you have pulled forward between parked cars and have parked backward, as you exit later, pedestrians and other drivers may not be looking in your direction, and *your backing lights will not be illuminated.* Do not underestimate the measures that other drivers and pedestrians will take to avoid you if you will simply alert them.

The CADETS BTW Grid No. 2 is dominated by parking lot parking and parking lot driving. If the beginning driver has demonstrated he/she is ready, the new driver may be allowed to drive to the various locations. If the new driver is not ready for advanced roadway and parking lot driving, the instructor or parent should drive the teen to these locations and describe the defensive driving and collision avoidance techniques you are employing during the process.

Angle Parking

Angle parking is typically a bit easier for beginning drivers than perpendicular parking. Almost all angle parking spaces are on the right. If the angle parking spaces are slanted forward on the right and backward on the left as you approach, your roadway is two-way.

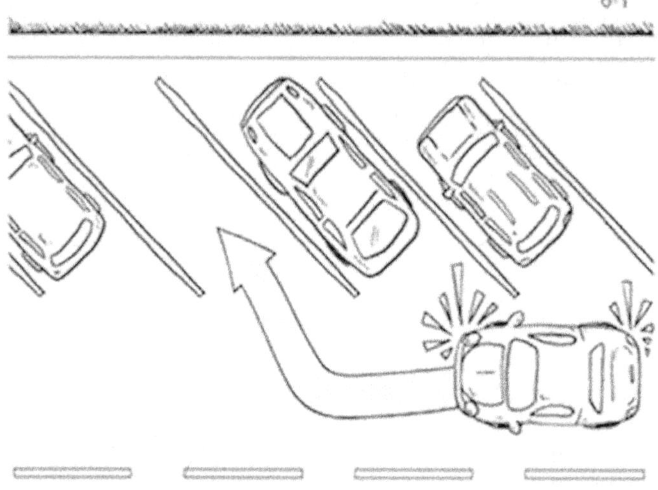

The spaces on the right are for your selection, and the spaces on the left are intended for vehicles approaching from the opposite direction. Some impatient drivers violate this intent at their own risk. A left turn into one of those spaces requires a turn of about 135 degrees. If cars are parked in adjoining parking spaces, the odds of scraping one of these cars increase significantly.

In a few parking lots, angle parking spaces are slanted forward in the same direction on either the right or the left of your driving lane. If the boundary lines are slanted *in the same direction toward your* car as you approach, you are driving on a one-way roadway, and you may turn right or left into available angle parking spaces. In any case, signal your intent as you approach, even if you believe it should be obvious which space you are selecting. Remember, other drivers and pedestrians are watching you trying to figure out what you are going to do next.

While slowly creeping (yes) into a parking space, the car is pivoted *around* the front boundary line of the parking space. As we teach during all parking maneuvers, precision is far more important than speed.

While training, our goal is to develop the new driver's confidence and skill such that they are able to repeatedly park in angle parking spaces without a wheel or any part of the vehicle crossing over a boundary line at any time.

The pivot point will vary a bit from vehicle to vehicle. For most vehicles, the pivot point is near the middle of the front door. Unless you are parking uphill, most cars with automatic transmissions will move at ample speed at idle as the brake pressure is released. In addition, while moving into the space, the car will continue to turn until the driver "tells" the car to stop turning. The wheel must be straightened while the car is moving into your parking space. This also takes some practice. The car must be stopped before reaching the end of the parking space boundary line. This sounds obvious now, but it is amazing how often it is violated.

Later, during actual angle parking situations (between parked cars), your right front bumper may pass within only a foot or two of a vehicle parked in the adjoining right-hand parking space. During the same parking sequence, your left rear fender may only pass within only a foot or two of a vehicle parked in the adjoining left-hand parking space. During training, this is why we treat boundary lines as if they are just as important to avoid as other vehicles. Do not leave the back of your car hanging out in the roadway either; if you do … well, you get the idea.

We consider exiting any parking space to be just as important as entering it. In fact, in most cases, there is less visibility while exiting and more danger. When exiting an angle parking space, put your foot on the brake, place the car in reverse, and signal before moving. Always signal in the direction the car will eventually turn. In most angle parking situations, this will be left. We train our students to clear left and clear right over each shoulder *before* they back. Initially, the car is backed with the wheels straight, the left hand at twelve o'clock and the right hand behind the passenger seat, looking behind the vehicle just as they learned during the first driving lesson.

During early driving lessons, we don't train our students while parking between cars; therefore, when we exit angle parking spaces, they *could potentially* exit without stopping because there are no adjoining cars for them to see around. However, our instruction is intended to prepare the students to enter and exit parking lots that have vehicles parked in each adjoining space.

The following sequence is recommended for your teen when he or she exits angle parking spaces in busy parking lots.

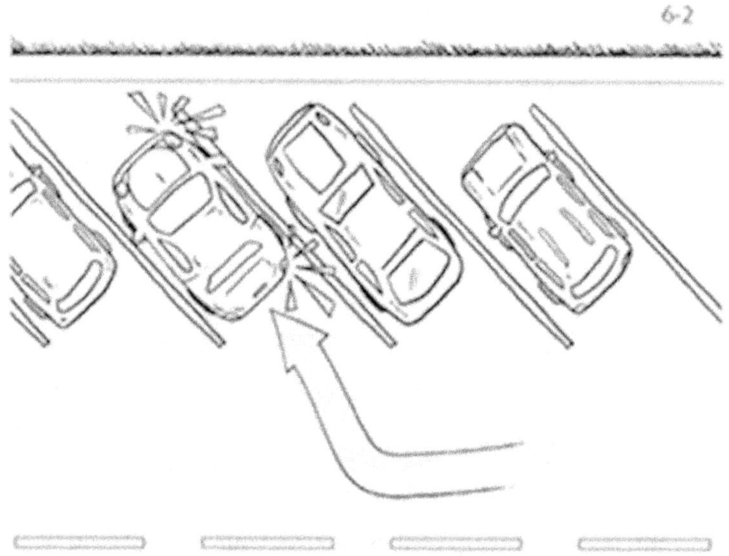

We have our students signal left before placing the car in reverse with the right foot on the brake. The driver must back up with the foot on the brake just far enough to see around adjoining parked cars before entering the roadway and before turning the wheel. Initially, the driver should be looking in the direction the car is moving (out the back window). The driver should stop the car as soon as he/she can see around parked cars. While the car is stopped, the head may be turned forward briefly to verify the location of the front of the car in relation to adjoining cars or spaces. This is a good time to verify that the right front bumper or any part of the vehicle is not going to contact another vehicle when backing is resumed.

Have your teen clear over each shoulder again before moving. While looking out the rear window, the wheel is turned only when the front of the vehicle is even with the bumper of the car on your right. At that time, the wheel is turned full left. The backing vehicle should be stopped when it reaches a forty-five- degree angle. The vehicle is placed in drive and the steering wheel turned full right before moving.

Perpendicular Parking

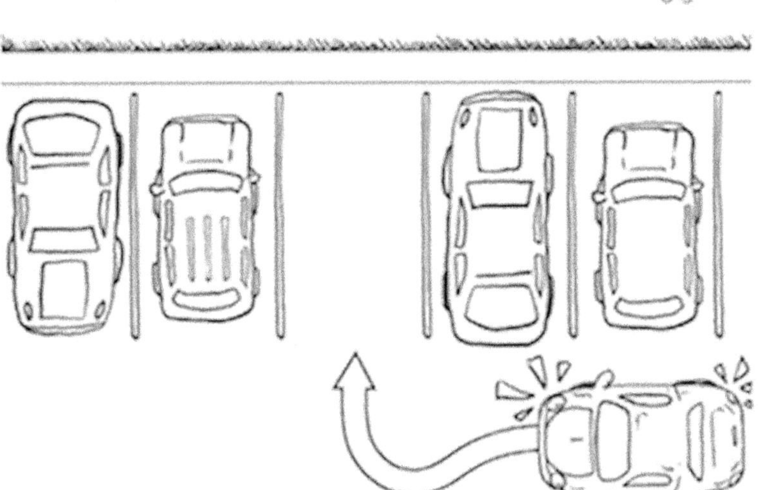

Beginning drivers must learn that cars are not designed to make sharp ninety- degree turns. When turning right into a perpendicular parking space, we teach our students to signal as they approach, clear oncoming traffic in the opposite lane, and then swing out with a pronounced arc during the entry.

Even though we do not teach perpendicular parking while parking between parked cars, our students are coached to enter such so that none of the four tires, bumpers, or any part of the body of the car passes over a boundary line at any time.

If the opposing lane is not clear as you approach, have your teen stop your car and wait until it is clear before completing the turn.

Many parents allow their teens to park in busy parking lots soon after their first or second professional driving lesson. Since cars don't turn at sharp 90 degrees, the above training procedures will significantly reduce the possibility of the right door or left bumper "touching" vehicles parked in adjoining parking spaces later. The precise requirements for angle, perpendicular, and parallel parking are just three of many reasons we emphasize precise steering and turning during the initial driving lesson.

Left turns into perpendicular parking spaces are actually a little easier than right turns because a relatively minor initial arc is required during the approach. During right and left perpendicular parking, the turn is completed at the pivot point of the car. For most cars, the pivot point is at or near the middle of the front door. Beginning drivers sometimes have more trouble safely and accurately perpendicular parking than parallel parking.

If your teen is having trouble determining exactly where the pivot point is, it is often helpful to use a different (second) visual key to assist the new driver. Have your teen turn the wheel at the *middle* of the parking space such that it *appears* that the right front tire is turning directly into the *middle* of the right- hand parking spaces, and left front tire is turned into *middle* of left hand spaces. As the car follows, the wheel must be straightened, or the car will continue to turn. Of course the car is turned into the parking space such that the car ends up with nearly equidistant space on each side of your vehicle. The vehicle must be slowed to a stop before the bumper crosses the end boundary line.

6-4

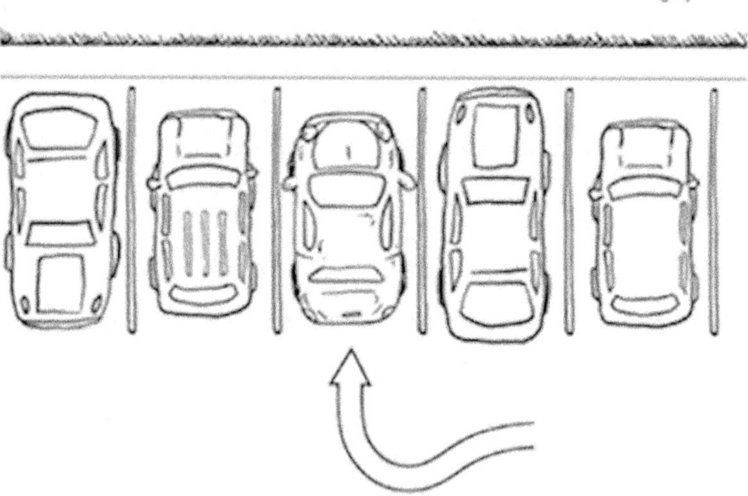

Once most beginning drivers are given this key, they are able to consistently and accurately perpendicular park into right hand or left hand spaces.

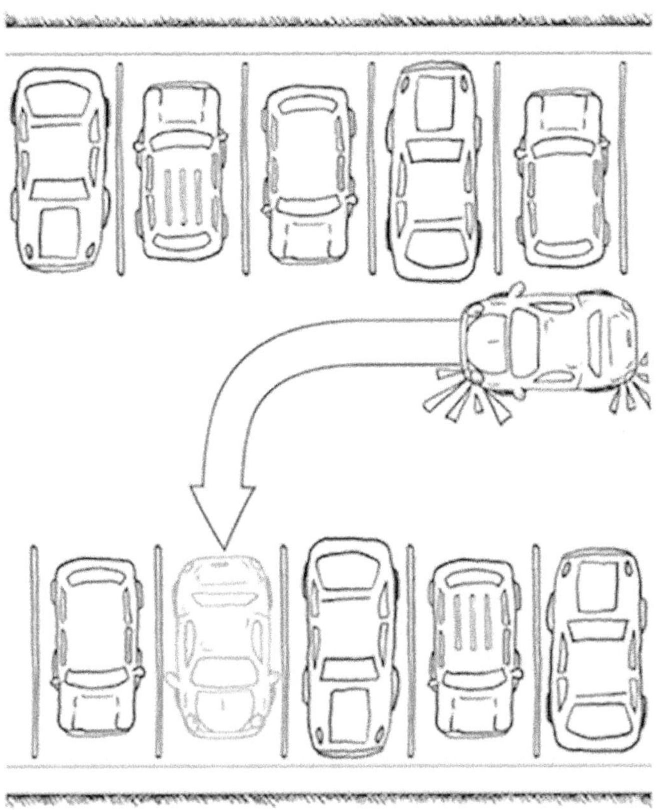

Perpendicular parking spaces must be exited with at least as much caution as exiting angle parking spaces. Since the driver may back left or right into the roadway, you must signal left or right before backing to alert other drivers and pedestrians of your intent before moving.

In preparation for exiting, the procedure requires clearing back, left, and right before moving, keeping the foot on the brake and not the accelerator while moving, and stopping halfway out or earlier to double-check around adjoining vehicles.

After clearance has been assured behind your vehicle and next to your vehicle, continue backing in the direction you have signaled until reaching a forty-five- degree angle. After placing your car in drive, turn your wheel either full right or full left while your vehicle is stopped.

Yes, these parking space exit procedures require a great deal of care. In addition, we will acknowledge that it is possible, even after taking every precaution that a "sniper" may suddenly appear in the roadway just as you begin to pull out of your space.

If this happens, you *must* be prepared to stop the car immediately as you observe the behavior of the other driver.

At this point, it doesn't really matter who is right and who is wrong. If the other driver does not stop while approaching, you must spring into collision avoidance mode, and you immediately stop your car. This should require just a fraction of a second because your foot is on your brake, and you are creeping out of your space. If the driver has finally seen your backing lights *and* your signal, the driver may allow you to complete your exit. If not, yield the right-of-way to the driver. Remember, the right-of-way may be yielded, but it should never be taken.

Review of the Standard "S Swerve" Procedure for Parallel Parking

In chapter 3, different parking techniques were reviewed. As noted in that chapter, the old *S* swerve is the technique most drivers have used to parallel park for years. The problem with the S swerve isn't that it doesn't work. It does work very well when executed properly. The problem is that a sixteen-year-old beginning driver (or any driver for that matter) must begin the *S* at precisely the right spot, reverse the wheel at precisely the right spot, reverse the wheel again at the right spot—all while moving and "guesstimating" speed and distance accurately.

Oh, by the way, a student driver must do this during a period of "mild stress" (taking a driving test) with a stranger in the passenger seat evaluating every move.

I have heard parents and teens complain bitterly about parallel parking even being included in a modern- day driving test because "no one parallel parks anymore." Of course this is not true.

It isn't that "no one parallel parks a car anymore"; it's that almost no one *wants* to parallel park a car anymore. Parallel parking is generally required "downtown" (and in many other locations) in even the smallest towns in every state. Most of the moms who bring their teens to our parking lessons (without being prompted) freely admit they cannot parallel park. The fathers usually mention that they can parallel park (also freely offered) but also admit that they are thrilled that they don't have to teach their teens how to do it.

6-6

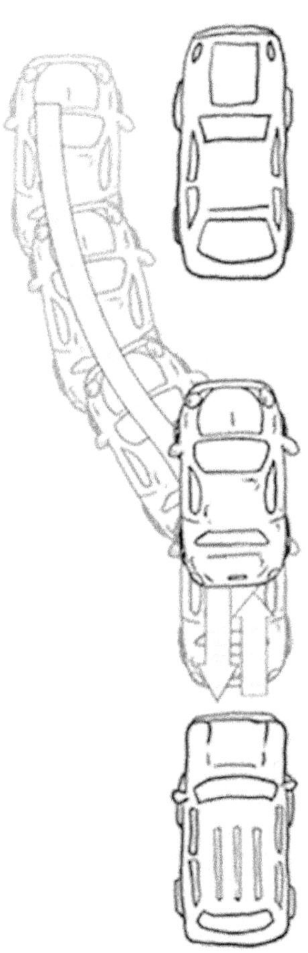

Many drivers I have observed parallel parking at various locations around the country somehow manage to "shoehorn" their car in there, but leave the car parked in such a way that it wouldn't pass a current department of motor vehicles driving test anyway. I tell my students that mastering parallel parking isn't only about mastering *parking*.

Parallel parking requires observation, judgment, technique, recognition, an awareness of the dimensions of the car, and an accurate sense of the boundaries the driver is parking his/her vehicle within.

Therefore, the CADETS parallel parking technique isn't magic. Like the old *S* swerve, it also requires the new driver to demonstrate skills in these categories too, but they may be applied in a systematic, safe, precise way.

The CADETS Parallel Parking Technique

The primary difference between the CADETS procedure and the old *S* swerve is that during the *S* swerve, almost all the key checkpoints must be checked and verified while the car is *moving*. We teach our beginning drivers to check most of their key checkpoints while the car is *stopped*. It gives them time to verify these specific checkpoints, collect their thoughts, and think about the next step before they execute.

Sometimes a parent will express concern that there may not be time to check and assess these checkpoints in an actual parallel parking situation. I remind these parents that on examination day, *speed* is not required. On examination day, precision is required. *In fact, while parallel parking, precision is more important than speed on any day.*

At CADETS, our instructors can parallel park training cars within six inches of the same spot nine out of ten times. No, we are not perfect. Sometimes we make mistakes, and sometimes examiners make mistakes. The following two sections include a condensed version of our parallel parking training sequence followed by a more descriptive version.

The procedures are not really as complicated as they may first appear. They are only wordy for instructional purposes in this text. In practice, we can generally train a beginning student to parallel park using the following procedure in about fifteen or twenty minutes. Once a beginning driver memorizes the steps and the keys, they can generally park the training car during each approach within one or two minutes during each parking sequence.

Mainly beginning drivers need to know what their keys are for each pause and which way to turn the wheel when they get there. After that, we suggest they practice the technique at the DMV in their parents' vehicle on a Saturday or Sunday when practice is allowed.

Once the technique has been mastered, the technique may be applied while parallel parking in a business district between cars too. It takes less time to complete this procedure *once* than is required to use a different procedure *twice*.

In all parallel parking cases, remember that precision and collision avoidance should be more important to you than speed is to the driver waiting for you. On examination day, students may use any parallel parking technique they wish. However, I can't recall any CADETS student stating, "Thanks for all your training, but I think I will use the old *S* swerve on my driving test anyway."

The Condensed CADETS Parallel Parking Technique

1. Signal approach.

2. Steer parallel to front car within one to two feet.

3. Stop car with no angle.

4. Back car to front barrier (rear bumper of front car) in middle of rear door window and then stop.

5. Full right wheel and back to right edge of rear barrier over left rear headrest and then stop.

6. Center wheel and confirm.

7. Back car to within two to three feet from curb and then stop.

8. Full left wheel and back to one to two feet from rear barrier and then stop.

9. Car in drive and straighten car within eighteen inches of curb while moving forward.

10. Center car equidistant between barriers and then stop and place car in park to signal parking complete.

11. To exit, back up to within one foot of rear barrier and then stop.

12. Foot on brake, car in drive, steering wheel full left.

13. Signal intent, clear entrance lane by looking over shoulder.

14. Perform steps 11 to 14 again only if necessary to clear bumper of car or barrier.

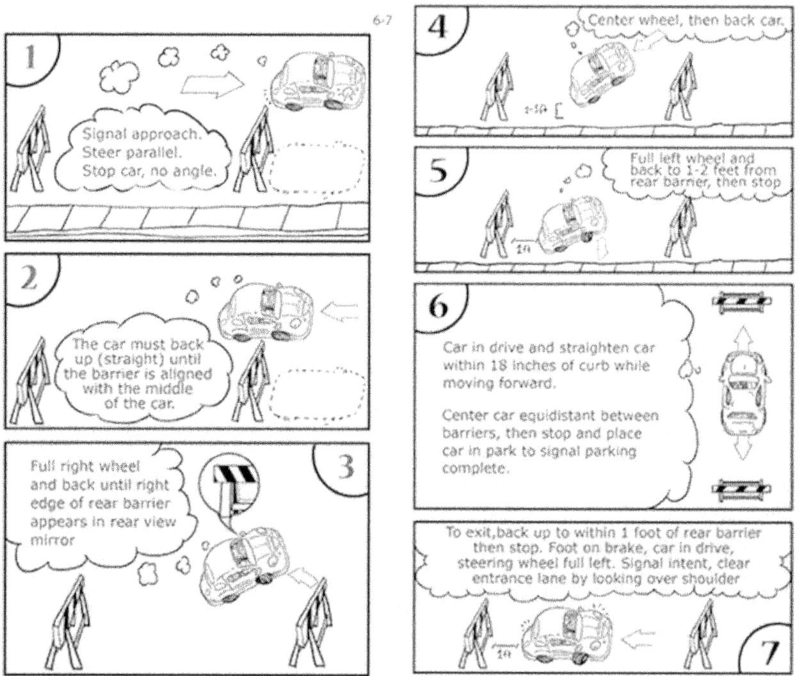

The Expanded CADETS Parallel Parking Technique with Descriptors

1. Signal with your right turn signal as you approach the parallel parking space.

2. Bring your car up alongside the front car (or barrier if practicing) so that the right side of your car is only one to two feet from the car or barrier.

3. Straighten your car so that your car is parallel to the real or imagined car in front, and then stop alongside. *Do not allow the car to remain at an angle or stop at an angle, or the parallel parking technique will be altered.*

4. Place your car in reverse and back straight back until the front barrier appears in the middle of your right rear window and then stop again. *No angle at the end of this step.*

5. Turn your steering wheel full right while the car is stopped. Begin backing with your wheel turned full right until the right edge of the back barrier swings over and is centered on your left rear headrest.

   If you don't have a rear seat, imagine where a left rear headrest would be, and stop the car from turning or moving as soon as the headrest aligns with the right edge of the barrier. Your car should be at about a forty-five-degree angle at the end of this step.

6. With your car stopped, turn your steering wheel and wheels back to center. *Lift your foot off the brake so that your car moves in reverse no more than a few inches just to ensure and confirm that your wheels are centered.*

7. When you have confirmed this, begin backing straight back toward the curb. Stop your car when you have judged that your right rear tire is between three feet and two feet of the curb.

   Please note that if you own a compact car with small wheels, this step requires you to stop a bit closer to the two-foot distance. However, if you own a large SUV, truck, or another type of vehicle with very large tires, you may be required to end this step three feet from the curb or greater before the next step.

   While backing, most state DMVs require drivers of passenger vehicles to look out the rear window while moving so as not to back into another vehicle or object. However, you may stop the car to double-check when you reach the three-foot to two-foot distance from the curb. At that time, with your foot firmly planted on the brake, look in your passenger mirror and out of your back window again. Verify your position now when it is still possible to adjust, not later when it is far more difficult to adjust. Also note that the car moves even closer to the curb during this step.

   If the driver backs in too far during this step, the curb will block the car from backing deep enough during step eight. If the driver does not back within two to three feet during this step, then the car will be greater than eighteen inches from the curb at the end of the step and often requires multiple steps to get it closer later. Most examiners will subtract many points or fail a new driver for alternating between forward and reverse multiple times in a futile attempt to move the car closer to the curb. Instead, during practice, have your teen confirm his/her keys (positions) during each pause of the vehicle.

8. When you are satisfied that your distance from the curb is correct, turn the wheel all the way left. Back while you are looking behind you until either your rear bumper is no closer than within one foot of the barrier representing the front bumper of a car or your tire *touches* the curb, whichever comes first. *Do not bang into the curb or the barrier. Some examiners will allow touching of the curb, but virtually no examiner will allow touching of the barriers, nor should they!*

9. Place your car in drive and allow the car to creep forward as you turn the wheel to straighten the car. *Do not allow your car to drift left away from the curb, and do not over correct right and run into the curb with your right front tire.*

10. Center the car roughly equidistant from front barriers and rear barriers. If not centered, adjust the car's position before placing the car in park. *Placing the car in park signals to the examiner that the parallel parking sequence is finished. The examiner should provide instructions to exit at this point. If not, ask.*

11. When given approval to exit, back up (straight back) to within one foot of the barrier representing the front bumper of a car and then stop.

12. With your foot on the brake, put your car in drive and turn your steering wheel full left before you move again.

13. Signal left that you are about to exit, and clear the adjoining lane by looking in your left mirror and over your left shoulder before you move. Exit the parallel parking space when your entrance lane is safe and clear.

14. While exiting, if it does not appear that you will safely clear the left front barrier, stop the car, place the car in reverse, turn the your wheel to center, back up a few feet, and repeat steps 11 to 14 again. *These extra precautionary measures are okay and may be required with larger vehicles. Remember the front barrier also represents the left rear bumper of a car. Better to be safe than sorry here.*

Parking Lot Driving

Angle, perpendicular, and parallel parking training are all typically conducted during a single two-hour driving lesson. We can generally complete training for all three types of parking in about an hour. The remainder of the time is used for our regular question-and-answer sequence and for driving to/from and within mall parking lots.

Parking lots are notorious for being dangerous. Other drivers often do not obey traffic laws, get tunnel vision when they see the space they want, do not signal their intent, and regularly drive around the parking lots at excessive and dangerous speeds. We have our beginning drivers drive around the parking lots at no greater that the posted speed and in many cases at less than the posted speeds at pedestrian crossings and other locations. If parking lots are so dangerous, why do we have our students drive in them? A busy parking lot is a microcosm of the driving world beyond.

In parking lots, we are usually driving at no more than five to fifteen miles per hour between parking activities. This is an excellent opportunity to develop and apply defensive driving skills at these very low speeds. We teach our students to scan the traffic scene at all times and look for pedestrians or drivers that may potentially enter our roadway. If it appears that a pedestrian is about to enter our roadway, we have our students immediately stop the car. The pedestrian may not have seen us or may not seem to care. In some states, pedestrians always have the right-of-way; but in any case, stopping the car is preferable to impacting a pedestrian and changing their life and yours forever.

While we are driving in busy parking lots, we often must deal with other drivers who exit their parking spaces without taking all the precautionary measures that we teach out students to take. These drivers present a different hazard, and they are dealt with a bit differently than pedestrians. If their backing lights are on and we see that they are about to move into our roadway, we have our students slow and tap the horn. In most cases when another driver knows he/she is about to enter someone else's roadway, they will stop and allow you to proceed.

If the driver doesn't respond, we have our student stop the car and apply the horn for a bit longer period of time. Since your car also should be stopped by now, collision has been avoided.

In these cases, a beginning driver must be taught when and how to apply the horn. Many beginning drivers are afraid to touch the horn because they are afraid to offend another driver. It is true. Some other drivers may get "offended" even as you prevent them from crashing into you. We remind our students that the purpose of the horn is not to intentionally make another driver mad. The purpose here is to use the horn to cause the other driver to *look at you and stop moving his/ her vehicle toward your vehicle.* This may be required in a variety of different future driving circumstances. It is a far better outcome to alert another driver and offend him or her than allow another driver to crash into you.

Intersections in parking lots are often more dangerous than intersections in residential neighborhoods. Many drivers conclude that stop signs, white lines, and all other traffic laws do not apply to them in parking lots.

Making matters worse, drivers often drive at odd angles through parking lot spaces when they see the specific space they wish to park in near the store. We call these drivers *snipers* because they are very dangerous drivers. Remember, a car can be a three-thousand-pound weapon. Many SUVs and trucks weigh much more. Here, collision avoidance is not only required; it is a necessity. Our passenger brake is applied more often in busy parking lots than at any other time.

Mall parking lots often have "inside track" roadways and "outside track" roadways. Getting to and from them safely is often tricky and requires proper steering, turning, application of gas and brake, defensive driving, collision avoidance, and the correct interpretation of the rules of the road at mall intersections. Theses parking lots may be used to verify the new drivers' performance before moving on to city driving. It is here in mall parking lots where we often confirm that additional coaching is required prior to city driving. Sometimes the coaching is physical (steering/turning the car), and sometimes the coaching is mental (rules of the road).

During this lesson, we ask additional rules of the road questions that were not covered in the previous lesson. We also discuss the following:

Wheel Parking on Hills

Which way do you turn the wheels during each of the four possibilities while parking on uphill/downhill streets? This question will be asked during the driving test. The acronym UCLA, besides referencing one of the most prestigious universities in the country, is also used as a memory jogger by many driver education schools. In this case, we use UCLA as an acronym that stands for **U**phill with **C**urb **L**eft **A**lways. Well, you may ask, "What about uphill without a curb, downhill with a curb, and downhill without a curb?"

In each of those cases, the wheels are turned right. What is the intent here? (This is the answer to the "why" part.) If the parking brake and transmission each fail while your vehicle is parked on a hill, the vehicle will either roll into the curb and stop, or it will roll off the road entirely so that it doesn't roll into another vehicle.

While parking uphill with a curb (UCLA) the back of the front tire rests against the curb and prevents the vehicle from moving, *even if the transmission fails and the parking brake fails.*

6-10

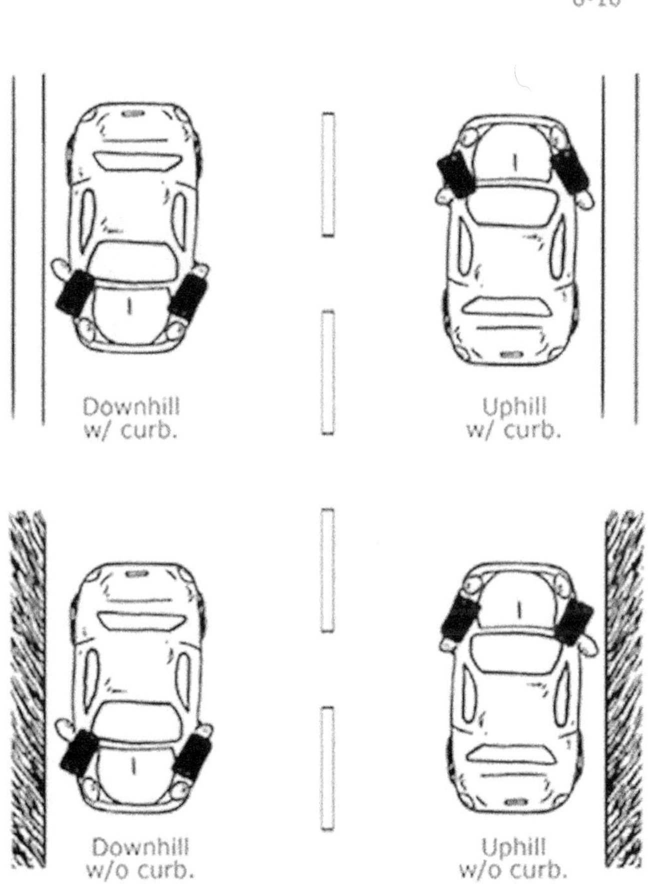

Lane Change Simulation (SMOG)

While parked in an angle or perpendicular parking place, we take the opportunity to have our student drivers *simulate* the four step process (signal, mirror, over the shoulder, and go) for lane changes into the left lane and right lane. This is more important than it might initially seem.

We have determined that if we have them simulate the process while parked in a parking lot first, there are far fewer errors later when we are moving in traffic.

Often, beginning students are confused about which way to signal, which mirrors to look in at a specific time, or which shoulder to glance over at a particular time. All this can be discussed while the car is stopped. Students are informed that while they are driving, they should be glancing in their rearview mirrors periodically. The frequency that they glance at the mirrors varies with traffic conditions. On a rural road, the glances may be less often.

In heavy stop-and-go traffic, the glances may occur a bit more often but not such the driver loses track of the brake lights of the car in front at any time.

Drivers should be aware of it when a driver directly behind them moves into an adjoining lane.

We coach that a lane change sequence is not initiated until our beginning driver has confirmed that a sufficient gap already exists for the lane change. During an actual lane change in traffic, there will be two additional opportunities to verify that the target lane is clear. During lane changes into the left lane, the left side mirror is checked, and a brief head turn to the left ensures that a vehicle has not moved into your blind spot.

During lane changes into the right lane, the right side mirror is checked, and a brief head turn to the right verifies that a vehicle has not entered the blind spot. In our state, the head turn must be completed as part of the lane change process during DMV testing or several points will be deducted. We caution our students that if they don't complete the entire SMOG sequence as instructed, the consequences in an actual driving situation could even be far more severe.

Introduction to City Driving

The introduction to city driving should occur only after a beginning driver has demonstrated that/he she has complete mastery of the car in parking lots *and* has answered all our right-of-way questions satisfactorily. Actually, the introduction to city driving began during classroom training and continues during all follow- up driving lessons. A beginning driver must know the rules of the road exceptionally well in order to demonstrate that knowledge while driving the vehicle in city traffic.

In addition, all the techniques and skills that were developed to control the vehicle safely in parking lots and residential neighborhoods must now be applied in traffic. The CADETS BTW performance grid for lesson 2 is provided on the last page of this chapter and is repeated in Appendix 2.

CADETS
843-651-6066
www.cadets4driving.com
DRIVER TRAINING

6·12
DRIVER

BEHIND-THE-WHEEL INSTRUCTION GRID NO. 2

Student Name:______________________ Instructor:__________________

ACTIVITY	INTRODUCTION	PRACTICE	MASTERY
LESSON DATE(S)			
Rules of the Road Review/Defensive Driving Q and A			
Angle Parking			
Perpendicular Parking			
Parallel Parking			
All Parking Space Backing			
Parking Lot Driving			
Right of Way Review			
Wheel Parking on Hills (UCLA)			
Lane Change Simulation (SMOG)			
Introduction to City Driving			

CHAPTER 7

The Advanced Driving Grid for Beginning Drivers

There is a first time for everything. In the driving world, there is going to be a first time your teen drives on the highway, drives through a controlled intersection, completes a left turn at a dangerous intersection, merges onto an expressway, and completes lane changes. Many beginning driver education students have never done some or all of any of these things before their parents enroll them in driver education. As noted in previous chapters, even if our students tell us earnestly that they have advanced driving experience, we must assume that they are not prepared until we *ensure* they are prepared.

The CADETS final driving lesson is two hours of advanced driving. Actually, it typically requires one hour and forty-five minutes of advanced driving and fifteen minutes of verification questions and answers before we begin. Our final lesson involves applying virtually all the skills learned in the classroom and preceding BTW lessons. The final lesson includes city driving, highway driving, expressway driving, and if possible, a trip to the DMV.

The trip to the DMV allows us to preview the actual driving test with our students. This includes a review of preliminary questions about the vehicle, basic auto setup, parking lot driving, three-point turns, parallel parking, and operating the vehicle safely at all times. If a student forgets a step or becomes confused during the process, we stop the car, review the step or procedure, and then have the student repeat the procedure. The following is a brief overview of grid no. 3 topics:

Advanced Driving Skills Q and A

Since many students have never driven in some or all these advanced driving conditions, we ask new questions pertaining specifically to grid no.

3 advanced driving. New drivers must have the *knowledge* to drive in advanced driving conditions before they can safely *demonstrate* mastery in advanced driving conditions.

One of our goals is to ensure that every student has the basic knowledge to perform every advanced driving activity on our performance grid before we move the car. Once the student begins driving, we coach and reinforce our students during the entire lesson.

Merging with and without Yield

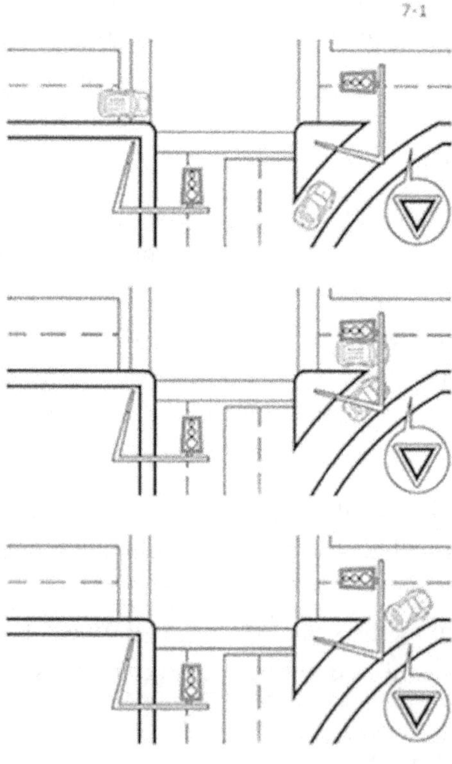

As described in previous chapters, at CADETS, we train our students to scan the traffic scene as they are approaching any merge. If a yield sign is visible in your feeder lane, the yield sign is giving you several messages in advance. First, that heavy traffic is common at that location. Second, the feeder lane is often very short or shorter than optimum for an ideal merge. Third, you may have to yield to a complete *stop* because all vehicles in the target lane have the right-of-way.

One of the reasons we have our students scan the traffic during all merges is because there may be no vehicles at all in the target lane. A driver of a vehicle following closely behind may be looking at the same target lane that you are looking at. If there are no visible vehicles in your target lane, you should keep moving,

albeit safely by completing SMOG before merging. The driver behind you does not expect you to stop if there are no vehicles in your target lane, and you are not required to yield if there are no vehicles for you to yield to.

Most merges without yield signs have longer feeder lanes, but be careful. They are not always longer, and they are not always safer than feeder lanes with yield signs. Part of your assessment while approaching is determining the merging gaps and the relative speeds of the vehicles you are merging with. If your target lane is populated by cars traveling at sixty miles per hour, that speed is also your ideal merging speed. If the target lane is populated by vehicles at or near forty miles per hour, that is your target speed. If your target lane is stacked with cars in "stop-and-go" mode, in order to merge safely, you may be required to merge after a complete stop.

We train our students to approach the target lane at or near the same speed as vehicles in the target lane and assess our vehicle as being in front of or behind specific target lane vehicles. Target lane drivers *may or may not* adjust their speeds slightly for merging drivers.

Beginning drivers must be trained to adjust their speeds for either type of driver. However, we also teach our students that if a driver in a target lane must noticeably *brake f*or us in order to allow us to merge, it is usually because either we didn't merge at the proper speed, or we didn't select the correct gap in traffic to merge into. Beginning drivers must be coached to merge properly in advanced driving conditions.

Highway Driving

New drivers also must be coached to adjust their acceleration speeds, slowing speeds, turning speeds, and braking distance for highway speeds and highway traffic. New drivers must be reminded to maintain space and visibility (referenced independently on our performance grid) and obey all the traffic laws they learned in previous lessons.

The first time a beginning drivers enters two-lane highways or four-lane highway, they sometimes drift out of their lanes slightly. Beginning drivers may do this, even though during previous lessons they were coached to steer properly and turn corners properly. In traffic, beginning drivers often must be reassured that all the skills they learned in previous lessons also apply to advanced driving conditions. This is one of many reasons that the final driving lesson is not simply an observation lesson.

Unless marked otherwise, left turns are completed in the nearest lane marked for vehicles moving in your direction. Right turns are completed in the nearest lane marked for vehicles moving in your direction. During these turns, watch your teen's hands and watch for drifting of the vehicle. There may be two lanes or more in the target roadway, but there is only one target lane. As coaches, instructors, and parents, we must remind beginning drivers that it is not okay to drift out of their current lane while driving or their target lane while completing a turn. After completion of the turn into the target lane, SMOG is completed prior to any subsequent lane change.

City Driving

Many beginning drivers drive with a level of tunnel vision initially. They must be coached to observe the traffic scene and use their eyes to scan. They should be scanning the traffic scene for signals, signs, brake lights, and telltale signs of intent of other drivers and/or pedestrians.

Give the beginning driver ample advance notice before preparing to exit your roadway or turning at intersections. Make sure your instructions are clear and precise. Avoid casual conversation. Make certain that the traffic conditions you are reading are the same traffic conditions that your teen is seeing and responding to. Also, observe your teen carefully at all intersections.

At stop signs, complete stops must be completed such that the driver stops behind the stop sign, and the car rocks back. Otherwise, it could be considered to be a rolling stop. A second stop is required at blind intersections.

Almost all four-way stops are set up such that you can see all four entrances. When four cars arrive at four different times, the four cars depart in the same order they arrive; 1-2-3-4. If your vehicle and another vehicle arrive from opposite directions and the other driver has not signaled, creep forward to ensure that the driver does not intend to turn in front of you. When two drivers approaching a four-way stop arrive at the same time perpendicular to one another, the car on the right has the right-of-way. However, remember that the right-of-way should be *yielded* to you; it should not be taken without the cooperation of your fellow drivers.

Most states allow right turns on red lights (unless marked otherwise) after a complete stop and an assessment of speed and distance of approaching vehicles. If there is a crosswalk in your target lane, the driver must ensure that a pedestrian has not entered the crosswalk.

Left turns are another matter. Any left turn without a green arrow is potentially dangerous, and some left turns *with* green arrows may even be dangerous. Speeds and distance of approaching vehicles must be assessed under green lights, yellow lights, and at unregulated intersections. There may be little or no margin for errors at busy intersections. Three safe right turns equals one unsafe left turn. However, recognize that when your teen is ready, the initial left turns should be completed with an instructor or a parent in the vehicle talking to the teen.

While no two drivers drive exactly the same way, you and your teen should have already discussed the appropriate responses to routine traffic conditions in advance.

If your teen is not judging speeds and distances of other vehicles as accurately as you feel is safe, have your teen pull into a parking lot (after the lesson) and discuss it while the car is parked.

As instructors, we never yell at teens. However, we are well aware that the parent-teen relationship is often emotional. We suggest that you express your expectations quietly but firmly. Later, refer to your state DMV manual and discuss the matter with your partner, the professional driving instructor. When parents partner with instructors, we can jointly assess unsafe driving practices and develop coaching strategies to overcome them.

Expressway Driving

If you live within twenty miles of an expressway, we urge you to have your teen drive on the expressway near the end of their permit period. We make every attempt to schedule our final lessons for late Sunday mornings. Sunday mornings are often characterized by having fewer drivers on the roads, fewer drivers in a tremendous hurry, and fewer distracted drivers. Drivers generally drive more safely with their families in their vehicles (on Sunday mornings) than they do when they are in a hurry to arrive home from their workdays.

During the expressway portion of the lesson, we have our student enter a long feeder lane and merge at the posted speed limit of sixty miles per hour. The few vehicles on the expressway at that time are driving at or near that speed. We coach our students to merge as they have been trained using SMOG and determining whether our vehicle fills a gap in *front* of a vehicle in the target lane or *behind* a vehicle in the target lane.

Once we merge seamlessly, we have our students complete several lane changes. Beginning drivers are cautioned that completing a lane change at sixty mile per hour is different than completing a lane change at thirty mile per hour. We ensure that preparation for the lane change is appropriate. We also ensure that execution of lane changes is safe and gradual at that speed. Any discernible drifting is gently pointed out and corrected during subsequent lane changes.

Generally, left lanes should be reserved for drivers who insist on driving above the speed limit. We don't drive in the far left lane unless we have a specific reason (lane change reinforcement) to be there. In any case, we don't drive in the lane for very long. The far right lane should be used for entering the expressway, exiting the expressway, and for slower moving commercial vehicles.

This means that we coach our students to drive in the middle lane or lanes the majority of the time. We coach our students not to pass on the right and not to enter the far right lane until preparation for exiting.

All Lane Changes (SMOG)

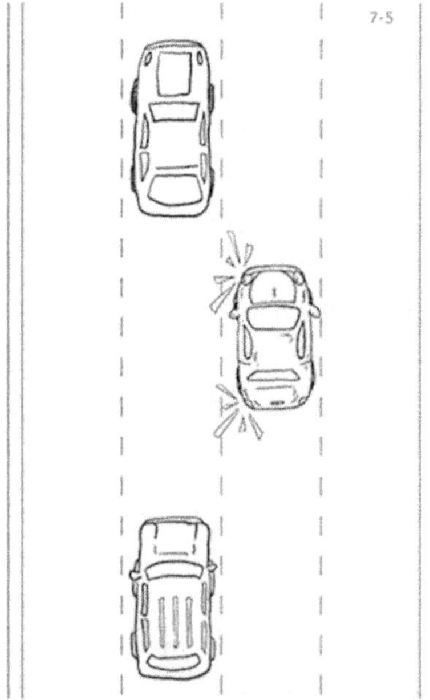

Signal, mirror, over the shoulder, and go (SMOG) is used for all lane changes. It is also used while pulling away from any curb, initiating three- point turns, exiting parallel parking spaces, and during all merges.

Exiting Highways and Expressways

As new drivers exit highways and expressways, they must be coached to respond to traffic signs that call for reduced speed. As previously referenced, the reduction in speed is often significant. We watch for these speed adjustment signs very carefully, and ensure our students respond appropriately.

The exit lanes from highways and expressways may terminate with a variety of different signs and signals depending on the type of road we are transferring to. The transferring vehicles in front of us may have been required to *stop*. Beginning drivers must be coached to slow the vehicle gradually and stop the vehicle such that passengers are not jerked forward in their seatbelts. Beginning drivers must learn that after driving at sixty- plus miles per hour, the requirement to drive at very slow speed or stop often takes place under an altered sense of speed and distance. Your positive coaching will help them adjust to these extremes safely.

One of our cloverleaf exits requires a new merge onto a busy roadway.

There is no yield sign at the end of the cloverleaf.

The feeder lane is short, the drivers are generally moving at fifty to fifty miles per hour, and our new driver must accelerate again to merge between vehicles within a relatively short distance. We coach our students to do this safely by pointing out the obvious gaps in traffic while we are on the cloverleaf. If we can see the target gap, the student should be able to see the target gap, but we assist them by pointing out the obvious. We also coach speed adjustment again, an important aspect of exiting one roadway and merging into another.

Maintaining Space

Make every attempt to maintain three-second following distance in good driving conditions. While driving in inclement weather, the following distance should be greater in the rain and much greater while driving on ice, sleet, and snow. We acknowledge that while driving in heavy traffic, if you leave a three-second gap, it is likely that another driver will pull into it. This isn't because your lane is actually moving faster; it is because misguided drivers often *believe* that your lane is moving faster.

In very slow-moving traffic, you may decrease your following distance slightly from the three-second standard, but you *must* keep part of your brain aware of the brake lights in front of you at all times. Your foot should be on the brake if you are moving at idle speed, thereby reducing the reaction time if a full stop is required. In stop-and-go traffic, you should stop your car no closer than half a car length behind the vehicle in front.

Maintaining Visibility

Maintaining visibility is stressed in each driving lesson. Some beginning drivers only think about what they can see, not what they cannot see. New drivers must be coached to recognize that part of the collision avoidance process is taking additional steps to ensure your vehicle is also seen by other drivers. The following are some examples, and there are many others:

- Always signal before every change of position of the vehicle.

- Do not follow large vehicles too closely, and stay out of the "no zone" of the driver.

- Avoid driving alongside the same vehicle for an extended period of time.

- Override your dusk/dawn light sensor, and put your low beams on during early stages of dusk and dawn.

- Turn on your fog lights or low beams during the early stages of fog.

- Avoid driving with your high beams on at any time other than in rural areas with no approaching traffic.

- At four-way stops, make eye contact with the other drivers. Eye contact helps reassure them that you see them and *helps* confirm that they see you. It also helps reassure other drivers that when the right of way is conceded to you that you will take it.

- Brake gradually into stops. Remember that as soon as you apply brake pressure, your brake lights illuminate for drivers behind. Most good drivers begin slowing immediately.

Blind Intersections and Blind Spots and No Zones

7-9

We encounter blind intersections during most of our driving lessons. At stop signs, if the approaching traffic from either direction is "blind" (if you can't see them, they can't see you), you must creep forward past the stop sign just until you can see and stop a second time. What you do next depends on whether the cross traffic has stop signs or does not have stop signs. You should have determined this while you were approaching the intersection. If cross traffic does not have stop signs, you must verify speed and distance of any approaching vehicle before crossing or turning at the intersection. If cross traffic also has stop signs, you should verify that the other vehicles are slowing to a stop in accordance with the stop signs before crossing or turning.

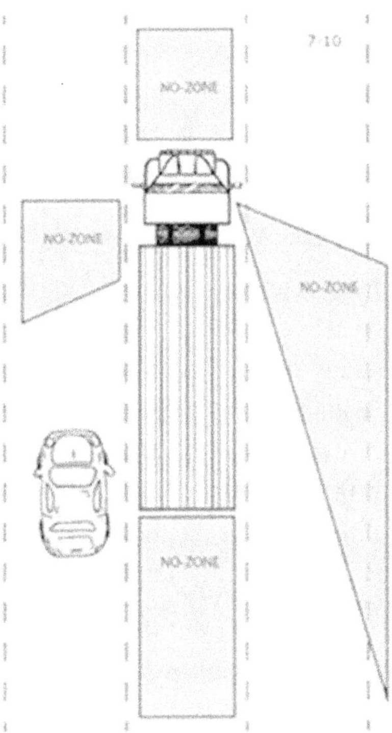

Blind spots are at the left and right rear fenders of passenger vehicles. Small vehicles and motorcycles can fit into those spots. All drivers should check in the rear view and side view mirror before the first step in SMOG for a lane change because those checks are routine periodic checks. However, SMOG is also required by DMV examiners. It has a practical reason too. A driver that is driving directly behind may suddenly pull around you without warning and accelerate.

This is also one of the reasons we coach our students to maintain a constant speed before, during, and after lane changes unless traffic conditions dictate otherwise.

Commercial vehicles and very large trucks have much larger blind spots and. If you are driving alongside an eighteen-wheel vehicle, the blind spot may be quite large for the driver. Even if the trucker has a convex mirror installed (many of them do), they often must glance at the convex mirror at the right time to see you. Avoid driving alongside the same commercial vehicle for more than a few minutes without adjusting your speed.

If you are following a large truck so closely that you cannot see the driver in his/her rearview mirror, this also means the driver cannot see you. This is as "no zone." Do not drive there and avoid stopping very close to commercial vehicles at intersections.

Point of No Return

The point of no return was discussed during the classroom chapter. During advanced driving lessons, your teen's understanding of the point of no return may be verified any time a light turns yellow during an approach. Ensure that your teen understands the relationship between speed and stopping distances. A car moving at twenty miles per hour requires the driver to perceive that something has changed (a yellow light), has assessed the time required to move the foot from the gas to the brake, and has considered the braking capabilities of the car.

According to the North American Alliance for Safe Driving, a typical passenger vehicle moving at twenty miles per hour requires sixty-nine feet to stop, including reaction distance, braking distance, and stopping distance. A car moving at forty miles per hour requires about 189 feet to stop. This requires about four seconds. This means that if you are only one hundred feet from the intersection while moving at forty miles per hour, you must keep moving and exit the backside of the intersection while the light remains yellow. You passed the point of no return safely.

A car moving at sixty miles per hour has those same elements, but the car is moving over a much greater distance during each phase of the total braking distance, and the car has much greater inertia. The same vehicle moving at sixty miles per hour requires 359 feet to stop!

When responding to "fresh" yellow lights or other routine driving conditions, new drivers should not brake so hard that the ABS engages, nor should they be "caught" exiting intersections during red lights. Drivers should not speed up before entering any intersection in order to "beat" a red light.

That leaves responding appropriately to the distance of the yellow light in relation to the speed of your vehicle as the only safe and proper option.

During our advanced driving lessons, we encounter yellow lights while approaching at a variety of different speeds. Experience will help new drivers adjust their braking and stopping distances for the speeds of their vehicles. However, coaching also helps.

Coach your teen so that he/she is aware of where the point of no return is for different speeds and distances from yellow lights. Also, never allow your teen to change lanes just before an intersection, accelerate near an intersection, or change lanes within an intersection.

1-2-3 Count

The 1-2-3 count is the time it takes to turn your head left- right-left. At stop lights, if you are the first vehicle sitting at the light, use the 1-2-3 left- right-left before you move. Drivers of approaching vehicles may have missed their light, or they may be running a stale yellow light or a quick red light intentionally. They may even be accelerating! If you are sitting at a crosswalk, you must also check for pedestrians that may have entered your crosswalk. If you are sitting behind another vehicle at the light, the 1-2-3 also allows you initiate the three-second following rule before you begin moving.

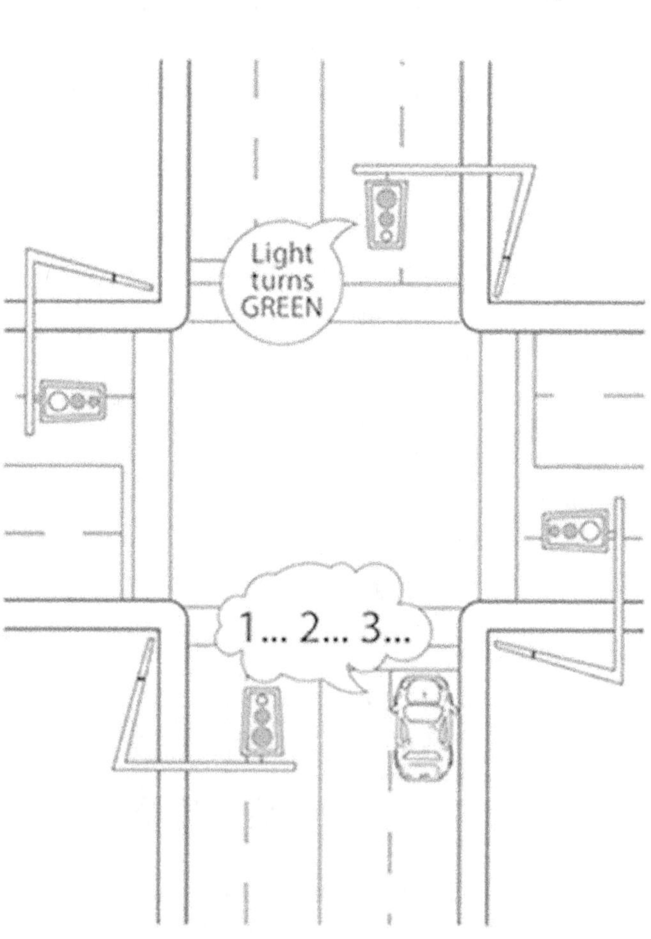

Three-Second Following

This has already been discussed in pervious chapters. Parents are urged to count the three seconds as one thousand one, one thousand two, and one thousand three after a vehicle in front has passed a stationary object (sign or telephone pole).

Your car should pass the same object after three seconds or greater. This method takes the place of the former "one car length for every ten miles per hour" rule that driver education instructors taught for years. The reason for the change was because at highway speeds (i.e., sixty miles per hour), it is a bit of a challenge to determine six-car lengths accurately. However, the three-second calculation is relatively easy to check, and it works for any speed.

Following distance must be adjusted greater for inclement weather. Rain, sleet, snow, and ice all require adjustments upward. Take it from me: error on the side of caution during inclement weather.

Wheel Visibility at Lights

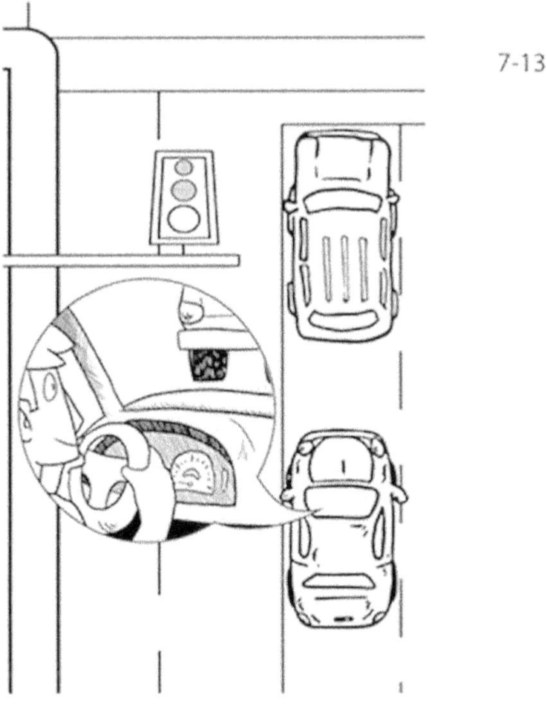

When a vehicle is stopped in front of you at an intersection, you should not allow your vehicle to inch toward the vehicle so close that you cannot see the rear tires of that vehicle. If behind a commercial vehicle, stay behind even further. Most commercial vehicles are manual shift and may roll back into your vehicle. In addition, if a driver behind you bumps your vehicle or crashes into it, you do not want your vehicle to be sandwiched into the car in front.

Reading of Intent of Other Drivers

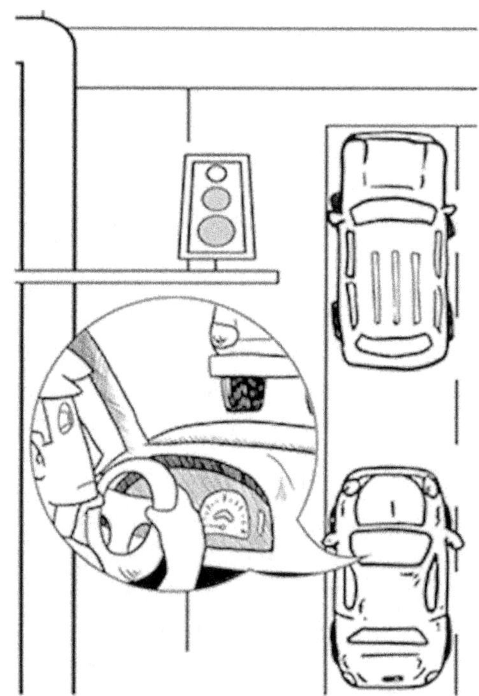

7-14

Other drivers do not always signal intent with turn signals, brake lights, and backing lights. However, almost all drivers will reveal intent with the wheels of the car, motion of the car, their heads, and their eyes. Drivers in parked vehicles will turn the wheels before they move. Drivers at intersections will turn usually turn their heads and eyes in the direction they intend to turn. The hoods of vehicles approaching intersections will dip down during braking but lift up during acceleration. Coach your teen to look for these types of telltale signs and respond accordingly.

Behind-the-Wheel Instruction Grid No. 3 is included at the end of this chapter. It is repeated in Appendix 3. Appendix 4 provides the full performance grid for all driving lessons and advanced driving.

We suggest to parents that after grids no. 1, no. 2, and no. 3 have each been completed at least once or even more, the full performance grid in Appendix 4 should be copied and referenced regularly during the remainder of the permit period. Remember that we usually only have a finite amount to time to teach. Meanwhile, even in our state, the entire permit period is six months long—plenty of time for multiple applications of the grid until they get it right! It is far better to have "over kill" than "under kill" with the reinforcement training. Know what I mean?

At CADETS, we do not place an *X* in the mastery column until the student has achieved a standard in accordance with our training. We are confident that the preceding and following chapters will help parents assess their teens' progress during the entire permit period.

BEHIND-THE-WHEEL INSTRUCTION GRID NO. 3

Student Name:_______________ Instructor:___________________________

ACTIVITY	INTRODUCTION	PRACTICE	MASTERY
LESSON DATE(S)			
Advanced Driving Skills Q and A			
Merging with and without Yield			
Highway Driving			
City Driving			
Expressway Driving			
All Lane Changes (SMOG)			
Entering and Exiting Highways/Expressways			
Maintaining Space			
Maintaining Visibility			
The Point of No Return for Yellow Lights			
The 1-2-3 Count for Entering Intersections			
Three-Second Following Distance			
Wheel Visibility at Lights			
Reading Intent of Other Drivers			

ADDITIONAL NOTES

191

CHAPTER 8

Full Performance Driving and Minimizing Risk

The contents of this chapter provide a bit more of the rationale behind our reluctance to use the word *accident* instead of the use of either the words *collision* or crash in describing, well … *crashes*. The word *accident* implies that you, your teen, or anyone else driving your vehicle has no immediate control over collisions, crashes, and the results thereof. Actually, just the opposite is true. Minimizing risk reduces the potential of your vehicle crashing into another vehicle or object or suffering the consequences of another vehicle crashing into you. Risk can be altered and reduced, but it can never be 100 percent eliminated.

The following are offered as suggestions for minimizing risk while your teen is driving and you are coaching. However, if all drivers of all ages followed these guidelines, thousands of lives, hundreds of thousands of injuries, and millions of dollars could be saved every year. Therefore, we suggest that these actions be taken by each and every driver in your family who is in possession of a driver's license or is in training to obtain a driver's license at all times.

At the end of chapters 5, 6, and 7, we introduced three training grids that we suggested you employ in order to supplement your teen's driver education. During the early permit period, repetitive coaching of your teen will be required for virtually all the activities listed on the three grids. However, once your teen has entered the advanced driving phase, we suggest that you gradually alter the training strategy as your teen advances. *Periodically,* reproduce the full performance grid in Appendix 4 and track your teen's performance in accordance with the grid. All the activities listed will not be required during every trip of course. However, you will be surprised at how many of the listed grid elements are required during a twenty-mile trip.

Look for safe habits, behaviors, and trends as well as performance grid elements you feel are in need of improvement. Remember that positive reinforcement is just as beneficial as negative reinforcement. Try to economize your words for use later during semiformal non-emotional feedback sessions after you have your teen's undivided attention.

Look for opportunities to balance your feedback with praise and guidance just as a professional instructor would. Also remember that your teen will be watching you and other drivers more closely now. Therefore, perhaps the most important thing you can do for your teen and younger siblings is to lead by example. Become a role model for your teen when you are in the driver's seat and a trusted advisor when you are in the passenger seat.

Seat Belts

Many North American drivers and passengers die every year without their seats belts buckled! These days, I can't imagine any driver or passenger riding in a car without having a seat belt on. Not only is it a state law within almost all states but also the seat belt just may one day save your life or the life of a passenger. Teens will not only watch their parents and mimic your behaviors; they will also often watch their friends and mimic theirs. Peer influence can be a very strong motivating factor. However, peer influence can be overcome with proper training, coaching, and repetition.

One of the very best female students that we trained several years ago was injured in a vehicle that was being driven by her boyfriend about six months later. He had flipped it into a drainage ditch when he took a sharp turn at a higher rate of speed than he was capable of executing safely. In addition, *he didn't have his seatbelt on.* Either her boyfriend had not been trained by a professional, or he had chosen to ignore the training. Sadly, he paid for it with his life. However, she had been thoroughly trained and coached repeatedly to wear her seat belt every time she entered a vehicle. It saved her life.

Please give your outstanding safety equipment a chance to do its job. Make certain that your teen not only buckles up before driving but also develops a habit of checking that other passengers have buckled up too. Your teen may not always be able to *control* the behavior of his/her peers.

However, your teen can often *influence* the behavior of other teens in a positive way.

Traffic Laws

Earlier in the book, we encouraged parents to refresh your knowledge of traffic laws and enhance your driving skills in order to help guide your teen through the driver training process.

By the time you are regularly riding with your teen in advanced driving conditions, you should be convinced that you and your teen have reached a common understanding of the rules the road. However, please remember that your teen will not be an *experienced* driver until after having driven for several *years,* not just a few *months.* During the entire permit period, be prepared to coach your teen when unique or unusual traffic circumstances arise. In order to be prepared to do this, you must stay thoroughly engaged. Do not turn into a passive or distracted passenger. Your teen should be responding to signs, signals, and other driving conditions in such a way as to inspire confidence from you and other passengers that your teen not only knows the rules of the road but is also in control of the vehicle at all times.

Intersections

Scan the traffic scene along with your teen while approaching intersections. Over time, your teen should begin to see the same things that you see and respond in a variety of different ways appropriate for the circumstances presented. As your teen enters the advanced driving phase, you also should be prepared to enter the advanced coaching phase. This means that you should be able to scan the traffic scene and take note of advanced driving conditions as they evolve rather than staring at your teen and looking for beginning driver mistakes.

Your peripheral vision and recognition of sights and sounds related to driving, perhaps previously ignored while riding as a passenger, now should stay engaged. While your teen is developing intermediate and advanced driving skills, your perception of slight changes in the motion of the vehicle, direction, acceleration, deceleration should have become more acute. For example, note gradual slowing of the vehicle for stops and gradual acceleration during departures to/from intersections. Use your peripheral vision and hearing to confirm that your teen continues to signal before every change of position of the vehicle. Your teen should signal at least one hundred feet before turning at an intersection unless a driveway is less than one hundred feet from the intersection.

All drivers should never speed up or make lane changes just before an intersection or within an intersection. Continue to confirm that your teen turns into the correct lane at each corner every time. Watch and feel for safe, consistent operation of the vehicle in accordance with all driving skills discussed in chapters 5 to 7.

Advanced Reading of Intent of Other Drivers

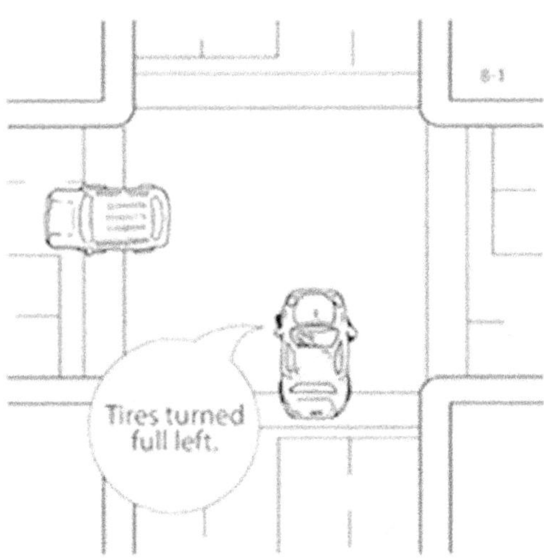

Ensure other drivers at intersections have seen your vehicle, signs, or signals by looking for "tells" in the movement of other vehicles. Your teen will not develop this skill unless you help identify "tells" during the permit period and verbalize them to your teen.

Advanced drivers pay attention to the direction wheels are turned from vehicles about to enter your roadway or waiting to enter your roadway. For example, at an intersection where a driver is waiting for clearance to turn left in front of your vehicle, the wheels should be straight until the moment clearance has been verified. If not, whoever is driving your vehicle should lift the foot off the accelerator as you approach the intersection and watch the vehicle very closely for movement. If the driver does not see you and turns left in front of you, your time/opportunity for collision avoidance will be minimal. In addition, if the approaching vehicle driver is tagged from behind, the vehicle may be pushed head-on into your vehicle!

Watch for other "tells" as other drivers are approaching your vehicle at intersections regulated by traffic lights. For example, when a vehicle is braking, the front of the hood will dip down. When a vehicle is accelerating, the hood of the vehicle will lift. You should also watch for this as you are about to enter any roadway from a two-way stop or driveway. An accelerating vehicle may not provide your teen with enough time to enter the highway safely, especially when entering a roadway from a dead stop.

Watch the head and eyes of the other drivers at four way stops. The head, eyes, and wheels will generally reveal where they intend to turn, even when their turn signals do not.

Parents riding as passengers in their family vehicle do not typically have an additional rearview mirror mounted on the passenger side. The additional rearview mirror is a very valuable tool for driving instructors. You may not be aware that a tailgater is behind your teen unless your teen says something about it or makes an abrupt lane change. Ensure your teen does not make an *abrupt* lane changes in order to avoid a tailgater. Impatient tailgaters often make abrupt lane changes without signaling.

You will see them as they drive by. We call them lane jumpers. Lane jumpers will endanger you if you do not take steps to avoid them. Also take note of situations where a series of vehicles pass your vehicle on the right. Is it because you are about to turn left, or is it for some other reason?

Is your teen driving below the speed limit, or is he/she driving in the left lane for an extended period of time without a specific reason? Tailgaters and lane jumpers cannot be avoided 100 percent of the time. However, take note of how your teen reduces the risk of being impacted by them. Tailgaters and lane jumpers often (eventually) crash into someone. Just don't allow it to be you.

Driving While Texting (DWT) and Driving While Phoning (DWP)

I have served as a professional driving instructor in for the past eight years. I can state unequivocally that the problem involves far more than texting while driving, and it involves a majority of the drivers out there, most of whom *are not* teenagers.

A driver *of any age* (including teenagers of course) cannot safely and efficiently operate a motor vehicle while phoning or texting on a cell phone. I know this after observing drivers who sincerely believe they can multitask driving up and down the Grand Strand of South Carolina all day. Usually I have a fifteen-year-old beginning driver behind the wheel with me when I see them. Sometimes I see them in front, alongside, and behind reflected from my specially mounted passenger mirror.

Watch for mobile phone use by drivers near you. The moment a driver near you picks up a mobile phone, the driver is going to begin making a series of mistakes. As I observe these drivers, I point out the mistakes so that my student driver can be prepared to apply defensive driving skills as required. I also mention the mistakes in the hope that our students won't do the same thing when they obtain their own driver's license.

Virtually all these drivers operate a vehicle as if they are driving under the influence of alcohol or drugs. Actually, they are driving under the influence. It doesn't take a driving instructor or a police officer to see it. Once the erratic driver is pointed out, the mistakes are so obvious that even beginning drivers can see them.

Fast Lane/Slow Lane

We suggest that you not refer to the lanes in terms of fast lane/slow lane.

Instead, we suggest that you refer to the far left lane as a passing lane and the far right hand lane as a merging lane or an exit lane depending on the location. If you designate the far left hand lane as a "fast lane" (to your teens), you will reinforce a common interpretation that the left lane is reserved for the fastest driver who wishes to drive in that lane that day! Those drivers usually pay for this line of thinking with speeding tickets, but there may be far greater consequences.

In many of the largest cities in the country, during nonpeak traffic periods, all the vehicles in every lane, except the merging/exit lane, will be running abreast at about the same speed. During peak traffic periods of the day, all the vehicles will either be moving at "slow and go" speeds or "stop and go" in all the lanes. Peak traffic periods may last for several hours in the morning and several hours in the afternoon. Once you move out of the merging lane into one of the middle lanes, avoid excessive lane jumping in heavy traffic. Lane jumping not only wears you out mentally and physically but also increases risk.

If you are driving on a highway that only has only two lanes on your side of the road, we suggest that you encourage your teen to drive in the right hand lane the majority of the time. Move to the left lane in order to pass large vehicles, pass vehicles moving below the speed limit, or in order to prepare for a left turn. Staying out of the passing lane the majority of the time reduces the opportunities for tailgaters to push you, cause near misses when they pass you on the right, or crash into you.

Many large cities with multiple expressways include diamond car pool lanes that require at least one additional passenger in the vehicle in order to qualify to drive in them. A diamond car pool lane is not a passing lane, although some lone drivers have attempted to treat it as one. Some Los Angeles commuters have been discovered to be so desperate to drive in the diamond lanes that they created "fake dummies" to ride along with them in their vehicles! This fools the highway patrol every time. LOL.

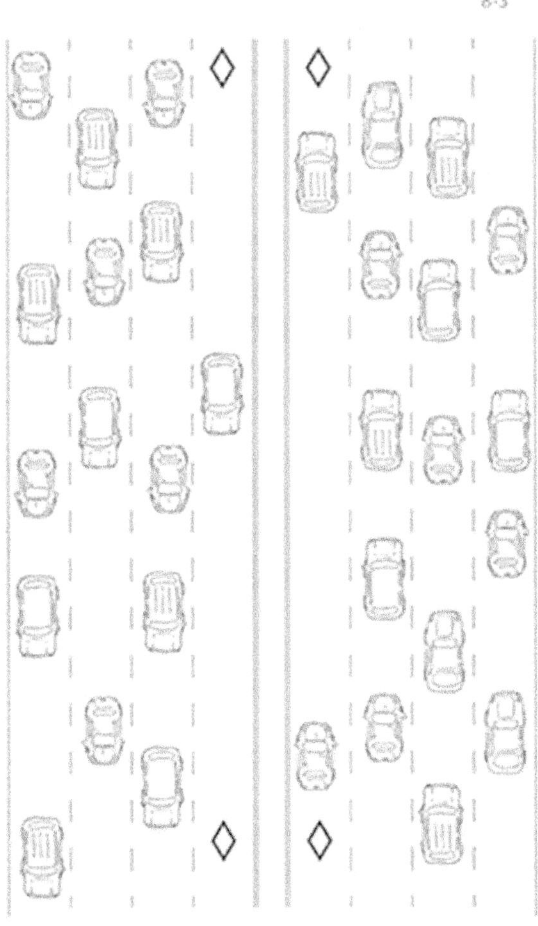

Advanced Merging

The previous chapter provided coaching guidelines for beginning drivers just learning to merge in routine traffic conditions. Advanced merging strategies are required for drivers of any age in most areas of the country every day.

Stop-and go traffic is common in most urban cities and suburban expressways near major metropolitan areas. We coach our students to merge as soon as a safe opportunity is presented. The following are some tips for advanced merging picked up during forty years of merging within forty states.

Sir Isaac Newton's first law of motion states that "an object in motion will stay in motion, and an object at rest will stay at rest unless acted upon by an external force." Newton's laws of motion are used to explain many things here on Earth common in our everyday lives. For example, trains require a very long time to get them moving and a very long time to get them stopped.

Typical eighteen-wheel trucks, midsize trucks, commercial and private pickup trucks and SUVs weigh more and sometimes much more than regular passenger vehicles. Newton's second law states that "f = ma." This means that force = mass x acceleration. Those vehicles are going to take significant *time* to get moving and significant *time* to get stopped.

There are some other factors involved in determining the rate of acceleration of course. However, when a truck driver is stuck in stop-and-go traffic with the rest of us, the first thing involved in getting his truck moving is *perception*. He needs to perceive that something has changed in front of him, and he needs to initiate action to get his vehicle moving. This takes precious *time* (especially if the driver is distracted).

If the driver is talking on a cell phone, a CB (Citizens Band) radio, or just looking out the window in sheer boredom, his perception time can be adversely impacted; more time elapses before the vehicle begins moving. Vehicles with manual transmissions also require precious time for the clutch to be released and first gear to engage. The larger the vehicle, the longer the time required overcome Newton's laws of motion.

Traffic moving at stop-and-go within a given one- mile stretch of expressway or highway may have as many as ten commercial vehicles in varying sizes in the target lane.

No matter how quick their reaction times may be, these drivers must reckon with the laws of physics.

They simply cannot physically get their vehicle moving as quickly as passenger vehicles in front. In addition, if they are carrying a somewhat fragile payload, they must do something I ask of all my students. They must accelerate and brake smoothly. The drivers of these vehicles create natural merging gaps, whether they wish to do so or not.

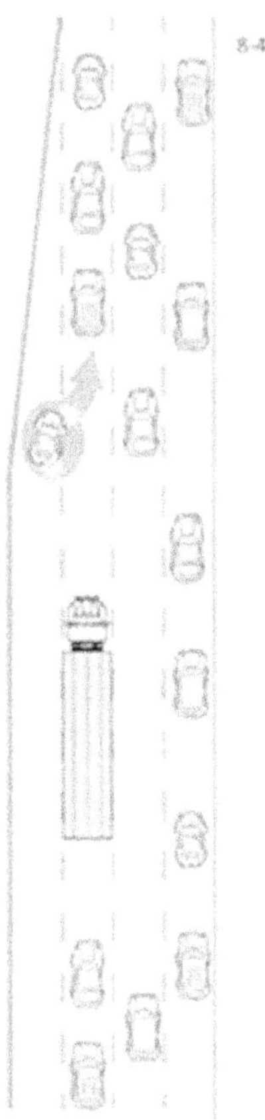

These are not dangerous gaps to merge into. In fact, they are among the safest. Let's consider that our merging time begins when the driver in front of the commercial vehicle begins moving. Within three seconds, the passenger vehicle may move as many as three car lengths. Those three seconds often take place while the trucker was going through his "perception" phase. The next three seconds take place while the trucker is going through his much slower acceleration phase. During that time, the gap between the truck and a typical family sedan in front opens up three more car lengths of space.

Meanwhile, well-trained or experienced drivers moving along safely in the feeder lane (at no more than five miles per hour) are looking for a safe opportunity to merge. These natural "gaps" created by the above laws of physics create safe merging spaces. Safe, patient drivers now have at least six car lengths of merging space to merge into in front of most of the large commercial vehicles as well as many smaller commercial vehicles with manual transmissions.

Drivers of larger commercial vehicles are still attempting to get their vehicle moving as you move into a six-vehicle space. Now that you have merged safely, the driver of the commercial vehicle will adjust temporarily to your new position. Besides, the driver knows something else; he knows that it is unlikely that you are going to stay in his lane for very long anyway. Regular movement of smaller quicker vehicles to the other lanes also opens up replacement gaps for new mergers. During the time it takes for ten vehicles to move concurrently from the target lane into the next lane, as many as ten more vehicles may potentially merge into the new gaps created.

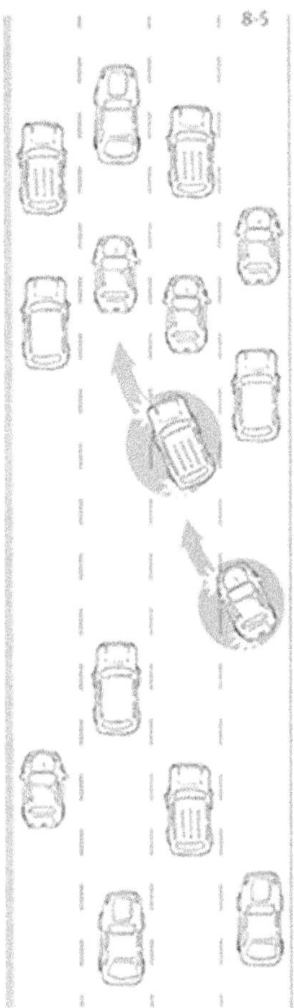

As speed increases on this expressway as "rush hour" fades, new mergers adjust their speeds to match. During peak traffic periods, you may be required to merge at no more than two miles per hour at that location. Just a few hours later, mergers at that same location may be able to merge at the posted speed limit of the expressway. One of the many favorable characteristic of an advanced driver is being able to adjust to varying traffic conditions as they are presented to you, not as you wish them to be.

Speeding

Advanced decision making begins before you drive and continues during your entire trip, regardless of how brief your drive is. In fact, studies have shown that most collisions occur within just a few miles of home, possibly because of our comfort levels and familiarity with roadways within our local communities.

Advanced drivers consider traffic, weather, road conditions, and route before entering the car. Your route may vary depending on the time of day, and your departure time may need to be adjusted depending on the time of day and weather. Speeding should never become a necessity, especially if you always preplan. Some drivers habitually speed regardless of planning or conditions demonstrating a disdain for traffic laws and safety. Remember, little or no skill is required to step on an accelerator.

There are many practical reasons for avoiding speeding at all times every time you drive. Yes, speeding is against the law, but there are even greater issues to deal with than your ticket. When you are speeding, you have less time to take evasive action to avoid distracted cell phone drivers, drivers with poor driving skills, reckless drivers, confused tourists, and *other* aggressive drivers. When you are speeding, other drivers have less time to avoid crashing into you too.

For example, in a residential neighborhood, when a resident is about to enter the roadway, they will most often look for vehicles approaching at the *posted* speed limit, not highway speeds.

Often, when speeding drivers are impacted in a crash, they refer to the mistake *the other driver made,* ignoring the fact that their excessive speed was a contributing factor.

Please remember that when you are speeding, you are already contributing a high degree of fault toward any potential collision, regardless of equally poor decision making exhibited by another driver. Your skid marks will tell the investigating officer how fast you were driving.

Tailgating

Tailgating is a common characteristic of aggressive drivers, careless drivers, and uninformed drivers. The drivers of these vehicles endanger other drivers and passengers all day. It usually has nothing to do with your speed. For example, aggressive drivers or drivers in road rage will tailgate you regardless of if you are driving above the speed limit or not. Aggressive drivers do not want *any* driver in front of them at any time.

In an earlier section, we noted that aggressive drivers will often pass you on the right at the last moment without signaling. Even if they don't pass you, the fact that they are following too closely means that if you must slow down or stop suddenly, the risk of collision has increased.

Many drivers simply do not understand the concept behind maintaining three-second following distances. Other drivers simply are not aware of the entire stopping distance required of their vehicle when braking at highway speeds.

Many tailgaters on highways don't consider that the driver immediately in front may be slowing down for a very good reason. For example, you may be preparing to execute a dangerous unprotected left turn. Signal these drivers early and begin slowing early so that the tailgater begins to respond with ample notice. Remember, tailgating doesn't really help you arrive more quickly; it just decreases the odds of you and your passengers arriving safely.

8-6

Dealing with Tourists

In our fair city, the population doubles every summer. Sometimes it triples. This phenomenon may not be as dramatic in your city or community. However, no matter where you live, you will often be exposed to drivers in your community who are unfamiliar with your local roads and highways. If you see a vehicle with an out-of- state tag in front of you, give that car an additional space cushion. You should be following at least *three seconds* behind all vehicles in front of you anyway. The driver may be looking at a GPS, a street sign, or searching for an unfamiliar place of business.

The driver may just be trying to figure out whether to make a right turn or a left turn ahead.

8-7

Don't become a tailgater or last second-lane jumper and become another "confusion factor" for the tourist or worse. Plan your lane change as you would any other lane change. All tourists are not necessarily bad drivers in their *own* home towns. Some tourists are only bad drivers in *someone else's* home town. The extra space cushion you provide for yourself and your passengers just may help you avoid an unnecessary life altering collision.

Passing on Two-Lane Roads

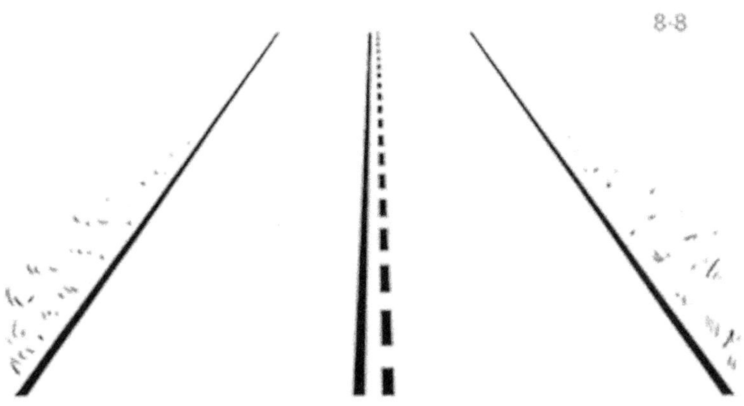

By now, your teen and all other drivers in your family should be thoroughly knowledgeable about the rules of the road regarding broken lines versus solid lines required for *legal* passing. Unfortunately, the ultimate responsibility for determining where it is *safe* to pass rests with drivers. This is where terrible tragedies occur. We train our teens not to pass on two-lane roads anywhere within the city. The odds are not in your favor in a city.

Usually, the legal passing zones are extremely short, and the visibility is very poor just before the zone begins and just after the zone ends. This is just one of several potential reasons passing is illegal on each side of the zone. Passing zones within the city or within suburbia means that traffic is near you too.

You may not initially notice or be able to see that a driveway or other type of entrance roadway is in a section where it may actually be legal for you to pass. If you can't see that entrance roadway clearly, a driver making a turn into "your" passing zone roadway may not see that you are *driving in his/her lane either!*

In a rural area, there may be justification for passing. The following are criteria that we suggest that you consider before you pass:

- The road markings clearly indicate that it is legal in the section where you wish to pass, or it isn't specifically prohibited by road markings.

- The vehicle you wish to pass is moving ten miles per hour *below* the speed limit or less.

- If you guesstimate that a pass will require a certain distance based solely on *your* speed, this means you must *double* the total distance required, if you see an approaching vehicle due to that vehicle's approaching speed.

- You must consider that the oncoming vehicle is moving toward you at your acceleration speed or *possibly an even greater speed.*

- For example, if you are moving at fifty-plus miles per hour and your vehicle requires about one hundred yards to pass, you actually require about two hundred yards or more of total distance. *One football field in length for your vehicle and another football field in length for the approaching vehicle moving toward you at fifty-plus miles per hour.*

- In addition, if your vehicle does not possess sufficient acceleration horsepower, the entire passing sequence may require significantly more time than first estimated.

- The vehicle you are passing should appear in your rearview mirror before you pull back into his/her lane.

Otherwise, the driver may swerve to avoid collision and create a different disaster.

We are not suggesting that drivers never have safe opportunities to pass. Passing is common in rural communities where tractors and other types of farm equipment are common.

However, we are imploring you to be very conservative in determining where you may pass and when it is justifiably safe. Patience is a virtue. Wait for a safe opportunity.

When you do decide that it is safe for you to pass, make certain your hands are positioned at 9:30 a.m. and 2:30 p.m. You will have better control of your vehicle during the entire passing sequence, and you will be better prepared to steer away from danger if an emergency develops.

Cruise Control

Cruise control is often overused in urban and suburban areas. Cruise control is terrific if you are driving out in the middle of Kansas. We suggest that you limit the use of cruise control to long-distance interstate and expressway driving. Even some sections of both types of roads may not be suitable for cruise control. You never want your interest in maintaining your speed and relaxing with your foot off the accelerator to supersede your interest in driving safely.

While driving in a variety of traffic and road conditions, these two interests regularly diverge. We do not allow our teen students to engage cruise control during our training program.

As noted in previous chapters, we may drive up to fifteen miles on a city expressway during the final driving lesson, but this distance and the traffic levels encountered do not justify engaging cruise control. In addition, we caution beginning drivers to avoid cruise control until they become experienced drivers.

This means that when the time is appropriate, you (the parent, grandparent, or guardian) must provide proper guidance in the application of cruise control in your family vehicle. Once again, you should do this by becoming a role model and coach the teen when to apply cruise control. The following are some suggestions for this process:

When you take an interstate trip with your teen, we suggest that you demonstrate how cruise control is to be used safely and efficiently. Make certain your teen is thoroughly familiar will *all* the methods to engage, adjust speed, and disengage cruise control. Most importantly, provide guidance for your teen concerning *where* it is appropriate to engage cruise control, *when* it is inappropriate to engage, and *how* it is to be disengaged immediately. Most cruise control systems disengage as soon as you touch the brake. However, there may be as many as three different methods to disengage cruise control on your vehicle.

If you must apply the brakes for any reason, do not become in a hurry to reengage cruise control. Take your time, reassess, reach your cruising speed naturally and gradually, and then reengage when warranted.

When cruise is engaged, experienced drivers routinely reduce speed at the slightest hint of danger ahead just as they would have if cruise had not been engaged. If you are driving under cruise control, you should be no less cautious when assessing potential danger ahead. The touch of the minus button slows your vehicle. I touch mine often. If I see or sense additional danger ahead, cruise is disengaged.

After your teen has observed you using this technology safely and efficiently, it is time for additional coaching with your teen behind the wheel. Remember that beginning drivers often drive with a level of tunnel vision.

Driving with tunnel vision, highway hypnosis, drowsiness, distracted driving, or driving under any type of impairment increases the danger of cruise control *significantly.* If you are paying close attention, you can feel every adjustment of cruise control from the passenger seat without even looking at the driver. If the driver does not disengage cruise control at appropriate times, you can feel this too.

Aggressive Driving and Road Rage

Aggressive driving and road rage are so common and so dangerous that I am devoting chapter 9 to the topic.

Near Misses

Air traffic controllers describe "near hits" as "near misses." The Federal Aviation Administration counts them religiously. They know how many near misses have occurred within controlled airspace each year. In our vehicles, we don't count our "near misses," do we? Ever wonder how many times each day you are required to take evasive action in order to avoid a collision with another driver? *Have you ever noticed how often other drivers have had to take evasive action in order to avoid crashing into you?* Have you considered how you can take proactive steps to reduce those numbers?

Once your teen has been trained properly, he/she should become much more acutely aware of collision avoidance procedures taken by you when you drive. You can help develop your teen's skills by talking to your teen about defensive driving and collision avoidance skills that you employ as you use them. Your collision avoidance techniques should be *preventative* the majority of the time, not *reactive* the majority of the time. However, some drivers routinely force other drivers to take immediate collision avoidance actions on a daily basis.

Watch how other drivers respond to your teen's driving and how your teen applies defensive driving skills in response to the actions of others. If your teen still drives with a degree of tunnel vision, point out obvious opportunities for your teen to drive more defensively and reduce risk. Ensure that your teen takes his/her foot off the accelerator *immediately* when another vehicle is about to enter your roadway.

The simple act of moving the foot from the accelerator to the brake saves precious time if circumstances dictate an immediate stop rather than slowing.

The next moment may require slowing, stopping, sounding the horn, or steering the car to the path of least resistance. Collision avoidance procedures are required in some manner virtually every time you drive. For example, when backing out of your driveway, your teen should stop at the end of the driveway, clear left, *and* clear right before backing into the roadway. This simple act must be done every time. Ensure that your teen responds to routine and unusual traffic conditions in a manner appropriate for the circumstances. Note that when all drivers in your family drive in this manner, "near misses" are reduced significantly.

Single Vehicle Crashes

Throughout the country, a common type of vehicle crash is the single vehicle crash. In many of these cases, the driver was driving alone; there were no witnesses, and precious little information is available. Now we have another major contributing factor: mobile phones. Although we have the technology to determine if a mobile phone was in use during crashes, currently this information is rarely released. At least one mobile phone carrier is now reporting this information in nationally broadcast commercials.

I would like to take this opportunity to implore the National Highway Traffic Safety Administration (NHTSA) to request this information from all carriers so that tracking data may be published in their annual *Traffic Safety Facts* publication.

Suppose the cell phone wasn't involved at all, and the driver merely became distracted by switching the radio, attempting to find a CD, inserting an iPod earpiece, or simply reaching into the console.

A common report when the driver or a passenger did not survive a single vehicle crash is that the driver "lost control" of the vehicle, left the roadway briefly, and then overcorrected while attempting to return to the roadway. The actual cause of a fatal single vehicle crash is more difficult to identify. How would an investigating officer determine beyond any reasonable doubt that one of these actions contributed to the fatal crash and not some other contributing factor?

In rural communities and midlevel size cities, veering over the double yellow center on the left may result in a head-on collision.

Veering over the solid white line on the shoulder (if one is actually painted there) may result in a fatal crash into a storm drainage ditches, fence, tree, parked car, telephone pole, and the list goes on. This is one of the reasons that we train our teens not to drift. It isn't the lines we worry about; it is the surface, vehicle, or object on the other side of the lines. Even drifting over grass on the shoulder can be deadly.

One of my favored cousins died in a one vehicle crash while driving his pickup truck at night on a country road in rural Missouri between Jefferson City and Russellville (a little town I spent much of my childhood in). The accident report revealed that his right front tire had briefly left the road on the soft right shoulder; he then overcorrected as he was attempting to regain control.

That night, he was driving on a road that he and I had grown up riding on with our parents, grandparents, uncles, and aunts. It was on a two-lane highway between Russellville and Centertown Missouri. As in the case for many crashes that happen within a few miles of home, he had been driving the route as an adult for many years and knew it very well. Why did he crash? It could have been a deer, or it could have been another equally plausible cause.

We will never know.

Delano Templeton was forty-three years old, a career professional tradesman, devoted family man and father. We will never know precisely why he crashed. However, we do know that he somehow lost control of his vehicle, and we also know that this otherwise very intelligent man *did not* have his seat belt buckled on that night.

I will never forget being informed of his death. I traveled one thousand five hundred miles from Washington DC to his funeral. It was one of the two most distressing trips to Russellville, Missouri, of my life.

Dealing with Senior Mature Drivers

This topic will be discussed in chapter 11.

Speeding through Construction Zones

When many drivers approach construction zones they do not alter their regular driving behaviors at all. Most construction zones have signs or flagmen or cones or a combination of all begging motorists to slow down and exercise extreme caution.

My father worked construction for Missouri State Highway department for much of his life. Several years ago, my father was handling the flag that implored drivers to slow down as they entered his construction zone. The son of a local dentist was speeding and distracted. Those are deadly combinations, especially in a construction zone. He plowed into my father and hurled him over fifty yards onto the adjoining farmland.

My dad lived that day but had multiple surgeries over the next several years. The doctors had such a difficult time resetting one of my father's legs and pulverized hip that they had to re-break his leg and reset it again a year later.

Two years after the "accident," my dad attempted to work construction for the highway department again. He was never ever able to stay on his hip/leg long enough to work again, so he had to "retire."

Dad, formerly very active and always on the move, could not hunt and fish anymore unless someone drove him to a spot and parked him in that one spot all day.

A couple of years after the accident, I traveled from Escondido, California (where I was living at that time), to Independence Mo to see my dad again. He and I attempted to go on a walk together, but after two blocks, we turned back. Dad was just in too much pain to continue. That's when I knew something was seriously wrong with my father… beyond physical ailments. I tried to help him. Nothing seemed to help. Dad committed suicide a few months after that. Dad didn't leave a note. He didn't need to. I don't need to have another reason for writing this book besides at least two in this chapter.

CHAPTER 9

Aggressive Driving and Road Rage

By now, you have probably figured out that I am an equal opportunity disser. Therefore, in this chapter, I'm going to diss lone male pickup truck drivers, lone male and female sports car drivers, and lone female SUV drivers. Stereotypes are often (but not always) developed for reasons. For example, note that all these drivers are described as driving alone. Professional driving instructors (and police officers) observe drivers driving alone very carefully. We have noted that when some drivers drive alone, without spouses, children, friends, or coworkers in the vehicle, they sometimes take on the characteristics of wild animals. In their zest to get from point A to point B, some drivers turn into wildebeests, wild hogs, and rabid dogs … and then we have the drivers in road rage!

All aggressive drivers are not in "road rage," and most of them are not teenagers. In fact, the majority of the *drivers* on the road are not teenagers either. How do you know if the driver near you is in road rage or just an aggressive driver? You really don't know. All you can do to avoid becoming part of the problem is by not becoming an aggressive driver yourself. This chapter describes some of the symptoms of aggressive driving and drivers exhibiting *some* degree of road rage.

Drivers in most of the largest cities in the country frequently experience highway and freeway gridlock. In some cases, within specific cities, rush "hour" is actually three or four hours or longer. How do these drivers manage without losing their minds? The overwhelming majority of them learn to adapt—psychologically, emotionally, and physically.

We ask our students in class. Who determines when or if you "develop a case" of *road rage* while driving? Some students quickly answer "the other driver." However, smart, thoughtful students realize that a different answer is more appropriate and far more insightful. These students answer "we do." Yes, this is correct. Ultimately, you, the driver, will determine if you exhibit (at least outwardly) that you are driving within a degree of road rage or with road/rage like symptoms. Good answer.

I have experienced and observed factors contributing to road rage within Los Angeles County, Riverside County, Orange County, and San Diego County within California and other northern California counties I did not regularly commute within but drove within periodically. I saw it on the Hawaiian Island of Oahu, and I saw it within the Beltway of Washington DC. These counties and the cities within them have a large number of tourists and foreigners. Tourists, foreigners, local drivers (and very often, road and highway conditions) mix to create a sort of "melting pot" to produce road and highway maniacs.

In an earlier chapter, I described some of my early California expressway experiences. At one point during the early commute years, I came to realize that just because I had lived through Vietnam, I wasn't necessarily "immortal." Bad physical things can happen to someone who otherwise appears to be young and healthy. For example, when I drove in a very aggressive manner, by the time I arrived home at the tiny apartment

I shared with my brother Gary, I was not much good for anything else. I may have somehow avoided one hundred or one thousand collisions that day, but by the time I arrived at home, I was a nervous wreck anyway.

I also discovered something else: when you commute for extended periods on very busy expressways every day, you had better pick a lane to drive in and relax. Forget cruise control! Besides, if you are stuck in heavy stop-and-go traffic, you can't or at least shouldn't use cruise control anyway. Instead of cruise control, put your favorite music on. No matter your musical tastes, listening to the music that pleases you will help sooth you … or it should sooth you. Forget lane jumping. You don't need to add to your stress level during a long distance commute that is already stressful. It isn't going to get you there any faster anyway!

During the many years I drove in heavy "expressway" traffic, I learned to relax as much as possible, without exceeding the relaxation limit. The "relaxation limit" is really defined by you. However, the following statement must or at least should be taken into account during any effort to reduce your stress level while commuting:

You may never, for a single microsecond, allow your peripheral vision and/or your cognitive awareness lose track of the status of the brake lights in front of you.

Experienced expressway commuters know that cars traveling on any major inner city expressway can be zipping along in all eight lanes at seventy miles per hour one moment, and in the next moment, all eight lanes may come to a screeching halt almost simultaneously!

Within Los Angeles and vicinity, there are (count them) about thirty-five freeways with different names and numbers. The reason I am including Orange County, Riverside County, and Ventura County freeways in this count is that many Los Angeles and vicinity commuters travel across two counties or more to get to/from work every day. In heavy traffic, sometimes your long distance scanning of the traffic scene in front actually enables you to *predict* that rapid deceleration (commonly called stopping) will follow. Please be advised that if you don't see the brake lights appear in these situations and take action *immediately,* the laws of physics must be reckoned with. Again, *they can be very unforgiving.*

In large metropolitan cities, drivers of sports cars that were designed to be able to move at over one hundred fifty miles per hour on the European Autobahn cannot propel them at one hundred fifty miles per hour in our HOV (high occupancy vehicle) lanes. In the NFL, the inside joke is that NFL stands for Not-for-Long, and it also stands for Not-for-Long if you drive at high speeds on heavily patrolled expressways. There may be huge gaps (of law enforcement) out there in the middle of "nowhere," but large metropolitan cities usually have at least three different types of law enforcement agencies lurking around ... and sometimes more.

Lone pickup truck drivers with huge power plants under the hood (often carrying no pay load) cannot tailgate at seventy-five miles per hour in HOV lanes in large cities. Those drivers are required to tailgate (if they must) in one of the other seven or eight lanes, just like everyone else. SUV soccer moms endlessly chatting on their cell phones while putting on their morning makeup must multitask in one of the other stop-and-go lanes too.

The city I now reside in and teach driver education within is an example of a city that is rapidly outgrowing its current road and highway system. The Grand Strand in Myrtle Beach, South Carolina, is also exhibiting several other early symptoms of several much larger tourist destination cities I have lived in.

As noted in the previous chapter, in midlevel cities, one of the biggest commuter problems is that many drivers have developed the mentality that the "fast lane" was constructed for their commute and theirs alone, at the highest speed they intend to drive that day. They also believe that the "slow lanes" are reserved for everyone else.

Compound this with the psychology of a driver who owns a vehicle with a huge power plant or a pickup truck or an SUV that is physically much larger.

Some of these drivers turn into road bullies and drive on the verge of road rage every day. Think about it this way: suppose the speed limit on a four- lane highway is fifty-five miles per hour. One driver wishes to drive sixty miles per hour, the driver just behind wishes to drive sixty-five miles per hour, the next driver wishes to drive seventy-five miles per hour. Meanwhile, the right lane has a series of eighteen-wheelers moving at about fifty miles per hour. The driver who wishes to drive seventy- five miles per hour will often attempt to bully the other drivers into driving behind the eighteen-wheelers so that he/she can drive seventy-five in the "fast lane."

Often, these drivers also feel that they are "pack leaders." This mentality works well if you are leading a pack of dogs—my hat is off to Caesar—but not so well if you are driving in the left lane on a highway with only two lanes to drive in. The problem of course is that these drivers can never quite make it to the lead of the pack where they wish to drive. For some reason, there are all these obstacles blocking their paths to leadership called other drivers.

In addition, some midlevel cities have a very limited number of left turn lanes and/or protected left turn arrows. Aggressive drivers, drivers on the verge of road rage or in a state of road rage, resent any driver who enters the "fast lane" in order to complete a routine left turn. In the driver education business, we have a polite name for these drivers that we can use with students: They are called chargers.

At one time, I believed that virtually all *chargers* were males driving alone, and it *seemed* like an inordinate number of them were driving pickup trucks.

If you get in "their lane," these drivers will tailgate you unmercifully, seemingly oblivious to the fact that no matter how much power they have under the hood, it requires a comparative longer period of time to stop a bigger heavier truck than a passenger vehicle, especially one that is carrying a payload.

If it isn't carrying a payload, then the vehicle is not "balanced"; and during emergency braking, the back-end swings around to match the front end. ABS helps this of course, but ABS alone cannot overcome idiot driving.

Now, we also have female SUV drivers who text or talk on their cell phones while they barrel down the "fast lane" oblivious to the fact that they are so close to the lead pack dog that they are actually drafting the vehicle a la NASCAR. Even in the unlikely event that they *are not* distracted by the phone, in an emergency, the drafter crashes right along with the draftee. These two vehicles either crash as a pair, or others are enlisted and crash *with* the pair. This is how some multivehicle crashes occur.

SUVs and pickup trucks, not only (generally) have bigger, heavier engines, but they also have oversized wheels that are bigger and heavier. True, more rubber on the road helps the antilock-braking system do its job in emergencies. However, no matter how good your brakes are, and no matter how sharp you think your reflexes are, physiological and physical laws say you must deal with perception, reaction time, and braking distance.

The fact is that without maintaining at least three following distance, in real emergencies, pickup trucks and heavy SUVs do not have sufficient space to bring these heavy vehicles to a complete stop, short of collision. This is the reason that a very slow-moving locomotive, pulling a fairly large number of box cars, may require as much as a mile or more to come to a complete stop. Newton's laws apply, regardless of whether you accept them or not.

After nine years of driving up and down the Grand Strand, often with 15/16fifteen- to sixteen-year-old student drivers behind the wheel, I think I can justify why the right lane of a four-lane highway (two lanes on each side) is the safest lane to drive in the majority of the time. The Grand Strand runs all the way from North Myrtle Beach, near the North Carolina border all the way down to near Georgetown. The precise ending spot seems to be in some dispute, but overall, the Grand Strand runs along about fifty miles of Horry and Georgetown County coastlines.

Highway 17 also runs up and down the southeastern seaboard throughout Horry and Georgetown counties and beyond.

Within those boundaries, we have the Coastal Grand Mall, the Myrtle Beach Airport, the Carolina Opry, Dolly Parton's Palace Theater, Broadway at the Beach, Legends in Concert, Brookgreen Gardens, Market Common, the Myrtle Beach Convention Center, Barefoot Resort, two factory outlet malls, and the Grand Dunes and the Murrells Inlet Marsh-walk just to name a few tourist attractions. We even have an east coast version of Huntington Beach that has even more pristine coastline than the west coast version, though not as famous. Most of these tourist attractions are located on or between U.S. 17 bypass and U.S. 17 business.

One day, I was driving one of the training cars back to Murrells Inlet from the Coastal Grand Mall. The CADETS Driver Training logo and Driver Training signs were still on the car. As I entered the now very familiar cloverleaf—it had been under construction for so long I thought all the "under construction" signs were permanent—I saw an exotic European model sedan in my right side mirror. The windows were so dark I couldn't see the driver. The driver had taken this beautiful exotic car and marred it by substituting some awful-looking oversized mag wheels that didn't look right on the car. This car looked like it was owned by a drug dealer because those are the only guys that drive those cars in this area, and it also looked like it was being driven by a pimp. Now how did I know that since I couldn't see inside? Stereotypes develop for a reason. They don't "evolve" on their own.

Hate is a strong word. But I hate dope dealers, pimps, and men who prey on young women by using drugs to entice them and control them. There is only one type of person that I hate even more than drug dealers and pimps and that's a *bad driver.* As usual, the pimp was tailgating my training car unmercifully; only this time, a student wasn't driving it. As we rounded the cloverleaf, I knew there were five total lanes to deal with. Eventually, five lanes would become two lanes. That's why I had all my students merge there during their final driving lessons.

As we rounded the final segment of the cloverleaf, he was right on my tail only a few feet behind.

I was driving at maybe five miles per hour above the actual speed limit posted for the cloverleaf because I didn't want to give him an excuse for being right on my tail. Besides, I knew how to bank a car.

About halfway around the cloverleaf, I did something I hadn't done with the training car in about four years; I floored the NHTSA five-star safety- rated Honda Civic! The car *lurched* to attention! It was as if the car had been waiting for someone, anyone to kick it in the ass for four years. In a matter of .5 seconds, I completed my first SMOG check, just like I had trained all my students to do it, and I had moved my car into the fourth lane, just like a race car driver does it.

He *had* to have had more power in his exotic roadster than I had in my *driver training car,* at least that's what he thought as he slammed his accelerator to the floorboard in a desperate bid to pass me. I could see the lift of his hood in my rearview mirror; that means rapid acceleration. However, in the time it took him to blink an eye, I had already glanced over my shoulder for my second SMOG and floored my accelerator again for lane 3. By this time, his pimped-out European roadster was kicked into overdrive, and he was right on my tail again. I could see he wanted to take lane 2 in order to regain some measure of self-respect (in his mind), but I had position, timing, speed, execution ... and forty-five years of freeway driving experience in my favor. I zipped into lane 2 and passed him some gas in the process.

By that time, he knew he couldn't take lane 1, *the fast lane,* unless I wanted to let him have lane 1 as a consolation prize. And so I dropped the little training car into cruising speed for Highway 17 Bypass and let him have lane 1. Of course, he not only roared by as expected, but I also caught him at the traffic light and pulled up beside him as I expected too. I didn't look over. I didn't need to. But I can almost guarantee you that *he* looked over at me … if for no other reason than just to make sure it wasn't a *student* driving the car.

Now why did I do that? Didn't I write earlier in never to get angry in a car? I wasn't angry. I was cool, calm, collected, and in complete control of my vehicle at all times. I did it to prove a point for this book.

Remember, when drivers tailgate you, it rarely has anything to do with your speed. It has everything to do with the psychology of the other driver and his or her interest in being the lead pack dog. Never forget that please.

Horry County has about two hundred fifty thousand permanent residents, but that number swells to about two or even three times that during peak summer months. Also, until recently, about three hundred thousand bikers (or bikers and friends) showed up every May for bike month. White bikers (think wild hags) would roar in to the southern part of Horry County during early May and black bikers (think ninja bikers) would roar into north Myrtle Beach during late May.

During early May, the Harley bikers would zoom in from the west and north; and once they got here, they would zoom from the south strand to north strand and back. During late May, the ninja bikers would zoom from Atlantic Beach in the north strand to Murrells Inlet on the south strand and back. Most bikers like to be seen and heard, especially if they don't have something called a "muffler" on their vehicle of choice.

In any case, within the Grand Strand, virtually anyone who travels any distance greater than two miles will end up on one or both Highway 17s. Sometimes we will drive on both 17s several times during the same day.

Like other many other metropolitan cities, sometimes truckers, soccer moms, tourists, and bikers end up driving behind or near a vehicle that has big bold letters on the back and side that say DRIVER TRAINING.

I don't know what *driver training* means to you, but *driver training* means to me that there just might be someone *inexperienced* behind the wheel.

We have discovered that displaying the words *driver training* on a vehicle, as required by most state laws when you are teaching, is like waving a red flag in front of a wild bull with an advanced condition of *rabies*. There are a lot of things I don't get, and I'll admit I don't get this. However, I'm just reporting the facts as I see them every day.

In the field of *driver training,* we do everything humanly possible to avoid wildebeests, wild hawgs, wild boars, and rabid dogs.

For example, as previously noted, we teach our students to drive in the right-hand lane of any four-lane highways (two coming and two going) the majority of the time. If we put a number on that, it would be about 80 percent of the time. If traffic is moving at or near the speed limit, we coach our students to drive at that speed too, but always strive to maintain at least three-second following distance regardless of the lane they must drive in at that particular time.

Students (and instructors) in a car clearly marked *driver training* occasionally must move over to the left lane to execute something called a *left turn*. This is where the trouble begins. When our students are asked to move to the left lane of a four-lane highway, they are also coached to drive the speed limit. Our students are also coached to maintain proper space and visibility at all times during their lane changes. These are completely foreign concepts to some adult drivers on the Grand Strand and within many major cities.

We have also determined that when a car moving in traffic is labeled *driver training*, many drivers conclude that the driver is clueless about how to drive a vehicle. This may have been true when the student *began* driver education, but this is not typically the case when a student driver is completing final lessons. In any case, when I am driving the car marked *driver training,* I see the same behaviors that my students see, and I have been driving for just a few decades. Nearby drivers often feel compelled to demonstrate how well they can drive by driving more aggressively. Some drivers even create new, previously unreleased rules of the road.

The following are examples of behaviors we have observed while driving our *driver training* vehicle at highway speeds:

- Chargers in our rearview mirrors tailgating within one-second following distance. As previously noted, most of these drivers don't want us to speed up as much as they wish to become the lead pack dog.

- While driving in the right-hand lane, we note that the faster the lead pack dog drives in the "passing lane," the faster the followers will drive. Remember, it doesn't really matter *how fast* you drive; there will almost always be a driver behind you who wants to drive faster.

- I'm not certain exactly how a soccer mom drives with one hand on a cell phone, another applying makeup, and another on the wheel while having *both* eyes trained intently on the rearview mirror *without* crashing, but somehow many of them do this. Perhaps these talented soccer moms steer with their knees?

- In any case, they roar past, merrily on their way, seemingly oblivious to the fact that they are propelling a five-thousand-pound missile that *must* be steered away from danger or stopped in an emergency!

- Rabid lead pack dogs will also use almost any technique imaginable to urge you to move back where you belong with 99 percent of the other dogs, er … cars.

- A common technique for a rabid sports car driver is to pass on the left, regardless of whether that segment of road is marked for legal passing or not. If the sports car driver misjudges, he (or she) may be returning to your lane at a *very inappropriate* time.

- A common technique for rabid pickup truck drivers is to pretend that your car doesn't exist at all. His vehicle will be on your bumper as the two of you barrel down the highway like a pair of X and Y chromosomes.

A "stale" yellow light may appear on the horizon. When it flashes, our student driver may not have passed the actual point of no return yet, which means of course that we should *stop for the stale yellow light and/ or the red light that will immediately follow.* However, if we have a rabid pack dog on our tail, we may need to revert to plan B, plan C, or even plan D. If our student driver has been instructed to complete a left turn to reach our destination, the following are some of the choices that our student driver must consider; none of them are very desirable:

- Our student can run the stale yellow light and fresh red light and have "hot-blooded you know who" to contend with at the next intersection anyway.

- Our student can change lanes at the last moment near the intersection *which we teach our students not to do.*

- Our student can stop the car at the light as he/she has been trained to do when there is sufficient time.

However, at this time, there is also the possibility that the rabid driver behind us will drive over our dead carcasses as he/she punches the vehicle into overdrive.

Soccer moms talking on cell phones while applying makeup have regular "near misses" every day, so we have learned not to take it personally just because we are in a *driver training* vehicle. The first "near miss" happens when we must slow for our left turn. The second "near miss" takes place as she passes us at the very last moment in the right lane as we approach the intersection. Then they (she) will often complete the "trifecta" by having another "near miss" as she accelerates back into the "fast lane" within the intersection.

Many drivers of any age or gender spend all day violating standard traffic laws but hope to avoid breaking a law precisely when a police officer happens to be nearby. Some drivers continually look out for police officers or install radar busters in their cars so that they can drive recklessly for most of the day without consequence, unless of course they crash.

When police officers observe reckless drivers, law enforcement officers have more latitude to take action than you might think. They are not just looking for drivers speeding, running stop signs, and making illegal U- turns. They can actually ticket you for something called reckless driving. There are all kinds of possibilities there.

When a police officer is near our training vehicles, I generally don't say anything at all to my student about the police officer being nearby. If the student expresses concern or anxiety, my reply is: "If you are not breaking any traffic laws, you don't need to worry about police officers." I have never personally experienced having a training vehicle pulled over by a law enforcement officer. However, if I had been following a few of my beginning drivers during their initial lessons, I might have concluded that some of the new drivers were "impaired." This is why we take our beginners to vacant parking lots.

Some drivers who *regularly* drive aggressively become angrier and angrier as traffic increases until they reach a degree of road rage that is unmistakable. Other drivers who normally drive safely enter a different psychological mind-set in heavy traffic.

Even if you personally have learned to control your own emotions and driving behaviors, you will sometimes find yourself riding along with someone who cannot or will not control his/her emotions or behavior in certain traffic situations.

It turns out that road rage is a common international problem too. I have a female friend who happens to be Russian. Believe it or not, she likes to tell jokes. Picture a woman who looks like the great tennis player Maria Sharapova but someone who sounds like Dolph Lundgren, you know, the Russian guy who beat up Rocky in *Rocky 35*. Use Dolph's voice in Maria Sharapova's body, and then you will have the delivery. Anyway, she tells me a common expletive that is hurled when two drivers already in road rage arrive at the same destination in Russia is: "May your wife make love to you in the way that you drive!"

There may have been something lost here in the translation, but it's the thought that counts, isn't it? I can also picture Arnold Schwarzenegger intoning this. Coming from *him*, this would be very sinister indeed. In some parts of the world, this world actually be considered to be either a *dare* or a *compliment*, but then there is no accounting for our international differences in delivering expletives and insults.

Then Dolph/Maria/Arnold told me another joke.

This one is rated R so parents who sincerely believe that their sixteen-year-old teen has never heard a blue joke can black this one out. I was informed that this particular insult is only delivered for the most serious offenses.

He, her, it intones: "May your 'private member' grow through a head hole!" Apparently, most of the offending drivers are male. However, after thoughtful consideration, I have concluded the expletive/insult works equally well for females. Now here's the *coup-de- grace*. The first time I heard Dolph/Maria/Arnold tell the joke above, I thought the punch line was: "May your 'private member' grow through your *corn rows.* " Now I don't care who you are. That's funny, especially coming from a Russian who looks like Maria Sharapova! I'll pick myself off the floor again and get back to business.

Before you *decide* to exhibit aggressive driving or road rage in a car, consider the following:

- Drivers in road rage or displaying symptoms of being in road rage will not generally reduce their commute time in any significant degree beyond drivers who remain cool, calm, and collected. On many occasions, I have seen lane jumpers arrive at a traffic lights at the same time as a driver (me) who simply stayed in one lane and relaxed.

- Drivers in road rage often make very dangerous driving errors in order to shave precious seconds off the clock, endangering all those around them.

- Drivers who tailgate have even less margin for error, especially in heavy traffic.

- If you allow yourself to exhibit the symptoms of road rage externally and through your behavior,

  physically your body changes accordingly.

- Your passengers will be watching you. Your expressions change while your body language also changes.

- If you are driving in road rage, most of your passengers will find you less pleasant to converse with and/or ride with.

- Some passengers will worry that since you have lost control of your own emotions, *that you have also lost control of the vehicle.*

- Drivers in road rage often focus on a single driver that has irritated them rather than maintaining awareness of the entire traffic scene, increasing the odds that they will not respond appropriately to other hazards.

- Drivers driving in road rage often influence other drivers who otherwise drive safely to commit unnecessary errors. For example, a tailgater may influence an otherwise safe driver to make a lane change at an inappropriate time or place in an attempt to avoid the tailgater behind. As a result, *either* driver could potentially initiate a crash.

- Many drivers, especially those who are *already distracted* or enraged, are expecting all *other* drivers around them to drive in accordance with the standard rules of the road. Aggressive driving *in combination* with another mistake may contribute *equally* to a collision.

Even locals who know where they are going and are used to getting from point A to point B in a specific period of time may become enraged when their normal commute time has been extended, sometimes by only a few minutes. As a result, a local driver or any driver at any time in any part of the country may exhibit one or more of the above symptoms while following someone who is perceived to be a nonlocal. Instead of driving in a manner described above, there are several alternatives. The following are offered as *suggestions* for reducing the potential of your vehicle crashing into another vehicle or suffering the consequences of another vehicle crashing into you.

These preventative measures are totally *under your own control* and are available to be taken by each and every member of your family who is in possession of a driver's license.

- Depart at an earlier time during peak traffic periods in accordance with traffic flow during that time of year.

- Allowing extra time will also minimize adverse impact of *unanticipated* changes in traffic flow such as those created by routine collisions.

- An alternate route may be longer in distance but shorter in time. Consider alternatives during peak traffic periods.

- Consider shopping at off-peak hours.

- Do not tailgate. Maintain at least three-second following distance in dry conditions and even more in inclement weather.

- Pick a lane and stay in it until you have a sound reason to change lanes.

- Respond to poor drivers by taking defensive driving evasive action at that time, but then move on.

- Forget about what the other driver did, and concentrate on your own business at hand which is safely driving your own vehicle.

- Scan the traffic scene ahead and watch out for distracted drivers.

- Never drive more than five miles per hour above the speed limit.

  You will find that if you drive in accordance with the policies above, at least several good things will happen regularly:

- You will have far fewer "opportunities" to tailgate; therefore, the space cushion in front of you (the most important one) usually expands.

- You will have more time to respond to all the poor drivers you will encounter each and every day.

- You will have more time to assess the traffic scene ahead as you are moving, especially as you approach busy intersections.

- You will have more time to take evasive action with your vehicle by steering toward an escape path during semi emergencies and emergencies.

- You are far less likely to run stale yellow lights and red lights.

- Your vehicle will provide you with better gas mileage.

- You will be able to demonstrate smoother acceleration and braking for your passengers, and they will *feel* the difference.

- When you are driving your vehicle at or near the speed limit, it has a positive impact on your emotional state as you drive.

- Your passengers will conclude that you are relaxed, calm, collected, and in control of your vehicle at all times.

- Your passengers will respond by also becoming more relaxed and more confident of your driving skills.

There are other side benefits. For example, there is no need to keep a lookout for police officers if you are not breaking traffic laws.

However, if a law enforcement officer does "light up" somewhere behind you, move over to the shoulder so the officer can stop another driver or respond more quickly to the emergency that some other driver has created. Relax, it won't be you!

Remember, even if you arrive home a little later than intended, you may save someone's life ... and it could be your own.

CHAPTER 10

Young Adults versus "The Cyclops"

A few years before CADETS was founded, a corporation by the name of Drive Square Incorporated was commissioned by the federal government to develop a very sophisticated driving simulator. The team was headed up by a German engineer (naturally) by the name of Konstantin Sisov. An entire book could be written about this topic. However, this is just one chapter that should help influence your conclusions about the relative merit of the previous nine chapters.

The primary function of the Coastal Academy for Driver Education, Training, and Safety (CADETS) was and is to promote and conduct driver education and training. Our purchase and eventual application of the very sophisticated virtual reality drive square simulator was originally intended for that purpose. We were also very much aware of other possible applications of the simulator. For example, it could also be programmed to simulate ten different levels of "impairment" for thirty different driving scenarios.

However, since we were planning to incorporate the simulator primarily for the purpose of supplementing our BTW training (for beginning drivers, we didn't initially intend for the impairment scenarios to be employed to any degree. As previously referenced, beginning drivers of any age have enough trouble controlling a vehicle without *any* real or simulated impairment!

However, primarily for promotional purposes, during the Grand Opening of CADETS Inc., we conducted driving, DWI, and DUI simulations all day at the Myrtle Beach Coastal Grand Mall.

Photos of that very successful opening event are included in this chapter. After the grand opening of CADETS, we attempted to incorporate the simulator into our training curriculum by *supplementing* (but *not* replacing any segment of) the state required minimum of eight hours of classroom and six hours of BTW training.

During this process, we discovered that the state of South Carolina did not have any provisions for any *pro-* driving school to introduce a simulator into the tightly structured highly regulated field of South Carolina driver education or any aspect of approved curricula.

At that time, only *high schools* could incorporate simulators into driver education curricula in South Carolina! Somehow this had been authorized by *public educators,* even though there are no log entry provisions on a standard South Carolina PDLA (Provisional Driver's License Application) for simulator time. This means that many high schools in South Carolina may have (potentially) logged simulator time as *either classroom or BTW time.* In our opinion, neither one is technically correct.

Part of the rationale for including this chapter is to appeal to the NHTSA to require *all* driver education oversight entities to create a *different* log entry category entirely for driving simulators. Sophisticated driving simulators are just as valuable in their own right for driver education, as the flight simulators I once certified are for fixed wing, and rotary winged aircraft are in flight education. Look at how valuable the NASA simulators were and are to the space program (remember Apollo 13!). However, no one in his right mind would equate landing on the moon in a simulator with… well, landing on the moon! That's why each activity is logged differently, not to mention viewed differently by the world.

During our research, we learned that some national organizations were already using similar but less sophisticated simulators (than the Cyclops) to conduct DUI simulations for university, college, and even some high school students throughout the country.

When I use the term *less sophisticated,* I mean *simulators* as primitive as goggles with distorted lenses have been used to simulate DUI at many public and private learning institutions at all levels.

Since we couldn't immediately incorporate the Cyclops into our driver education program, we decided to set about determining if there were any other suitable public and private institutions that would be interested in taking full advantage of the full DUI, DWI, and Driver Education capabilities of the Cyclops. The answers were yes, yes, and no!

Most college administrators have concluded that their students *must* already know how to drive, or they wouldn't be there. Their thinking has been manifested by their desire to employ ever more creative ways and means to keep them sober! College administrators are confounded by the need to guide and protect their students while continuing to provide an environment for personal growth, life experience, and a formal education.

Few issues complicate their lives more than the volatile consumption of alcohol (and many other drugs) by young college students that are away from home for the first time and feeling frisky.

Let's face it; partying is pervasive in and around all colleges and universities, from "formal" socialized drinking activities to all night frat and sorority "keggers" in the dorm rooms. Students may stagger from room to room in their quest for the ideal party. However, usually, eventually one of the revelers presents the brilliant idea to *travel* somewhere else for an even better party. As a result, students drive to parties, drive away from parties, and sometimes they even drive *while* partying.

School alcohol policies and local traffic laws are not enough to prevent inappropriate levels of libation. When someone *drives* to a party, then someone must (or at least should) be sober enough to drive the party animals back to their frat or sorority house unless they literally and figuratively crash wherever they land. In order for this to happen—this is the hard part—*the owner of the vehicle must be convinced that the "designated driver"* (often recruited at the very last moment) *is a better driver than the drunken pack leader that usually drives.*

Obviously that last part hasn't happened as much as college administrators and parents had hoped.

We became sought after by college administrators because we could employ "the Cyclops" to effectively contrast *before, during, and after* performance characteristics of DUI and DWI without endangering lives.

Also students could experience this with their own eyes ears and senses while stone-cold sober! Some of them may be dumb when they are numb, but they are not entirely stupid beforehand.

During this period, CADETS was the only professional driving school in the country in possession of this particular simulator and the only one (that we were aware of at that time) employing *professional driving instructors* to conduct the DUI and DWI seminars. This gave us a degree of credibility that few other simulator organizations could claim.

Eventually, the Coastal Academy for Driver Education, Training, and Safety (CADETS) conducted DUI, distracted driving, and driver improvement "presentations" at many institutions around the country but mostly in the southeast. The simulator never went anywhere without my partner and lead simulator specialist John Kurywchak at the helm. I joined him for about half of the "seminars." We actually called them shows after a while because that's what they ended up becoming.

During a three-year-period, we were contracted by institutions as large and prestigious as the University of Georgia, the University of Central Florida (enrollment 46,000), the University of South Carolina, and the Loyola College in Maryland, corporate giant BP America, and many others. As a public service, we also conducted much smaller "shows" at few local high schools (i.e., Saint James High School in Murrells Inlet, South Carolina, and Johnsonville High School near Conway, South Carolina).

The simulator hardware consists of a laptop computer, a virtual reality headset, multiple vehicle control sensors for gas, brake, and steering wheel, two huge forty-pound disks that rest under the front wheels, and a large observation video screen. Once a vehicle is hooked up to the simulator, the vehicle's engine is never turned on; but the steering wheel, front tires, gas, and brake each *seem* to be operational to the "driver," especially when the virtual reality headset is placed over the head and eyes.

When the "driver" enters the vehicle the headset is placed over the head and the screen surrounds the eyes. These aren't "goggles!" The animation is displayed on the screen of the headset and one or more video screens being fed by the computer. Both hands are placed on the steering wheel (or at least both are *supposed* to be there), and the right foot operates the gas and the brake just as in an actual vehicle.

Of course the software provides the virtual reality simulations, just as they do for sophisticated video games. The computer convinces virtually all your senses that you are driving, and the vehicle is moving! When a "human" puts the headset on (I use this term broadly), the large video screen substitutes for the eyes, and it looks to observers as though your two normal-sized eyes have been replaced by one giant eye. Therefore, eventually, and perhaps inevitably, I named the entire contraption "the Cyclops!"

I must admit that no one at CADETS seemed to like the name Cyclops very much. Neither did the German engineers who designed it. No one seemed to have a sense of humor about the absurdity of "the Cyclops." I was usually the most serious one in the bunch. Go figure!

However, all "the "kids" seemed to like the name, including adult "kids" of all ages that were compelled or coerced to "drive" it. All these hapless candidates of any age seemed to get a kick out of trying to master the Cyclops. John and I had driven it many times ourselves of course, testing out all the scenarios and our presentation strategies. We discovered that if you didn't show up with your "A" game, the Cyclops would win … and you would *crash!* The first time I ever drove it, even I, professional driving instructor extraordinaire, crashed the Cyclops!

This was not because the Cyclops was poorly designed. This was because we (all of us) don't realize just how often we screw up when we drive and the *other* driver, pedestrian, or bike rider, etc., takes evasive action in order to avoid crashing into us! The Cyclops, either through sheer genius or by mastermind design, wasn't engineered to correct for your screw-ups. When you drive the Cyclops and you screw up, *you crash;* it is really that simple. Lesson learned and game over. The same thing happens when you "fly" sophisticated flight simulators. I know because I have crashed them too.

An additional entertainment and educational aspect of the Cyclops was the fact that it could be preprogrammed into thirty different driving scenarios with degrees or levels of impairment from one to ten possible for each scenario. All this was and is possible by only a few keystrokes on the keyboard. If we were confronted by a particularly cocky potential driver (often males at "higher learning" institutions), we made sure that said driver crashed spectacularly! Then for good measure, we would give him a second chance, and we made certain that the offending creature would crash again! We were not bashful about this.

I had been to Vietnam and had served as sergeant of the guard on the perimeter of the Two-Hundred-Forty- Second Assault Support Company at edge of Cu Chi at the ripe old age of twenty-one. John had set up the air traffic control tower in the war zone of Bagdad, Iraq, after we ousted Saddam Hussein. Besides, John was every bit a typical air traffic controller from his head to his toes. No shrinking violets we. We wanted these adult "kids" to know that this was no disco, and we weren't there to amuse them.

John took the lead for all the Cyclops seminars. As referenced earlier in the book, John had not only controlled traffic for Burbank TRACON but was also a former manager at Southern California TRACON and at Oakland Air Traffic Control Tower. He was and is an outstanding driver education instructor and an outstanding simulator specialist.

I assisted John at about half the seminars he conducted. Another CADETS associate assisted John at several other seminars. Usually, John and I partnered to guide drivers through two or more of the virtual reality simulations described below. During a full seminar day, our syllabus allowed about one hundred "drivers" to demonstrate that they could drive a moderately challenging scenario "unimpaired" and at least one or two more scenarios under different degrees of virtual impairment.

On show day, the Cyclops required about three hours to set up in the morning. In order to attract maximum attention, the beginning of the show was generally arranged to begin before the lunch period. Usually within a matter of a few minutes, an appropriate scenario from those listed below was selected by John. After an appropriate number of crashes, the brave ones suffered further humiliation by allowing John to "program" impairment levels from one to ten drinks and simulated driving time from one to ten hours after the alcohol has been consumed. Since I was briefing and screening the candidates in line, I would sometimes tip John off if I had a smart aleck on deck. John would save the "special" scenarios just for them.

The virtual reality environment of the Cyclops included but was not limited to the following:

1. Basic auto setup	6 Passing and being passed
2. Right of way at four-way stops	7 Defensive driving in normal conditions
3. Traffic signal intersections	8. Defensive driving in hazardous conditions
4. Lane changes	9. Merging onto highways and expressways
5. Heavy traffic scenarios	10. Yielding to pedestrians

*The drug and alcohol driver impairment scenarios were available for all of the above except no. 1. Impairment option no. 1 was reality based.

When we contracted with a university, state college, private corporations, or another entity, we generally provided at least five hours of virtual reality driving, and we generally ran dozens of students through the simulations with hundreds more observing the large video screen at some point during the day. The Cyclops could be attached and interfaced with the CADETS training vehicle, a student's sports car, SUV, Hummer, or any other vehicle up to and including a vehicle as large as a fire truck.

While one student was "driving," many others could watch the big screen video interfaced with the computer. Everything a driver sees on the Cyclops screen observers also see on the big screen.

Usually, the following sequence of events would transpire. A group of friends would arrive together to observe whatever was attracting the crowd. Eventually, one of the boys would urge his girlfriend into the vehicle first (brave boys that they were).

She would attempt to drive the Cyclops through an entire scenario without any impairment dialed in … and crash. The virtual reality "crash" made spectacular audio noises over a small audio system, like those heard on commercial radio and TV. We discovered that most of the students at the major universities of the land found these spectacular crashes to be hilarious, especially when the driver had been earnestly attempting to drive the scenario *without* crashing. After all, this was just a game, right?

Usually the boyfriend was anxious to get behind the wheel after the girlfriend crashed, especially if she crashed with *no impairment* dialed in. The boyfriend figured that she was just as bad a driver as he had always imagined. Now he had proof! Then the boyfriend gets in and suits up.

Since he has already seen the previous scenario, he believes that the new scenario will look exactly like the preceding one he just observed. However, real life isn't like that, is it? Just like in real life, some situations may *look* the same initially, but they *are not* exactly the same. *This is why most crashes occur within just a few miles of home.*

As the young man approaches the intersection, he is looking for the same sequence of events that tripped up his girlfriend. However, business partner, former air traffic controller, and off-the-charts extrovert John has cleverly dialed in a *different* scenario that *looks* exactly like the first one but *isn't* the first one. He now sort of looks like the Road Runner rigging up some sort of booby trap for Willy Coyote.

Part of the reason the young man crashes is dealing with the reality of the difference between what he *expects* and what he actually *gets*. This happens in real life too. This is how virtually all collisions happen. We know from having driven all the scenarios ourselves that the crashes can be avoided, but you have to be "on your toes," even while driving unimpaired. In almost all cases, overconfident males crash their first scenarios spectacularly … with all the telltale bells and whistles going off for all the happy camper observers. Some of them had been waiting months for "you know who" to crash land.

After a few male and female friends have crashed and at least one has successfully navigated a complete scenario *without* crashing, *then* we introduce a mild level of impairment. Generally, only a few simulated beers are required, not the ten that we *could* program in. At that point, "the victim" drives again, believing that he/she has now "mastered" the Cyclops, and then he/she crashes spectacularly again!

Sometimes John and I would play good cop and bad cop. Before the driver entered the vehicle, I would ask some questions about what the driver should do under certain circumstances for defensive driving purposes. I would then tell the new "victim" to strap on the seat belt so they would know we were not kidding when we said "virtual reality."

I would even coach them on how to place more than one hand on the wheel. Some college students were completely confused by this concept and never really recovered from the shock. Victims soon learned that *both* hands were actually required for expert collision avoidance in order to keep from crashing the Cyclops … just like in real life.

I would also make certain that they knew what to do at the intersections (duh). I quickly discovered that many college students, otherwise fairly smart in some ways, don't necessarily know common rules of the road. In fact, we soon realized that most of the college students who drove the Cyclops didn't know the basics that we had been teaching our teenage drivers. If they didn't crash because of the poor mechanics of operating the Cyclops, they would certainly crash when anything unusual was presented.

After a while, John and I figured that the only way we could get them through an entire unimpaired scenario *without crashing* was to give them tips on what they were going to see before they even saw it. This sort of defeated the purpose of the Cyclops, didn't it?

We were interested in providing golden opportunities for at least one hundred students to crash the Cyclops rather than teaching just ten how to drive one or more scenarios without crashing. After a while, we realized that even though most of the participants and all the observers laughed at the crashes, they also got the message loud and clear. Some of the students may have been a bit young and dumb (pre-graduation), but they weren't stupid!

Some of the more responsible young adults were very shaken by their performances in the Cyclops. They sincerely didn't have a clue how poorly they operated a motor vehicle … even *before* they went to happy hour!

The DUI simulations are literally and figuratively sobering. This is important to you because during our travels, we determined that driver impairment was and is only a fraction of the problem. First of all, as previously referenced in the book, many young adults have not been trained to drive properly. Moreover, driver distraction, especially now because of the invention of something called the mobile phone, *is at least as responsible as DUI for contributing to the loss of thousands of lives each year.*

Eventually, your teen will become a young adult, and he/she will be convinced that he/she knows how to drive. In fact, many of them become so convinced that they can drive expertly under virtually any circumstances that they also believe they can drive when they are moderately to severely impaired. Along the way, we also discovered that college administrators, in their infinite wisdom, wanted us to run the DUI simulations, but they were *not interested in having us refresh young minds with anything related to driver education and driver training.*

After all, virtually all college students already have their driver's licenses when they begin college, haven't they? Seriously, this was the reasoning of the faculties at virtually all the learning institutions we dealt with who were and still are responsible for the health and well- being of eighteen- to twenty-two-year-old semi-adults!

Conclusions and Issues of Concern

During the early DUI/DWI Cyclops shows, John and I simply put on the show that we were contracted to deliver. After all, college faculties were the clients, and we were the customers being paid to deliver the product (DUI entertainment) that they requested. However, after a while, during the period John was prepping the Cyclops or running a scenario from the passenger seat, I would be talking to each "student" waiting their turn to take a crack at the Cyclops.

After a while, I also began to ask rhetorical questions about driver education and safety. It was at about this time that I discovered that college students don't know any more about driving than high school students do

They just *think* they know a whole lot more.

John and I had a bit of a difference of opinion about how to deal with this phenomenon. I wanted to spend a reasonable amount of time educating each student during the limited time we had. John wanted us to focus on the job we had been hired to do. Finally, after a few trips out where we both expressed our opinions before, during, and after the shows, we decided to put our difference of opinion to the test. John and I coauthored a new solicitation letter where we offered college administrators a choice of either approach or both approaches during an entire "show day." We even offered to set up presentations in their classrooms, gymnasiums, or auditoriums where we could essentially present a condensed version of Gumby Bay Studio's multiple awards winning *Rules of The Road* and AAA's *Managing Space and Time*.

As previously referenced, the Gumby Bay Studios release of *Rules of the Road* was used in our classroom religiously over the four years we provided classroom training. The *Rules of the Road* training video was developed for teenagers, which half of the college students technically still were. The other half may have believed that they were adults, but many of them quickly learned that they still had some learning and ciphering to do.

AAA's *Managing Space and Time* was actually developed for an *adult* driver improvement program. As referenced earlier in the book, different states have a different name for the same training. In South Carolina, the course is called "Four-Point Reduction" because, well, when you spend all day in class being trained by an AAA certified driving instructor (as Beth Templeton and I both were), you are eligible to have four points knocked off your DMV traffic violation record. In other states, it is simply called driver improvement; and in still other states, it is called something else entirely.

Then there is something called fleet training. Beth Templeton and I were both certified to provide fleet training, although we never contracted to do so. Fleet training, as the name implies, is for commercial driving companies. Have you ever ridden with a commercial driver in any capacity anywhere that was so good he or she *didn't require* any aspect of this training? I didn't think so. How about taxi cab drivers? Do you think any of them would benefit from this training? How about their passengers?

Is it any wonder that college administrators basically said "thanks for all your concern about the safety of our students, but we think we will pass on driver improvement?" *After all, college students already know how to drive, don't they?*

CHAPTER 11

The "Super Seniors"

In the United States Tennis Association, the term *super senior* is designated to a player over sixty years old. The term *senior* refers to a player over fifty years old. Virtually, all other players are ranked according to their USTA ratings. If you are a "senior" or a "super senior," you are entitled to both the USTA rating and the other designation that tells the tennis world how old you are and at least part of the rationale for the way that you play. Not so fast! Pros become seniors, and they eventually become super seniors too. If you ever meet one in a tennis tournament, you will soon discover that age is just a relative consideration. Underestimate one of these players, and he or she will "clean your clock." They all still play; they just don't play in prime time anymore.

In 1984, I had something new called radial keratotomy (pre Lasik) performed on my left eye at the Dean McGee Eye Institute of Oklahoma City, Oklahoma. After a year of allowing my left eye to heal (that's how long it took in those days), I had my right eye done in 1985. I had been a "pro" since I was in my teens, but I use that term very loosely because no one wins any money at table tennis even when you win tournaments.

My last table tennis hurrah was at the Tropicana Hotel for the United States Open Table Tennis Championships in early 1984. What does all this old guy table tennis and tennis stuff have to do with driver education and safety? Well, humor me please. When I flew to Vegas, I met one of the best friends of my life there. His name was Bart Lawson, and he was a tournament level table tennis player too. I had met him years before when I was fresh out of the army, only twenty-two at that time.

Bart was twenty-six, had a thriving family of a wife and four children, and owned his own high-fidelity store right on Beach Boulevard in Huntington Beach California where I had gone to high school. It was called Lawson Sound. I hadn't yet started college at age twenty-two. If fact, I had no idea what I was going to be doing when I first got out of the army. Who was there to tell me?

I admired Bart as a family man, as a person, and as a friend. I used to call him Black Bart after the old cartoon character, but there was nothing "black" or dark about Bart. Bart was the funniest man I have ever known. Bart was always late for everything, and I was always early for everything, and I would always be sitting there twiddling my thumbs, for it seemed like hours waiting for him. When he would walk in, he would start telling jokes or funny stories, and I just couldn't stay mad at the guy … never could. I never saw Bart without a smile on his face.

Bart and I agreed to enter the tournament out at the Tropicana Hotel in Vegas more because we wanted to see each other than either of us having any false illusions about what we were going to do in the United States Table Tennis Open. We each had United States Table Tennis ratings of about 1,750 points. That was good for me being rated ninth in the state of Oklahoma, and both of us maybe in the top five hundred in the state of California, if we were even that high. We each lasted about a couple of rounds before we went down in flames, but we had a good time doing it.

One time, Bart rode a motorcycle from Huntington Beach California to Oklahoma City to see me … in the middle of August. I was working as an instructor at that time at the FAA academy. I knew he had ridden across the desert of course. I had done so several times myself … but I had always been in a car.

When Bart pulled into the driveway, I could hear his big Harley as he pulled in. I went to the front door and opened it as he was pulling off his helmet. I swear … I wasn't prepared for this. When he pulled off his helmet, he looked like a giant … lizard! His face was all swollen and horribly disfigured from the ride through the desert. I said, "Geeeeez! Next time wear a face mask, man!" I know it wasn't a very diplomatic thing to say to a guy that had just ridden one thousand five hundred miles through a desert to see me, but he had already seen the look on my face, and he was expecting it. He had a smile on his face. How he did that, I will never know

...

Bart was best man at my wedding to Beth Templeton in 1989. The wedding took place overlooking Dana Point Harbor in Southern Orange County, California.

We have photos and a video that prove Bart was there, but I think I had to drive *him* to my wedding in order to make sure he showed up before the ceremony was over ... and to hand me the ring.

In 1991, while Beth and I were living on the east side of Oahu in Hawaii, I received a phone call from Bart's oldest son Lee. None of his children had ever called me in Hawaii or in Oklahoma before. Bart had always made those calls. I knew there had to be a reason that Bart had not made the call. There was. Bart had been killed by a drunk driver after being hit head on. Apparently, he had died instantly. I had just returned from a six-week detail at the FAA Regional Office in Los Angeles, and I just had too much pressing business at my regular sector office to depart again. I had to send my regrets and could not attend his funeral ... something I will regret until the day I die. All our table tennis buddies used to joke that Bart would be late for his own funeral. Maybe he was ...

And now you know the third reason I decided to write the book.

At first glance, it may seem like the "super senior" tennis and the table tennis introductions were unrelated to "super senior" driving. I believe differently. "Super senior" drivers who have been trained properly can drive better than twenty-five-year-old adults who have not been trained properly, even considering the natural process of aging and deterioration of some motor skills. In fact, they can be so much better that there isn't even a comparison. A sixty-year-old 4.0 "super senior" tennis player can blow a twenty-five-year-old 2.0 player off the court and a sixty-year-old driver who knows what the hell he or she is doing can blow a twenty-five-year-old idiot off the highway with driving skills too.

This super senior chapter could have included more than the few anecdotes about driving lessons I actually did conduct for some "super seniors, besides the seventy-

five-year-old grandmother and the two that I have chosen below. For example, an eighty-five-year-old pastor came to me and asked me to be "assessed" because he wasn't sure he still "had it" anymore. He not only still "had it," but after a first lesson "tune-up" and a second lesson *that he requested,* he turned out to be a better driver than any other adult I personally ever gave a "tune-up" to.

The wife of an eighty-three-year-old called us to set up lessons for her husband because he had let his driver's license lapse … and he had failed the driving test. When I took him out, I could see why she was concerned about him; he was all over the place. He figured that if I would just show him how to parallel park again, then the rest of the road course would be a breeze. That's what they all think. Anyway, he couldn't back a car straight, so the least of his problems was parallel parking. He canceled the second lesson she had already paid for because, after all, he already knew how to drive and had been doing it for fifty years, right?

He went up for round two at the DMV after a few weeks of practice on his own. I found out later that he failed that one too … for a different reason. Remember this too please. The only way you can "teach an old dog new tricks" is if the old dog is sufficiently motivated to learn a few new tricks. If not, it is a waste of everyone's time.

The remainder of this chapter is also going to be devoted to "super seniors" from the perspective of classroom training and behind-the-wheel training. Please remember that in sports, proper training supersedes youth *or* experience ten times over as it does in every sport. This is also true in driver education and training.

So if you are a "super senior" and, like the pastor, you are no longer certain if you still "have it" or if you ever "had it," read the entire chapter please. What have you got to lose now? Well, you can still lose your life in an unnatural way. Roads and highways don't care how old you are or how long you have been driving.

Included in this chapter is a written quiz. My initial submittal for this book included the correct answers to the quiz questions, in bold type.

However, after due consideration, I removed the bold-typed correct answers. This quiz may be completed by any driver in the country of any age. The actual correct answers may be debated between those administering the quiz and those being subjected to the quiz. This is the new purpose and intent of the quiz.

Some of the answers are more than a little obvious. This was intentional in preparing the original version for teens and the later version for seniors.

In our opinion, a good quiz or exam should help reinforce the material that the student (or someone who claims to thoroughly know the subject matter) should already know.

In early mid-2007, not too long after CADETS opened and before we seriously considered training seniors, the owners and operators of CADETS were offered the "opportunity" to conduct a *free* presentation to senior "mall walkers" at the Inlet Square Mall, Murrells Inlet, South Carolina. This was an opportunity we couldn't refuse, so all three owners and the wife of John Kurywchak, Brazilian beauty queen Claudia Kurywchak, also showed up with her CADETS shirt on and her game face on.

The press release and original agenda for that event are as follows:

PRESS RELEASE

10125 Hwy 17 Bypass South * Box 12A Murrells Inlet,
South Carolina, 29576

For Immediate Release	
Contact:	**Carol Fallon**
Company:	**Inlet Square**
Phone:	**843.651.6990**
Email:	**Carol.fallon@am.jll.com**

CADETS to Provide Inlet Square Mall Walkers*
with a Driver "Tune-Up"

Murrells Inlet Mall Walkers* will be receiving a driver education/training "tune-up" assessment to determine where their driving skills are today compared to where they were when they first received their driver's licenses. The owners and operators of CADETS will be discussing how senior drivers' fatality rates compare to other age groups. CADETS will be giving our seniors an update on current driver education safety practices which is something worthy of addressing for any age group.

*This event will be open to all seniors in the vicinity of the southern Grand Strand interested in attending.

Topics will include:

- A brief overview of relevant statistical data provided by the National Highway Traffic Safety Administration.

- The administration of a written quiz so that attendees can assess their own current knowledge of South Carolina and national rules of the road, as well as general defensive driving procedures.

- A brief overview of the CADETS Senior Driver Assessment Program.

- A brief overview of the CADETS Senior Driver "Tune Up" Refresher Training Course

- A brief description of the Cyclops, one of the most sophisticated driving simulators in the country.

- A question-and-answer period. The question- and-answer period will allow attendees to ask any questions regarding driver education and safety that may arise during this event.

Agenda

- Thanks to Carol Fallon (marketing director of Inlet Square mall) for inviting us

- Introduce owners of CADETS, John Kurywchak, Mike Templeton, Beth Templeton, and Claudia Kurywchak

- Who we are as a driving academy

- Description of today's activities

- Statistics from the National Highway Traffic Safety Administration

- Administer quiz

- Answers to quiz (conducted by Beth)

- Question-and-answer period (Mike)

- A description of the Cyclops driving simulator (John)

- A brief overview of the CADETS Senior Driver Assessment Program (Beth)

- A brief overview of the CADETS Senior Driver "Tune-Up" Refresher Training Course (Beth)

- Additional question-and-answer period (All)

As referenced in the agenda, we decided to determine what the seniors knew about driving safely, at least on paper, by administering a quiz that was very familiar to us. It was essentially the same quiz we administered to our fifteen- and sixteen-year-old teens at the end of their classroom day.

As previously noted, the quiz was not developed to fail anyone. In fact, after all our teens received our classroom training, only two teens in four years failed the quiz. However, during the presentation of the quiz to the senior mall walkers … and other interested observers on the day referenced below, about 50 percent of the respondents failed the quiz (seventeen correct or less).

It should be noted that a pro-driving instructor from the school that I had previously been employed by showed up to observe and take the quiz. He was the only one to score 100 percent correct, proving that there is remarkable correlation between the thinking of pro- driving instructors, as opposed to everyone else. Also, the AARP graduates performed much better than all the other seniors, most of whom failed the quiz.

The pro-driving instructor who showed up to listen to the presentation and take the quiz, a former coworker, had never seen our quiz before. He showed up because he wished to be the first pro-driving instructor to be hired by CADETS. For a variety of reasons I don't need to convey here, our first driving instructors were a former fireman who trained his firefighters to drive fire trucks and a female public educator. Both of them turned out to be terrific. We chose wisely.

In the meantime, the overall results of the quiz turned out to be shocking! We didn't get surprised often, but we were absolutely astounded by the poor results. We were even more astounded by this; we had offered a two-hour behind-the- wheel "tune-up" to each attendee for a very nominal discounted fee … as a local public service. None of the senior mall walkers who failed the exam accepted. It turns out that many seniors believe if they have somehow escaped serious harm in a vehicle all these years, they are "immortal too."

There is a message here. In fact, there should be several messages here.

Adult/Senior Classroom Quiz

*Name:*_________________________ *Date*: _________________________

Phone Number: _____________________

Have you previously completed AARP classroom training?

Yes_________ No ___________

Number of correct answers – CADETS Quiz: ___________________

1. When a school bus has stopped with its red lights flashing you must:

   A) Stop if you are directly behind the bus.

   B) Stop if you are about to pass the bus.

   C) Stop if you meet the bus while it is loading at an intersection.

   D) All of the above.

2. If you arrive first at a four-way stop, when should you proceed?

   A) You can go right away.

   B) You must wait for another car to come.

   C) You must make a complete stop first, and then proceed when you have verified that another driver is not running through one of the other three stop signs.

   D) If no one is there, you don't have to stop.

3. Which of the following is the best definition of the point of no return when approaching an intersection with a stale green light?

   A) Stop as soon as you see the light turn yellow regardless of where you are.

   B) Speed up to make it through the intersection as soon as the light turns yellow.

   C) Brake to a stop on yellow even if the end result is that you skid into the intersection.

   D) The point of no return is dependent on speed and distance. If you have passed the PNR, you drive through the intersection when the light turns yellow.

4. To improve visibility while backing:

   A) Look at your mirrors as you are backing.

   B) Clear the area behind you first by checking over each shoulder. Turn your body so that your right hand is behind the passenger seat. Look directly behind the vehicle as you continue to back.

   C) Open the driver's side door and check for a clear path.

   D) Adjust seat position further from the steering wheel.

5. Check blind spots to the side or rear of your vehicle by:

   A) Using the rearview mirror.

   B) Using side mirrors.

   C) Using rearview and side mirrors.

   D) Looking over your shoulder.

6. You intend to turn at the next intersection. What is the minimum distance from the intersection where you should turn on your signal?

   A) Signal just before entering the intersection.

   B) Signal at least one hundred feet before the intersection.

   C) Signal as you enter the intersection.

   D) Your signal depends on the point of no return.

7. Which is the correct lane change procedure?

   A) Check mirrors, signal, and go.

   B) Signal, check your mirrors, check over shoulder, and go if clear.

   C) Check over your shoulder, glance in mirror, signal, and then go.

   D) Check mirrors, signal, and then glance over your shoulder.

8. You are parking on a downhill grade with no curb. You should:

   A) Center your wheels.

   B) Turn your wheels left.

   C) Turn your steering wheel right.

   D) Turn your steering wheel right, but your tires will be pointed left.

9. When approaching an intersection at fifty miles per hour, the light turns yellow. If you have *passed* the point of no return, where should your car be in relation to the intersection when the light turns from yellow to red?

   A) Just entering the intersection.

   B) In the middle of the intersection if you skidded past the crosswalk.

   C) You should stop immediately regardless of how far you are from the intersection.

   D) If you have judged your speed and distance correctly, you should be through the intersection when the light changes from yellow to red.

10. Your car *does not* have ABS brakes, and your car is beginning to skid as you brake. You should:

    A) Turn your wheels in the direction the rear of the car is skidding. Release pressure on the brake slightly until your steering correction straightens the car. Reapply brakes as firmly as possible without introducing another skid.

    B) Keep the brake pressure firmly on and turn your wheels away from the direction the rear of the car is skidding.

    C) If your car is skidding, you have no control of the direction of the car. Simply keep the brakes locked.

    D) Don't brake or steer. Wait for the car to stop skidding.

11. The best way to allow an escape path in case of an emergency is:

    A) Maintain space and visibility in front.

B) Maintain space and visibility on each side.

C) Maintain space and distance from cars behind you.

D) All of the above.

12. When passing another car on a two-lane highway, how can you decide when it is safe for you to return to the right lane?

A) When your front door reaches the front bumper of the other car.

B) When the road ahead is clear.

C) When you can see the entire front end of car you are passing in your rearview mirror.

D) After applying your right turn signal.

13. Your car is *equipped with ABS brakes,* and you must brake to an emergency stop on wet pavement. You should:

A) Pump the brakes until you feel the ABS kick in.

B) Brake with your emergency brake.

C) Brake until you feel the ABS kick in and then release the brake until you coast to a stop.

D) Keep your foot on the brake very firmly until you feel the ABS pulsing sensation. You may also steer the car away from danger while braking hard.

14. You are driving on an expressway with three lanes on your side of the median. Which lane is the safest lane to drive in the majority of the time?

A) The right lane because it is the slow lane.

B) The left lane because you can easily pass all the drivers that are driving the speed limit in other lanes.

C) The middle lane.

D) The right lane allows you to slow for mergers.

15. Every time your car is in the shop for a tune-up, it's a good idea to check:

A) The exhaust system.

B) The cooling system.

C) The brake system.

D) All of the above.

16. At a four-way stop, four cars arrive, one after the other. What is the sequence for each car to proceed?

A) 4, 3, 2, 1.

B) Depends on which car is on the right.

C) 1, 2, 3, 4

D) Wait for each driver to motion with their hands which car should proceed next.

17. You wish to turn left at a four lane intersection, and you have a green light.

You should:

A) Turn because you have the right of way.

B) Turn only after the light turns yellow.

C) Only turn left at an intersection when you have a green arrow.

D) Turn when oncoming traffic clears and you clearly have enough time to complete your turn without impeding the progress of oncoming traffic.

18. What is the best way to prevent fatigue when driving?

A) Change drivers from time to time.

B) Get plenty of rest and avoid driving before sunrise or after midnight.

C) Stop for rest and stretch your legs every two to three hours.

D) All of the above.

19. The sign above means:

A) Always stop in the feeder lane.

B) Expect other traffic to yield to you.

C) Always yield to a stop when you see this sign.

D) Always yield to other traffic but keep moving if there is no traffic.

20. The sign above means:

A) Vehicles must not exceed the shown speed limit when the yellow light flashes.

B) The speed limit should only be observed when children are seen.

C) Only school buses must observe this sign.

D) Always drive twenty miles per hour.

21. The sign above means you should:

A) Detour immediately.

B) Slow and watch for workers and machinery.

C) The sign is for construction workers only.

D) Maintain your speed.

22. You have a green light at an intersection where you wish to turn left. However, the driver of the car directly in front of you also wishes to turn left and is waiting for clearance in the middle of the intersection before turning. You should:

A) Wait behind the white crosswalk line until the driver has turned left from the intersection. If the light is still green, you may enter the intersection and wait for the next clearance to turn.

B) Pull up directly behind the car in front of you. When the driver turns left, you may also turn left.

C) Stay behind the crosswalk line until you see a light with a green arrow.

D) Wait for a yellow light. As soon as you see the yellow light immediately turn left because you know that all oncoming traffic will stop.

23. Right-of-way laws are important because:

A) They help prevent collisions.

B) They provide for an orderly flow of traffic.

C) They help eliminate the guesswork of who should go next.

D) All of the above.

24. You are waiting to turn left on a four-lane highway, and you are the only car in the intersection. The green light facing your lane suddenly turns yellow. You should:

A) Immediately turn before the light turns red.

B) Wait until the light turns red and then turn because you know all cars will be stopped by that time.

C) Verify that oncoming traffic is braking by watching the dip of the front of the cars as driver's brake. Once you have satisfactorily verified that all oncoming cars either have braked or are braking, you may complete your turn.

D) Stay out in the intersection until you get another green light.

25. Communication with other drivers is recommended by each of the following except:

A) By maintaining eye contact at four-way stops.

B) By signaling your intentions before every turn.

C) By tapping your horn when another driver is about to invade your space.

D) By calling another driver on your cell phone.

The following pages pertain to an assessment of a volunteer senior driver. She was a seventy-five-year-old grandmother and had been driving for almost sixty years. I must say that although I knew her, I hadn't previously seen her drive. I had no previous knowledge of her driving behaviors or capabilities.

As the lead driving instructor for CADETS, I had specifically requested that she allow me to simply observe her driving as I would during typical second and third teen driving activities *without offering any training advice or guidance.* In other words, I wished to establish a baseline of her knowledge and skill before any training took place.

It should be revealed (and is very relevant) that prior to Mrs. Doe completing the CADETS assessment and follow-on training, she had completed classroom AARP training during two previous training periods. Mrs. Doe's introduction to CADETS training began with her completion of the CADETS driver education quiz normally administered to fifteen- and sixteen-year-old beginning drivers.

Mrs. Doe, with some help from her husband (which she cheerfully acknowledged), answered twenty-two of twenty-five questions in the above quiz correctly. Fortunately, her husband had also attended AARP training during two previous years.

During the initial driving assessment that took place on September 7, 2007, Mrs. Doe was assessed in thirty- two categories. Five other performance grid categories (normally required of teens) were not assessed during the two-hour period. Of the thirty-two categories assessed, Mrs. Jane Doe demonstrated mastery of six. During the performance assessment, Mrs. Doe also demonstrated moderately successful performance in twelve of thirty- two categories.

During assessment of the remaining fourteen of thirty-two categories, Mrs. Doe demonstrated a clear and obvious need for hands on behind-the-wheel training.

On September 26, 2007, I personally provided two hours of applied behind-the-wheel coaching and training for Mrs. Doe. As a result of the training, Mrs. Doe's replacement performance grid notations were revised for the following grid. This notations in this grid indicate that at the end of just a single two hour training period she had demonstrated mastery in 12 additional categories. She also improved her performance in 10 categories from "training required" or "not safe to observe" to "partially successful".

Most of the "TR" deficiencies were corrected during the two-hour lesson. However, parking lot driving in particular and her answers to hill parking questions revealed that additional training beyond the two-hour lesson was required in those two specific categories.

After the two-hour training session and upon reflection a few days later, the instructor and the senior driver agreed that (for the intended purpose of the study) the training had achieved the desired result. It should be noted that the performance grid developed for Mrs. Doe was similar to but not an exact duplicate of those developed solely for beginning drivers. *For example, parallel parking is obviously absent.* Parallel parking was not intended to be included in the study or training program. However, as a result of Mrs. Doe's response in the other CADETS training categories, I was very confident that she could have easily been coached to parallel park. As referenced earlier in the book, CADETS Inc. incorporates an exclusive written parallel parking technique that is quite effective with beginning teen drivers. Mrs. Doe was a much more accomplished driver than an average beginning teen driver.

Conclusions

Mrs. Jane Doe demonstrated some minor loss of motor skills and flexibility. However, there were no obvious physical deficiencies that precluded her from driving safely, at least in the immediate future. More significantly, she demonstrated *measurable improvement* as a result of the one thing almost all adult drivers could use more of … hands on behind- the-wheel training delivered by a professional driving instructor.

I authored the following letter to Mrs. Doe. Please forgive the informal and personal tone of the letter. I knew her well and sincerely did not wish to offend her. However, I learned long ago that in order for feedback to be effective, it must be credible; otherwise, its effectiveness is severely diminished.

Therefore, the good, the bad, and the ugly must be conveyed, no matter how painful some of it may be to the recipient. In this case, I felt "the good" far outweighed "the bad" and especially "the ugly."

Dear _________________

Enclosed is your driving assessment. I know you didn't ask for this (ha) … It was my idea, and I want to thank you again for it. As the lead instructor for CADETS, the insight I gained has already proven to be extremely valuable toward our efforts to develop a comprehensive senior training program.

In fact, the first draft of the attached new adult senior performance grid was not in existence and would not have been possible if you had not agreed to be "assessed." More importantly, as a professional driving instructor (at least, at this stage in my life), I am perhaps in a better position to assess the driving skills of _________________ than someone else; at least I hope so.

*I could have "dialed it in" and rated you terrific in every category. I wouldn't have had an ounce of credibility if I had done so because **I know you knew** when you had trouble with a maneuver or task.*

As intelligent as you are, I know you also must have realized that I would see some driving performance deficiencies that only an experienced instructor might catch. In any case, please don't consider this assessment to be too overly critical. The fact is that virtually all the performance issues that I observed can be significantly improved upon during a single two-hour lesson.

*I would like to offer my services for this lesson free of charge of course. By the way, twenty years ago, I discovered that my own mother had never learned to drive on an expressway. For over a year, **she had driven on side streets** for thirty miles (from Huntington Beach, California, to Laguna Niguel) to get to her nanny job. This choice was made primarily due to fear, despite the fact that the San Diego Freeway (I-405) connected the two locations and was an obvious choice, especially during nonpeak hours.*

Finally, I was able to convince her to allow me to train her to merge, drive, and exit an expressway properly.

She thanked me many times for it during the next ten years of her employment. Author's post script: Mother worked for the attorneys as their nanny after the births of each of three children.

However, in 1992, she had the first of two major strokes. She was no longer physically able to drive after her first stroke ...

Please be reassured that I don't see any significant deterioration of motor skills, physical skills, or mental skills that would inhibit your current capability to be an outstanding defensive driver. In my opinion, a little additional training is all that will be required to increase your driving skill level from "moderately satisfactory" performance levels to the "excellent to outstanding" performance levels. This will help all your family members feel a bit more secure about you driving safely for years to come.

Thank you for giving me the opportunity to do this!

Sincerely,

Mike

Adult/Senior Driver Assessment Program

Adult Driver's Name: Jane Doe (a seventy-five-year-old grandmother)
Instructor: Mike Templeton

ACTIVITY	**Unsatisfactory**	**Satisfactory**	**Mastery**
Assessment Date 9/7/07			
Rules of the Road Confirmation			X
Basic Auto Setup			X
Right Turn Series		X	
Left Turn Series		X	
Wheel Release		X	
Gas and Brake	X		
Three-Point Turn		X	
Backing	X		
Residential Driving	X		
Right-of-Way			X
Cul-de-Sac			X
Blind Intersection	X		
Stop Signs	X		
Cornering	X		
Defensive Driving Confirmation	X		
Angle Parking		X	
Perpendicular Parking	X		
Parking Lot Backing	X		

ACTIVITY	Unsatisfactory	Satisfactory	Mastery
Parking Lot Driving	X		
Parking on Hills (UCLA)	X		
City Driving		X	
Double Lane Turns	X		
Lane Changing (SMOG)		X	
Lane of Least Resistance			X
Lane Control		X	
Speed Control		X	
Merging with and without Yield Signs			X
Intersections		X	
Unprotected Left Turns			
Three-Second Following			
Wheel Visibility at Lights			
Maintaining Visibility			
Maintaining Space			
Yellow Lights		X	
Highway Driving		X	
Exiting Highways		X	
Advanced Collision Avoidance Procedures	X		

X = Training Required

MS = Moderately Successful

Mastery = Observed or Confirmed

THE WRITTEN ASSESSMENT*

MASTERY

1. Very good auto setup and mirror adjustment

2. Excellent figure 8 hand over hand

3. Fairly good wheel release

4. Smooth gas but jerked brakes a bit (not familiar with the outstanding brakes on the training car)

5. Three-point turn very good but could be improved to excellent with training

6. Cul-de-Sac turns outstanding

7. Merging described correctly and well executed

8. Very good to excellent overall understanding of rules of the road

9. Very good perpendicular parking between lines but left front end over grass (representing front boundary)

10. Good knowledge and execution of lane change procedures but turned head too far

TRAINING RECOMMENDED

1. Accelerated while backing instead of applying controlled idle/braking

2. Did not back in straight line

3. Used mirrors for backing in parking lot (resulting in off center backing) but turned head around (too far) for lane changes and other backing maneuvers

4. Did not use correct (left) hand on wheel and body turn during backing

5. Attempted to turn left across three lanes of heavy traffic from parking lot (after being given a choice for an alternate safer route)

6. Hands at 10/2 versus 9/3—okay if by choice and all other performances. Okay but not preferred because of potentially air bag deployment. Consideration must be given to long time 10+2 drivers.

7. Did not signal for turns in parking lots

8. Cut two corners too short (drove over grass)

9. Rolling stops at several stop signs

10. During perpendicular parking left front of car over grass

11. Double lane left turn—turned into incorrect lane

12. In mall parking lot, drove across several white lines at angle and higher than safe speed in order to reach intended target and backward park

13. Lane change procedure satisfactory but turned head too far resulting in possible premature wheel turn

14. Removed right hand off wheel while driving on Highway 707 resulting in the weight of left arm pulling the wheel left and car drifting over center yellow line

15. Drove eight miles per hour under the speed limit for an extended period on Highway 707 resulting in multiple tailgaters behind

The following grid was completed during a subsequent two-hour training session that took place on September 26, 2007.

Adult/Senior Driver Training Program

Adult Driver's Name: Grandmother, Jane Doe

Instructor: Mike Templeton

ACTIVITY	Unsuccessful	Moderately Successful	Mastery
Training Date 9/26/07			
Rules of the Road Confirmation			×
Basic Auto Set-up			×
Right Turn Series			×
Left Turn Series			×
Wheel Release			×
Gas and Brake			×
Three-Point Turn			×
Backing			×
Residential Driving			×
Right-of-Way			×
Cul-de-Sac			×
Blind Intersection			×
Stop Signs			×
Cornering		×	
Defensive Driving Confirmation		×	

Angle Parking		×	
Perpendicular Parking		×	
Parking Lot Backing		×	
Parking Lot Driving	×		
Parking on Hills (UCLA)	×		
City Driving		×	
Double Lane Turns			×
Lane Changing (SMOG)		×	
Lane of Least Resistance			×
Lane Control		×	×
Speed Control		×	×
Merging With and Without Yield Signs			×
Intersections		×	
Unprotected Left Turns		×	
3-Second Following		×	
Wheel Visibility at Lights		×	
Maintaining Visibility		×	
Maintaining Space		×	
Yellow Lights		×	
Highway Driving		×	
Exiting Highways		×	
Advanced Collision Avoidance Procedures		×	

X = Training Required

MS = Moderately Successful

Mastery = Observed or Confirmed

Senior Driver Assessment/Training Program Training Grid Template

Driver's Name:________________ Observer:__________________

ACTIVITY	Unsatisfactory	Satisfactory	Mastery	Notes
Rules of the Road Confirmation				
Basic Auto Setup				
Right Turn Series				
Left Turn Series				
Wheel Release				
Gas and Brake				
Three-Point Turn				
Backing				
Residential Driving				
Right-of-Way				
Cul-de-Sac				
Blind Intersection				
Stop Signs				
Cornering				
Defensive Driving Confirmation				
Angle Parking				
Perpendicular Parking				
Parking Lot Backing				
Parking Lot Driving				
Parking on Hills (UCLA)				

City Driving				
Double Lane Turns				
Lane Changing (SMOG)				
Lane of Least Resistance				
Lane Control				
Speed Control				
Merging with and without Yield Signs				
Intersections				
Unprotected Left Turns				
Three-Second Following				
Wheel Visibility at Lights				
Maintaining Visibility				
Maintaining Space				
Yellow Lights				
Highway Driving				
Exiting Highways				
Advanced Collision Avoidance Procedures				

X = Training Required

MS = Moderately Successful

Mastery = Observed or Confirmed

Assessment Comments

Training Comments

Mastery Comments

*Additional sessions may be required either in a simulator or behind the wheel or both. Observers shall advise all drivers of deficiencies and recommend appropriate additional training as required. Based on this advice, drivers may elect to choose the simulator or actual behind-the-wheel training. The assessment grid, the feedback, and the blank training grid may be copied and utilized by other training schools, other agencies, or other private parties for any adult of any age. The advantage of having them used far outweighs the reality that they are out there now … and no longer in our domain. This seems like a small price to pay. Use them please.

CHAPTER 12

Driver Education for the Twenty-First Century

The most dangerous driver on the road today is not a "wildebeest," a "wild hawg," or "rabid dog." It isn't even a driver in road rage. The most dangerous driver on the road today is the driver of a moped! How could this be? Well, let's look at the facts. We can also draw some additional conclusions based upon what we have seen and what we know:

- Most mopeds only reach a top speed of about thirty miles per hour, which makes them unsuitable for most highways and expressways, although it is legal for them to be on most highways.

- Since they can't achieve regular cruising speed, most of them "cruise" in the far right section of the "slow lane," creating a lane that really doesn't exist at all.

- Drivers of mopeds are "driving" the moped for good reason. However, the reason isn't normally a reason of their choosing. This is one of several reasons that most of them *do not* look like they are having a grand time on the moped.

- Most moped drivers do not have a regular driver's license, although some of them *might* have a moped license.

- Many moped drivers once had a driver's license but lost it because of some unfortunate behavior(s).

- Some adult moped drivers have never obtained a driver's license at all.

- Most moped drivers are not insured properly.

- For some inexplicable reason, the overwhelming majority of moped drivers, at least in this state, do not wear helmets. We could debate all day about the *rationale* for this, but it is what it is.

- We guess moped drivers figure that if they go down, they are going to die anyway, so what the hey!

  Now how does this potentially affect you? If a moped driver wishes to "go commando" on a suicide commute, how could this potentially impact *you?*

- Most moped drivers move over to the far right section of two-lane and four-lane highways, thereby creating a new lane that isn't there at all. Then … wait for it.

- From there, the moped driver can experience the pleasures of being passed by wildebeests," "wild hawgs," and "rabid dogs" … and those aren't even the ones in road rage.

- If the moped driver has the audacity to move over to the middle of the lane, *then* he/or she will quickly have a close encounter with a driver in road rage.

- Moped drivers understand the concept of "the path of least resistance." I'm not sure how they all learn this; perhaps from previous crashes. Anyway …

- Moped drivers have calculated that is far less risky to force *you* onto oncoming traffic than it is for *them* to veer off the right shoulder. This is especially true in states that haven't yet developed the concept of "breakdown" lanes. If there is no place for auto drivers to "break down," there is no place for moped drivers to drive semi-legally in either.

- The only state in the country that has more than two roads adorned with bike lanes seems to be California. However, even in California, they have discovered that mopeds don't "comingle" very well with skateboarders, pedestrians, and those pedaling their way to work on real bicycles. Besides, a California bicycle commuter often pedals faster than a moped rider's two-horse-power motor will carry him, thereby requiring the moped driver to select an even "slower lane" if one is available.

- Moped drivers know that if they lose control and veer only two feet left they *might* die. However, if they lose control and veer two feet right, they *will* die. In many states (like this one), there are almost no breakdown lanes. The white boundary line at the edge of the only lane going your way on two-lane blacktop is drawn perilously close to a weeded shoulder, gravel ramp, rut, or pothole. *Dealer's choice!*

- Weeded shoulders, gravel ramps, ruts, and potholes are a "whole lotta fun" for the monster truck demolition drivers in the area that create them. For moped drivers, these unnatural phenomena act as launching pads for the next phase of their careers.

- Just a few feet beyond will be something commonly referred to as a "drainage ditch."

- I picture a "ditch" as being no more than a few feet wide. Our "drainage ditches" running alongside most of our state roads are more like the ravines and moats you see protecting castles.

- When the hapless moped driver "weed whacks" the shoulder and hits the launch pad, his initial feeling might rival the initial surge of adrenaline that Evel Knievel once felt as he launched over the Snake River Canyon. However ...

- It's that sudden "jolt" on the other side of the ravine that really gets their attention. Picture Willy Coyote after the Road Runner has booby trapped him.

Now here is something that Evel Knievel and moped riders *do not* have in common. Evel Kneivel had sense enough to wear a helmet. In South Carolina, the state legislators, the state judiciary, and the South Carolina Department of Motor Vehicles have somehow concluded that it is semi-safe for moped drivers to drive or ride without a helmet! This is almost true as long as you can steer the thing within a one-foot wide strip, *give or take an inch* ... all day.

Now think about this in advance please. You are following a moped driver, keeping your vehicle three seconds back and minding your own business when the hapless moped driver in front of you veers two inches to the right and front wheel catches the mud rut next to the white line. The moped driver turns his wheel sharply left to get his little undersized tire back over the lip, and he loses balance as his moped lurches over the curb.

He goes ass over tea kettle, and *you* have three options that you must assess in about .5 seconds flat:

1. You can veer right into the ravine or the moat. The moped rider didn't like that option, and you won't either.

2. You can veer left and hit the oncoming driver head on. Helmetless moped riders don't like that option, and you won't either.

3. You can look down at the helmetless moped rider and now headless moped and calculate your launch distance in advance. If your left tire launches over his head, and your right tire launches over his bike, chances are still good that you can remain in your lane for a four-point "touchdown" that even Evel Knievel would envy.

Still wonder why moped riders are the most dangerous drivers on the road … for you? You get to go back and inspect the damage while dialing 911. Just tell them to send the coroner while they are at it.

It gets worse. About five years ago, the mayor of Myrtle Beach attempted to reduce the number of wild hawgs roaring into and throughout the Grand Strand during the entire month of May each year. At one time about three hundred thousand would roar in and populate Horry and Georgetown counties, a population of about two hundred fifty thousand under non- tourist circumstances. Yes, we were outgunned and outnumbered, and so were the cops.

The mayor instituted at least three ordinances designed to reduce, if not entirely eliminate the workload.

1. Require that all traffic laws be obeyed. (This was a novel concept to some bikers.) This included obeying a couple of laws the bikers had never heard of before.

2.   A noise ordinance was introduced. This meant that when all the bikers convened outside an "establishment" at 2:00 a.m. for a "burn out toast," they were required to do so at sound volumes of 104 decibels or less. This was in contrast to the "burnouts" exceeding the volume of a 747 engine as had been allowed previously. Owners of nearby residences rejoiced but not too loudly, lest they disturb the bikers.

3.   This next one almost sealed the deal. The mayor declared that within the city limits of Myrtle Beach, South Carolina, bikers must wear something called *helmets.*

This meant that bikers that had arrived in Myrtle Beach for the express purpose of partying as they roared from the north end to the south end showing off and then turning around and roaring from south end to the north end showing off would have to pause at the entrances to Myrtle Beach proper. Here, they had to do something that is an antipathy of many bikers. They were required to install the useless helmet they had been hauling on the side of the bike all these miles and then take it off again when they reached the end of the city line. Man, these guys are just too smart for the mayor!

Of course, since this ordinance only pertained to Myrtle Beach proper and not the entire Grand Strand, most of these same bikers would come to town and "hang out" in the *suburban* areas surrounding Myrtle Beach, such as those where I taught driver education, training, and safety. In other words, I couldn't escape them no matter how far I drove with the kids.

I must say here that most of the bikers I have encountered (here on the Grand Strand) are about my age and have real jobs at home. Three of the best friends of my life have owned them and traveled to see me on them. I have owned two motorcycles in my lifetime myself. Many bikers are quite courteous on the road and off of it. However, some of us have wondered why they don't just convene out in the middle of South Carolina by night and have burnouts at one hundred ten decibels out there in the middle of nowhere. Then the next day, they can sleep it off at a Myrtle Beach hotel on the beach and play in the surf when they get up at 4:00 p.m. It seems reasonable to me, but then no one asked me.

You can imagine how the two groups (grizzled bikers and beginning drivers) with conflicting missions, goals, and objectives actually mix in reality. Yes, reality sometimes bites.

Then the bikers found the right ACLU judge (someone always does), and this "judge" ruled that requiring a motorcycle rider or a moped rider to wear a helmet was *unconstitutional.* Oh really? How is it "constitutional" to require drivers and passengers to wear seat belts, but it is "unconstitutional" to require motorcycle riders to wear helmets? How is it "constitutional" to require a mother to strap her baby in a baby seat, but "unconstitutional" to require a moped rider to wear a helmet? Please!

It seems to me that someone needs to read the United States Constitution again. I have a copy of it hanging in my hallway. It doesn't say anything about seat belts, child seats, motorcycles, mopeds, and helmets because horse-drawn carriages were common in those days. A governing body needs to interpret the United States

Constitution for modern road and highway transportation systems just as the Federal Aviation Administration has been doing for air travel for decades.

For about a decade, the FAA's little brother, the Transportation Security Administration, has been doing it for *flight preparation security.* This is a continuation of the responsibility a branch of the FAA had for the previous half century.

Activist judges normally don't determine or attempt to determine when the FAA is being "constitutional" or not. When the FAA makes a determination about a safety practice, the airlines do it, and the passengers do it, or they can pack up and go home.

Even mega stars like Alec Baldwin do not tell the FAA what they will do or what they won't do, at least NFL (Not-for-Long). It is either "do it the FAA way or go back to the highway and don't let the exit door hit you in the rear end on the way down the chute."

People have proven time and time again that they can't police themselves.

Meanwhile, there are several troubling aspects of attempting to teach quality driver education in South Carolina or any state for that matter.

Because of the fact that national standards and a national governing body does not exist and all fifty states have their own rules. Imagine how that would work for airline travel? How would you like it if the rules changed as you flew across each state? I can hear the flight attendant now.

I think this is best represented if you think in Ellen DeGeneres's voice since she used to do a "flight attendant" bit.

Ellen (delivered cheerfully): *"During the first half of the trip across the Pacific, you have to wear a seat belt as if we are going to crash because we are still under California flight rules. However, once we get past the point of no return, those of you from Texas, New Mexico, and Arizona can **unbuckle** your holster belts and your seat belts as we prepare to crash into the Pacific."*

A passenger in the front row wearing an Aloha shirt raises his hand. *"What about those of us from California and Hawaii?"*

Well, Ellen pauses. *"Those of you from California and Hawaii will need to **buckle** your seat belts, then bend over, put your head between your knees, and prepare to be kissed by a Texan! Thank you for asking!"*

Fortunately, the FAA has forged international agreements with most countries that promote a high degree of continuity for airline travel over oceans and between other countries too. This has somehow been achieved despite many political, cultural, religious, and economic differences, not to mention that we also have a few different ideas about how to achieve national security which certainly includes airline travel.

Contributing factors to this extraordinary level of cooperation are some undeniable facts the international community cannot deny:

- The American Wright Brothers invented the airplane. Without this invention, we wouldn't be discussing airline travel at all, at least not as we know it today.

- Most of the top aircraft manufacturers in the world are still here … in the United States. We haven't let China or anyone else wrest that from us yet … and we shouldn't. Keep pouring the coals to 'em boys!

- The FAA's air traffic control system, though flawed even now, is still undeniably the very best in the world, and everyone else in the world seems to know it … except Americans!

Now back to automobile travel throughout America in general and South Carolina in particular. An individual state must be used as an example because this is the only way we can define what it wrong before we can define how to fix it.

South Carolina is a perfect example (if I can use that word) and representative of what can happen when individual states are allowed to "govern" themselves regarding something that has national implications.

Some of these have been alluded to earlier in the book, but I thought it might be helpful to summarize them here again just in case someone who can make a decision actually reads them:

1. A *different* set of driver education, driver training, and driver training standards are used for high schools versus professional driving schools.

2. Now the PDLA (the Provisional Driver's License in South Carolina) *must* be handed over to the parent regardless of if the student can drive safely or not. When I was informed of this ruling by a GS-5 bureaucrat at the state DMV, she said, "Well, we believe some of you guys are requiring more lessons just so you can get paid more money!"

3. That's when I knew that the bureaucrat involved in the decision had never conducted a *single lesson* in a training car.

If she ever had, she would have known *beyond any shadow of a doubt* that the last person you really want driving your training car with you in the passenger seat is a student who requires extra driving lessons … *at any price and for any fee!* We do it out of necessity! *Hello, does anyone up there get this?*

4. During our last year of running CADETS, for those parents who could afford quality driver training or for those parents who were not avoiding driver education for their teen entirely, I figure I was teaching for about $5 per hour. Probably less than the bureaucrat was earning, but I'm not sure.

5. The high schools were allowed to charge as little as $50 for driver education for each student. How could they survive without being subsidized? The answer is that they couldn't survive without being subsidized ... by tax revenue. So ...

6. A year after we closed the doors on CADETS, when tax subsidies got lean, most of the high schools in Horry and Georgetown counties and throughout most of South Carolina also closed their doors on driver education. In South Carolina, the professional schools are now doing it almost exclusively. That's the good news. However ...

7. The SCDMV in their infinite wisdom (again) decided that the pros now had so much integrity that they could not only *train* their students but *test* the same student in their cars in lieu of the state having to pay those pesky DMV examiners hefty salaries to do it.

8. Major league baseball managers have a high degree of integrity too but would you want the manager of the New York Yankees calling balls and strikes against *your* team ... while managing the Yankees? Well, you would if you were a Yankees fan. How about the manager deciding who is safe and who is out at the plate, *for his own team,* when the decision is made in a fraction of a second?

9. Teachers, managers, and coaches are human. We *want* our students to succeed. Sometimes we wish for them to succeed so badly it clouds our judgment. Someone else besides a parent must judge a parent's teen behind the wheel, and someone else besides the instructor should judge that instructor's student.

10. Therefore, in my not-so-humble opinion, when training is conducted by one school, public *or* private, the actual DMV performance test should be conducted by a *different* school, and it should be conducted in either the family car or the car the beginning driver will drive the

majority of the time. This would have a side benefit of reducing the tendencies of driving schools to employ unusual little *subcompact* toys that very few people actually buy or drive, especially teens.

I hate to bring it up again, but I can think of no better example. Every single system, subsystem or piece of equipment utilized within airway facilities of the FAA requires a corresponding performance exam for those of us charged with *certifying* that the systems meet performance standards that are uncompromising. When you fly, would you want it any other way? During the past fifty years, how many crashes have been attributed to faulty equipment, services, professional airway systems specialists, or incompetent air traffic controllers? Can you remember any?

If there needs to be a national governing body, governing all fifty state DMV programs, all state public driver education programs, all state professional driver education programs, and the insurance agencies that have decided to get into the driver education business, shouldn't it be an organization like the National Highway Traffic Safety Administration? Potentially, this could become reality and could take place throughout the entire country. This concept needs a "reason" to exist, as well as the "right" to exist. If not, within the driver education industry, we will have the same thing ten years from now that we have today.

Wouldn't you like to know when you drive from one state to another that you can turn right on a red light after stopping and clearing the lane or whether the NHTSA determines otherwise for all states, not just one? If you are a parent, wouldn't you like to know for certain that your kid's instructor was certified by the best driving school in the land, one that can't be bought, influenced, bribed, coerced, or politically influenced to do anything other than follow the letter of the guidelines of the NHTSA?

Are you really willing to let your child enter the driving world as it exists today when a potential alternative is not only possible it is plausible? I didn't think so.

Appendix 1

BEHIND-THE-WHEEL INSTRUCTION GRID NO. 1

Student Name:____________________ Instructor:____________________

ACTIVITY	**INTRODUCTION**	**PRACTICE**	**MASTERY**
LESSON DATE(S)			
Basic Auto Setup			
Figure 8 (R/L Series)			
Right Turn Series			
Left Turn Series			
Wheel Release			
Gas and Brake			
Three-Point Turn			
Backing			
Serpentine or Backing Turns			
ABS Braking			
Basic Rules of the Road Q and A			
Residential Driving			
Cul-de-Sac Maneuvering			
Right-of-Way Confirmation			

ADDITIONAL NOTES

Appendix 2

BEHIND-THE-WHEEL INSTRUCTION GRID NO. 2

Student Name:_________________ Instructor:_________________

ACTIVITY	INTRODUCTION	PRACTICE	MASTERY
LESSON DATE(S)			
Defensive Driving Q and A			
Angle Parking			
Perpendicular Parking			
Parking Lot Backing			
Parking Lot Driving			
Parallel Parking			
Wheel Parking on Hills Q and A			
Lane Change Simulations			
Review of Residential Driving			
Introduction to City Driving			
Parent Option			
Parent Option			
Parent Option			

ADDITIONAL NOTES

Appendix 3

BEHIND-THE-WHEEL INSTRUCTION GRID NO. 3

Student Name:________________ Instructor:________________

ACTIVITY	INTRODUCTION	PRACTICE	MASTERY
LESSON DATE(S)			
Advanced Driving Skills Q and A			
Merging with and without Yield			
Highway Driving			
City Driving			
Expressway Driving			
All Lane Changes (SMOG)			
Entering and Exiting Highways/Expressways			
Maintaining Space			
Maintaining Visibility			
The Point of No Return for Yellow Lights			
The 1-2-3 Count for Entering Intersections			
Three-Second Following Distance			
Wheel Visibility at Lights			
Reading the Intent of Other Drivers			

ADDITIONAL NOTES

Appendix 4

BEHIND-THE-WHEEL INSTRUCTION BEGINNING/NEW DRIVER
PROGRESS GRID

Student Name:_________________ Instructor:_________________

ACTIVITY	INTRO.	PRACTICE	MASTERY
LESSON ONE DATE(S)			
Basic Auto Setup/Moving/ Complete Stop Demo.			
Figure 8 Series			
Right Turn Series			
Left Turn Series			
The Wheel Release			
Acceleration and Braking Pre- and Post-Turns			
Three-Point Turns in Accordance with the DMV			
Backing in Accordance with the DMV			
45-Degree–90-Degree Backing Turns			
Eye/Foot/Hand/Horn /Accelerator/Brake/Wheel			
Right-of-Way Q and A Confirmation			
Residential Driving with Blind Intersections			
Cul-de-Sac Entrance and Exit Reinforcement			

Unprotected Left Turn Series Q and A			
LESSON TWO DATE(S)			
Defensive Driving Q and A Follow-Up			
Angle Parking			
Perpendicular Parking			
Parking Lot Backing			
Parking Lot Driving			
Parallel Parking			
Wheel Parking on Hills (UCLA Acronym Assist)			
Signal, Mirror, Over Shoulder, and Go (SMOG)			
Introduction to City Driving			
LESSON THREE DATE(S)			
Advanced Driving Skills Q and A			
Merging with and without Yield			
Highway Driving			
City Driving			
Expressway Driving			
Advanced Lane Change Performance			
Exiting Highways and Expressways			
Maintaining Space			
Maintaining Visibility			
Blind Spots			
Point of No Return While Approaching a Yellow			

1-2-3 Count from the Front			
Row			
Three-Second Following Distance on Dry			
Wheel Visibility at Lights			
Reading of Intent			

ADDITIONAL NOTES

Appendix 5

The CADETS Exclusive Parallel Parking Technique

1. *Signal* with your right turn signal as you *approach* your parallel parking space.

2. Steer your car close to the front barrier or cone/pole representing the left rear bumper of a car and pull alongside *parallel to within one to two feet.*

3. Stop your car parallel to the imaginary car with your wheels straight and *no angle* remaining in the direction of your car in relation to the front car or cone/pole.

4. Back your car straight back so that the rear of your car is *one-third past the front barrier or cone/pole.*

5. Note location of right rear barrier or cone/pole (at or near right rear headrest or speaker). *Turn wheel full right and back car until right rear barrier or cone/pole appears directly behind left rear headrest or speaker. (Car will be positioned at 45 degrees in relation to curb.)*

6. *Center your wheels* (verify that they are centered) and *back your car to within two to three* feet of the curb.*

7. Turn your steering *wheel full left* and *back* your car until either your rear bumper is no less than *one foot from the rear barrier or cone/ pole or until your right rear tire TOUCHES the curb.*

8. Place car in drive, turn your *wheel full right,* and creep toward curb until front of car and back of car are *equidistant from curb. Straighten wheels until front of car and back of car are parallel with curb.*

9. Center car *equidistant between front and rear barriers* or cone/ poles representing cars. Place car in park (or first gear if manual

transmission). Place parking brake on and turn engine off. If parking in an actual parallel parking space, the car is parked properly when both tires are within eighteen inches of the curb and front and rear bumpers are equidistance from front and rear vehicle.

10. When preparing to exit an actual parallel parking space or a DMV-designated parallel parking space, *signal left to signal intent* before moving.

11. *Back up to within one foot* of the rear barrier or cone/poles.

12. *Check mirror and over left shoulder* to clear before exiting.

13. Place car in drive and turn wheel full left. *Creep forward and verify.*

14. Verify that your right front bumper will *clear the left front barrier or cone/pole. The barrier or cone/pole represents the left rear bumper of a car.* If you are not certain you will clear, turn wheel full right, back up approximately two feet, and repeat steps 12 and 13 again.

*A vehicle with very small tires may be required to be backed a bit closer to the curb. A vehicle with very large tires such as a truck or SUV may need to be backed to within three to four feet from curb before the final left wheel turn.

Appendix 6

Senior Driver Assessment/Training Program Training Grid Template

Driver's Name:_________________ Observer:_________________

ACTIVITY	Unsatisfactory	Satisfactory	Mastery	Notes
Rules of the Road Confirmation				
Basic Auto Setup				
Right Turn Series				
Left Turn Series				
Wheel Release				
Gas and Brake				
Three-Point Turn				
Backing				
Residential Driving				
Right-of-Way				
Cul-de-Sac				
Blind Intersection				
Stop Signs				
Cornering				
Defensive Driving Confirmation				
Angle Parking				
Perpendicular Parking				
Parking Lot Backing				
Parking Lot Driving				
Parking on Hills (UCLA)				

City Driving				
Double Lane Turns				
Lane Changing (SMOG)				
Lane of Least Resistance				
Lane Control				
Speed Control				
Merging with and without Yield Signs				
Intersections				
Unprotected Left Turns				
Three-Second Following				
Wheel Visibility at Lights				
Maintaining Visibility				
Maintaining Space				
Yellow Lights				
Highway Driving				
Exiting Highways				
Advanced Collision Avoidance Procedures				

X = Training Required

MS = Moderately Successful

Mastery = Observed or Confirmed

Performance Grid Comments

Assessment Comments

Training Comments

Mastery Comments

*Additional lessons may be required either in the simulator or behind the wheel or both. Observers shall advise all drivers of deficiencies and recommend appropriate additional training as required. Based on this advice, drivers may elect to choose a simulator or actual behind-the-wheel supplemental training.

The assessment grid, the feedback, and the blank training grid may be copied and utilized by other training schools, other agencies, or other private parties for any adult of any age. The advantage of having them used far outweighs the reality that they are out there now ... and no longer in our domain. This seems like a small price to pay. Use them please ...

Appendix 7

Acknowledgments and Accolades

*The **CADETS** and *ProDriver* logos were created by Wraps Incorporated of Murrells Inlet, South Carolina. The ***ProDriver*** logo is a silhouette of the 2013 Hyundai Genesis 345 HP Turbo. The 345 HP Turbo is not appropriate for teens or any other beginning drivers of course. However, this car and a few others similar to it *could* be used to teach professional drivers who wish to feel what a 345 HP vehicle actually feels like, how to control it, and most importantly, how to make it do what you wish .